Making Big Money Investing in Real Estate

Making Big Money Investing in Real Estate

WITHOUT TENANTS, BANKS, OR REHAB PROJECTS

Peter Conti & David Finkel

Dearborn™
Trade Publishing
A **Kaplan Professional** Company

Editorial Director: Donald J. Hull
Acquisitions Editor: Mary B. Good
Senior Project Editor: Trey Thoelcke
Interior Design: Lucy Jenkins
Cover Design: DePinto Studios
Typesetting: Elizabeth Pitts

© 2002 by Dearborn Financial Publishing, Inc.

Published by Dearborn Trade Publishing, a Kaplan Professional Company

Printed in the United States of America

02 03 04 10 9 8 7 6 5 4 3

Library of Congress Cataloging-in-Publication Data

Conti, Peter.
   Making big money investing in real estate without tenants, banks, or
rehab projects / Peter Conti & David Finkel.
        p.   cm.
Includes index.
   ISBN 0-7931-5415-4 (7.25 × 9)
   1. Real estate investment. 2. Real estate investment—United States.
3. Real estate business. 4. Real estate business—United States. I.
Finkel, David. II. Title.
   HD1382.5 .C656 2002
   332.63′24—dc21

                                                          2002002080

Dedication

To Heather: Thank you for your love and support. I love, value, trust, appreciate, and respect you and look forward to building our life together.

David Finkel

To Joanna: Thanks for being the woman of my dreams.

Peter Conti

Foreword: How a "Stay at Home Mom" Bought 14 Properties and
How You Can Too!   xi

Acknowledgments   xv

Introduction: Welcome to Purchase Option Investing   xvii

1. GETTING STARTED   1

Why I Almost Gave Up on Real Estate before I Even Got Started   1

Anyone Can Make Big Money Investing in Real Estate   3

Why So Many People Fail Financially   5

Why Real Estate Is So Powerful   10

What Stops Most Investors Cold   16

The Power of Mentors   16

Six-Figure Freedom   19

How I Grew $3,500 into $350,000 with Just Three Deals and
How You Can Too!   20

The Big Picture of Purchase Option Investing   24

Our Bias in Real Estate Investing   24

The Three Main Steps in All Purchase Option Deals   28

2. FIVE PURCHASE OPTION BUYING STRATEGIES   29

The Four Biggest Barriers to Traditional Investing   31

Purchase Option Buying Strategy One: The Lease Option—How to
Buy Homes in Nice Areas with Nothing Down   34

Purchase Option Buying Strategy Two: Equity Splits—How to "Partner Up" with Your Seller 54

Purchase Option Buying Strategy Three: "Subject to" Purchases—How to Get Long-Term Bank Financing without Ever Talking to a Banker 59

Purchase Option Buying Strategy Four: Big Money Cash Close—How to Pay a Seller with Borrowed Money 85

Purchase Option Buying Strategy Five: Owner-Carry Financing—How to Turn the Seller into Your Bank 90

3. 23 NEGOTIATING TECHNIQUES TO GET THE BEST DEAL POSSIBLE 107

The Five Steps of the Instant Offer System 107

The Single Most Important Negotiating Skill 109

What Really Drives Home Sellers 111

The Power of the "Take Away" Close 112

Language Patterns of Reluctant Buyers 113

The Five Keys to Closing the Deal 116

Four More Secrets to Phrasing Your Offer So the Seller Says, "Yes" 126

Three Surefire Techniques to Get the Best Price 132

The Four Most Common Seller Objections and How to Handle Them 136

Negotiating Wrap Up 144

4. 14 LESSONS TO LOWER YOUR RISK 145

Lesson 1: Always Build an Escape Hatch into Every Deal You Do 145

Lesson 2: Do Your Due Diligence So You Don't Get Burned 149

Lesson 3: Do It with Nothing Down 164

Lesson 4: Never Commit to a Deal unless You Have Found Both Buyer and Seller 168

Lesson 5: Avoid Recourse Debt Like the Plague 168

Lesson 6: Pass the Maintenance onto Your Buyer and Seller 169

Lesson 7: Quickly Record Your Agreement 170

Lesson 8: If You're Going to Have a Delayed Closing, Escrow Your Closing Documents Up Front 171

Lesson 9: If You're Buying on a Lease Option, Record a Performance Deed of Trust or Mortgage 174

Lesson 10: Remember to Recommit the Seller to the Deal 175

Lesson 11: Use Corporations and Trusts to Keep Your Wealth Safe 177

Lesson 12: Always Maintain Adequate Insurance to Cover Property Damage and Lawsuits 178

Lesson 13: Disclose! Disclose! Disclose! 179

Lesson 14: Do Business with Integrity 180

5. SELLING YOUR PROPERTIES FOR TOP DOLLAR   181

How to Get the Best Deal from Both Buyers and Renters without the Traditional Downsides   182

How to Turn Your Properties into Hands-Off Money-Makers   185

Why Tenant-Buyers Mean Cash Flow   187

The Right *Attitude* to Take with Your Tenant-Buyers   188

The Three Magic Words to Find Your Tenant-Buyer   188

The Single Best Way to Find Your Tenant-Buyer   189

The Three Keys to Finding Your Tenant-Buyer   192

How You Make Sure Your Tenant-Buyer Is a Renter *Not* a Buyer   200

Seven Simple Steps to Sell Your House on the Spot   203

The Three Hows of Selling Your Property   223

6. WHAT NOW?   231

Three Techniques to Find Your First Deal in 45 Days or Less!   232

A Simple Five-Step Action Plan to Launch Your Real Estate Investing Business   236

How Five Ordinary People Created Extraordinary Lives by Investing in Real Estate and How You Can Too!   241

A Few Closing Thoughts   251

Index   253

About the Authors   257

Special Bonus Offer   259

How a "Stay at Home Mom" Bought 14 Properties and How You Can Too!

My name is Cheryl, and I am just an ordinary mom. My husband works at our church a few blocks from our home, and I home school my three teenage kids. If you were to tell me three years ago that I'd also be a successful real estate investor who had already bought 14 properties, I would have told you that you were crazy!

My very first experiences in buying real estate were the homes my husband and I bought over the years to live in. I always played the role of his right-hand helper. At the closing he would point to the line and say, "Sign here," and I would. I didn't understand any of the details of what was going on. Banks and loans and escrow and title companies were like Greek to me. Then about two-and-one-half years ago things changed for me. My husband had resigned from his job, and we were getting ready to move. I had always had a fascination with real estate. Maybe it was because of all the friends I had had over the years who had made money investing in real estate that I decided to learn how to invest.

It was at this point in my life that I first met Peter and David. I saw them in a roomful of 700 other investors at a two-hour workshop they were teaching at the Ohio Real Estate Investors Association's Annual Convention. The more I listened to their ideas, the more I said to myself, "This is it. I have found what I want to be doing."

I became one of their mentorship students. While I was waiting for the live training part of their program, I began studying their home-study materials. Over the next two months I began looking for my first deal. I started calling For Sale By Owner ads in my local paper using Peter and David's scripts. Less than four weeks later, I found my first deal. I talked with a husband and wife who were what I call "empty nestors" because their kids had moved out. On top of that, the husband had been transferred with his job to another city where they had already purchased a new house. Now they were stuck with an empty house about two hours distance and double payments to cover each month.

When I went to meet with the sellers, I was so nervous. I kept thinking to myself that the sellers were going to know I was a fake. I had this fear that the husband was going to take one look at me, laugh, and say, "You're not an investor, you're just a mom." But it actually went much easier than I thought. When I went inside the house to meet with him and his wife, I left my two teenage sons in our minivan to wait. We talked for a while, and then he turned to his wife and said that selling me the house for $2,500 down on a lease option (something that you'll be learning about in this book) was a good fit for them. He signed and then pointed to his wife and told her where to sign. I thought, "Isn't this ironic, it's like things came full circle here. I used to be the one whose husband told her where to sign, and now I'm buying my first investment house."

I fumbled through signing up the deal. Actually, it seemed like the seller knew a lot more about real estate than I did, and he kind of coached me through the deal.

I walked out to my car using all my self-control to stay calm and poised. I sat down, slowly backed out of the driveway, drove down the street and out of sight of the house. There I pulled over and let out a victory yell. My sons and I traded high fives and shouted out in our excitement. I ended up making $35,000 of locked-in profits when I sold that house to my buyer a few weeks later.

I remember going to the three-day real estate investor training in San Diego for the mentorship program and bringing my minialbum of photos of the house. Peter and David and the whole class probably got bored with all the photos of that house and my rehashing of that story, but I couldn't help myself. I was so excited to have done my first deal and to have made money at it that I couldn't sit still. It was a light switch that was turned on inside of me that said, "Yes, I *can* do this!"

My husband always believed in me. He just was a bit skeptical that a person could really make money investing in real estate without $50,000 cash sitting in the bank to start with. For him, it took my second deal, a house that I bought for nothing down, before he realized this wasn't a fluke.

I found this deal through a response to a small classified ad Peter and David told me to put in my local *Thrifty Nickel* newspaper that said, "I Buy Houses." I got a call from a seller who was about 45 minutes away from where I live. I remember thinking to myself as I drove out to meet with the seller that I didn't want a house this far away from where I live. I kept saying over and over, "I don't want this house; it's too far."

When I arrived at the house, I spent the next hour trying to convince the seller that I didn't want to buy the house and going through all his other options to sell. The seller kept telling me all the reasons why I had to buy the house. Finally, I gave in and bought the house for $800 down and at $15,000 below market value. It was a great deal. I just didn't think I wanted a house that far from me. The seller gave me the title to the property, the coupon book for his lender, the keys to the house, and just walked away from it. I am now in the process of selling that house through a real estate agent that I now work with and will net $10,000 to $15,000 on the property.

Over the next two years, I just followed Peter and David's system, buying a variety of houses using their Purchase Option strategies. All totaled, I picked up 14 properties over this two-and-one-half-year period. It has been an incredible feeling to be building a future for my family.

My favorite deal was a $162,000 house that I bought with nothing down and owner financing. I made over $40,000 on this one deal alone. The bottom line is that these ideas work. They worked for me, and they'll work for you.

For me, it isn't just about the money. Don't get me wrong. The reason I do this is to make a profit, but I also really enjoy investing. My whole family is behind me. When my daughter was 11 years old, she was being given a ride home by the mother of one of her friends. When she walked into the house, she handed me a stack of flyers on houses for sale in the area. It seems that she kept asking her friend's mom to stop whenever she saw a house For Sale sign so she could get a flyer for me to call on to see if there might be a deal there.

My oldest son, who is 17, kept asking me when I was going to teach him how to invest this way. I finally gave in, and he spent a few months listening to me talk with sellers over the phone and going on appointments with me. I introduced him to the real estate agent I work with named Vic.

Vic brought a lead on this foreclosed house to my son. Together they put in an offer for half the after-repair value of the house. It was accepted! My son spent the next six weeks working on the house and overseeing the cleanup of the property. He just sold it to another investor in town who wanted it for a rental. The other investor got a great deal on the house and my son netted $10,000. Of course, he's not happy that his dad and I are insisting that he reinvest the money in his next property and not just spend it on any teenage toys.

I urge you to pour over every word in this book. Take the time to learn these strategies. Then, go out and put them to work. Because they do work, if only you will invest the time and energy to make them happen. Ultimately, the freedom and sense of security you will build for yourself and your family will far outweigh any of the temporary challenges that you will face. You couldn't have found two more caring mentors to guide you on your journey than Peter and David. They have been a blessing in the lives of my family. I wish you great success.

Cheryl Hastings

We would like to thank the following people for adding to the success of this book project and helping us touch lives out there: Our entire Mentor Financial Group, LLC team of Mike, Cheryl, John, Theresa, Renata, Julia, and Bernice—you are all integral to what we do; our mentorship students for proving daily that real people can make a lot of money investing in real estate; Mary and everyone at Dearborn Trade for believing in the project and making it happen; Marcia, Gary, Reddy, Frank, and our Inner Circle students for showing what happens when an investor decides to take his or her investing to the next level and really goes for it.

All of the stories we share in this book tell of real deals that we or our students have done over the past several years. In some cases, for the privacy of those parties involved, some of the names and descriptions have been changed. All of the relevant details of each deal, however, remain true and accurate to the best of our knowledge. We thank you and want you to know how much we appreciate and value your contributions.

And, finally, we would like to give a special thank you to the readers of *How to Create Multiple Streams of Income Buying*

Homes in Nice Areas with Nothing Down. Your letters, e-mails, and phone calls inspired us to invest the energy and time to do this book. We are thrilled to hear of your success with these ideas and hope this new book will give you even more strategies to profit from.

Welcome to Purchase Option Investing

Thank you for picking up this book. We're not sure if you bought it after attending one of our workshops, or after hearing us interviewed on television or radio, or if a close friend of yours gave the book to you as a gift. Maybe you were just browsing in a bookstore and picked this book off the shelf. However you found this book, it was no accident. Something drew you to learn more about making money investing in real estate.

Perhaps you are already investing in real estate and want to pick up a few more ideas to help you fine tune your skills, or maybe you are beginner and want to learn exactly how to get started investing. Whether you are a seasoned investor or a fresh beginner, this book will help you make more money investing in real estate without the hassles associated with traditional real estate investing, such as tenants, banks, or rehab projects.

How can we make such an outrageous claim—and even put it on the cover? Is our claim just hype to trick you into buying the book? No, it isn't. Over the past six years, we've been fine tuning our Purchase Option System so that we now do almost all of our deals without ordinary renters, without risky bank financing, and without involved rehab projects. In this book, you'll learn how you can put all that we have learned into action to make money investing in real estate.

Rather than putting a renter into your investment property, you will learn how to sell your properties on a rent-to-own basis to a tenant-buyer. Your tenant-buyer will give you a large chunk of cash up front for the opportunity to buy the property later and will be responsible for the day-to-day maintenance of the property. Your tenant-buyer will have an ownership mentality that will free you up from the headaches and hassles of traditional landlording.

And rather than putting 20 percent to 30 percent down and signing personally on conventional financing, you are going to learn how to get owners to be your bank. You'll learn about how to put tried-and-true buying strategies to work for you like "lease options" and "subject to" financing. You are going to learn the exact language patterns you need to use to get sellers to say, "Yes!" to financing your deals.

And rather than spending long hours and lots of money overseeing involved rehab projects, you are going to learn how to buy homes in nice areas with little or nothing down. While you still might be tempted to do a rehab project now and then, we're going to show you how you can make a lot of money by buying nice homes that don't need fix-up work so that you get your profits easier and with less risk.

Treat this book like a cafeteria line of insider tips, tricks, and techniques. As you go through it, put the items you feel are most valuable on your tray and use them. Leave whatever isn't a fit for you behind. The ideas and strategies you decide to put into action will help you make money.

The book is laid out in six chapters that give you the full picture of Purchase Option investing. Purchase Option investing is a simple and systematic approach to buying nice homes in nice areas with little or nothing down. It uses a variety of creative financing strategies to get ownership or control of properties with attractive, low-risk terms to you—the buyer. The focus of the Purchase Option System is to keep you in your highest paying role, that of an investor, *not* the role of a handyman, landlord, or loan supplicant.

In Chapter 1, you'll get introduced to the big picture of Purchase Option investing. You'll learn what stops other investors and how you can make sure you succeed.

In Chapter 2, you'll learn all five of the Purchase Option buying strategies. You'll learn to use these powerful techniques to finance your deals so that you can safely leverage your way into each purchase.

In Chapter 3, you'll learn about the Instant Offer System—the cutting-edge negotiating system that will help you get sellers to say, "Yes!" to your creative offer. You'll learn 17 specific language patterns and negotiating tactics that you'll need to close the deal.

In Chapter 4, you'll learn 14 ways to systematically lower your risk when you are investing in real estate. This chapter will give you the peace of mind that you will be able to keep all the money you will be earning with your investing.

In Chapter 5, you'll learn how you can turn your properties into a hands-off stream of income by selling them on a rent-to-own basis. You'll learn how to price, market, and show your properties so that you can turn your real estate portfolio into hassle-free income.

And finally, in Chapter 6, you'll learn how to put it all into action. You'll learn three ways to find your first deal in 45 days or less. You'll also get a five-step action plan to give you a road map of what to do next.

After you've given our ideas a try, we'd love to hear from you. Maybe your story will be so good it will go on our Wall of Fame on our Web site at <www.resultsnow.com>. Please e-mail your stories to us at: mentor@resultsnow.com. We wish you the best of luck in your investing!

Getting Started

Why I Almost Gave Up on Real Estate Investing before I Even Got Started

■ Peter's Story

I felt like I was stuck in my tracks, even though I had barely started investing in real estate. I had bought a duplex using a real estate agent five months earlier and was now officially a real estate investor. The problem was that I didn't feel like a real estate investor. I would make calls and go out and look at properties, but I was terrified when I made offers. In fact, I was so scared of making a mistake that I would self-sabotage and make my offers so low I knew the seller would never accept them.

It was no surprise to me that all these offers were rejected, and the sellers would later tell me that they sold to someone else. Was I missing something? Were all these other people making "stupid" buying decisions and I was the only "smart" one? I didn't feel very smart about the fact that I wasn't getting any more properties. And I knew that when I looked at a deal, I had no idea, despite what the real estate agents said, whether I would make money or lose money.

1

I remember the little classified ad to this day:

> Real Estate Investor Training.
> Easy, Lucrative, and Fun!
> Call Keith 303-555-1212

I found out that Keith was a successful local investor who wanted $5,000 for a five-day class on investing. That was a lot of money for me then. As an auto mechanic, I made about $50 on average for each car that I worked on. $5,000 for me meant fixing 100 cars. That's quite a bit of work. But when I thought it through, I realized that either way I was going to have to fix those 100 cars. At least if I took the class, I would have a real shot of getting out of having to fix cars forever.

I was in a position where I wanted to change things and change them fast. I was struggling with the emotional turmoil created by going through a divorce from my wife, after seven years of marriage. I had moved into a tiny two-bedroom condo and was at a low point in my life. Despite all of this, I knew that things could only get better. I knew that thousands of other people had made a lot of money investing in real estate, and I also knew that what I was doing wasn't going to get me there. I was ready to do something, anything, to turn things around for myself. So I took the chance. It turned out to be the right decision for me.

The class was in Keith's 4,000 square-foot home located in a prestigious neighborhood in the hills west of Denver. He explained how he had bought the home without using any of his own money and how I would soon be able to do the same thing. I didn't believe him, of course, but I thought that if I could use his ideas to buy a house even half as nice, I'd be doing okay. Little did I know at the time that in less than three years I would move into a home in the same neighborhood.

I listened closely as my new mentor shared his secrets with me. "There are only two ways to buy a property so that you end up making money," he explained. "You can either buy on price or on terms, but you can't give the seller both his price and all cash. When you're paying all cash for a property, you'll need to make sure you aren't paying more than 60 percent to 65 percent of the value of the property to leave enough room for you to cover all of your costs and still make a profit. But buying based on getting a low cash price can be risky," Keith explained. "You need to be able to know the exact value of a property, the cost of any fix up required, and know all the carrying costs that you will have to pay while you're fixing up the property. If you make even a small mistake in choosing the price you'll pay, you can end up working long and hard on the property without making much of a profit, or worse, you end up losing money. I'm going to show you how to let the seller have his price as long as you get your terms. If you buy on the right terms, you won't always make money, but you will never lose money."

This made sense to me, and I spent the next five days listening as Keith taught me many fundamentals about investing in real estate. Over the years I've used those ideas as a strong foundation to put deals together.

I wish I could tell you that I never got scared to make offers after that or that everything went smoothly, but I can't. After the class, I was still scared, but I had the knowledge I needed to overcome my fear. Getting started is never easy. But I think about what my life would be like today if I were still fixing cars and I thank God that I moved forward with my investing despite the fear. What will it ultimately cost you if you don't get started with your investing? ■

Anyone Can Make Big Money Investing in Real Estate

What would it mean for you and your family if you were able to earn an extra $25,000 this year by investing in real estate? How about an extra $50,000 or even $100,000? Wouldn't it take much of the stress and worry out of your life? Would it improve your sense of freedom and security?

We're just two ordinary guys—one an ex-mechanic and the other an ex-jock. Yet, by using the ideas in this book, we've been able to create both healthy monthly cash flows and large net worths by buying homes in nice areas with nothing down. Throughout this book we'll share with you many of our firsthand stories of what worked for us and what didn't. The bottom line is that if we were able to start where we did—with nothing—and do what we did, you will be able to do the same thing. It's our hope that you'll be able to do it faster and easier than we did.

But what if you don't make a million dollars during your first year of real estate investing? So many beginning investors want it all overnight. Like any other skill, investing takes time and practice to learn. So when you are setting out your investing goals, make sure you think in the long term too.

One of our students, Will, set a goal to make $100,000 in cash profits from his real estate investing. It took Will over two-and-one-half years of investing on a part-time basis before he reached that goal. He found his first deal while he was at our three-day real estate training. He found an owner of a rental property who sounded motivated. Will and another student at the training arranged to meet him. They ended up buying the house on a three-year lease option, a method you'll learn about in Chapter 2. The way Will tells it, he just stumbled through the paperwork with the seller, figuring out what belonged in which blank as he went. Five weeks later he had the house sold to a tenant-buyer for a $10,000 profit. While this is one of the smallest deals he's done, it was his first. And first deals, like first loves, are something special. They are the deals that let you know, "Hey, I can do this! This is real." Can you imagine what it will feel like when you have the check in hand from selling your first house? What will you do with your profit?

Will went on to do other deals. He never did more than four in any one year, but in the end he reached his $100,000 goal. We want to be clear here—it takes work. No one is going to go out and sign up deals for you. But in the end, it's worth it.

We can already hear what you're thinking, "If it's so easy, why doesn't everyone do it?" The only response we have is that most people were programmed for financial failure from the beginning. And here is our best observation as to why.

Why So Many People Fail Financially

Have you ever wondered why so many people fail financially? Living in a world with so many opportunities, the overwhelming majority of people end their days dependent on their family and the government for their main source of income.

One day we heard a story of how they catch monkeys down by the equator that helped us to understand why so many people are struggling with their money. It seems that clever hunters have learned a simple way to catch monkeys. They hollow out a coconut and make a small opening in one end. They then attach a leather tether to the other end. Inside the coconut they place peanuts.

Next they put out the coconut in a place they think a monkey is likely to come by and sit down to wait. Before long a monkey comes by, drawn by the irresistible smell of the peanuts. The monkey easily fits its hand inside the coconut and grabs the peanuts. But with it wrapped around the peanuts, the monkey's hand no longer can fit back out. The monkey pulls harder and harder, working himself into a panic, never realizing the one simple step he would have to take to go free—letting go of the peanuts.

How many people do you know who are working for peanuts, too scared to stop what they're doing to free up some of their time to build and create what they want? How many people are holding so tight to what they know to be true that they never step back and look for other ways of accomplishing their ambitions?

Many people hang on to those peanuts for dear life because they are afraid of losing what they have. Many blindly cling to modest incomes so that they don't have to step out into what they consider to be the blind terror of the unknown.

■ **David's Story**

When I was younger, I trained to play field hockey in the Olympics. I spent my early life chasing this dream, moving off to live and train at the Olympic Training Center and to play in foreign leagues around the world.

I was rewarded by a successful career on the United States National Team. On my way to playing in the Olympics, I started having strange back problems. Shooting pains and muscle spasms would keep me in bed for days. It was one of the scariest times of my life. I was so afraid of losing my dream that I locked my sights on the diagnosis of the doctors and the daily routine of physical therapy. The problem was that none of this was working. So I clung to this routine tighter, went to physical therapy twice a day, saw the doctor more and more often.

It took me over a year and a half to realize that none of this was working. I ended up having surgery that cured the problem (a small fatty tumor was pressing on a nerve in my hip—fortunately, it was benign). If only I had been willing to face the reality earlier that the routine of doctor visits and aggressive physical therapy wasn't working, I may have been able to heal from the surgery in plenty of time to play in the Olympics.

My "peanuts" wasn't money from a job, but it was the routine of blindly following a plan that clearly wasn't working. When faced with the reality of losing my dreams of playing in the Olympics, I clung to my routine with all the desperation of a drowning man holding onto a lifeline. At the time, I simply didn't realize that the lifeline was really an anchor, and it was pulling me down.   ■

Think about all the would-be real estate investors who cling to what they know rather than taking the steps to acquire and fine tune better investing strategies they could use to create massive wealth. So keep an open mind as you read this book in order to grab new ideas and tools. But remember, only keep holding these ideas for as long as they are helping you get what you want. Be willing to drop them and pick up better ideas along the way.

When you see someone locked in the monkey trap, you can't help but feel a gentle sense of compassion. After all, they are merely stuck in a place where you may have once been. But you had the courage to step out on faith. You decided to invest the energy and time to learn and grow into a successful real estate investor. And whether you plan to invest full-time or part-time, you are to be admired because at some distinct point in your past you chose to loosen your hand and let your peanuts fall to the floor, choosing instead to build a better future.

■ Peter's Story

Have you ever had anyone tell you that you wouldn't amount to anything? I've found that the world is full of people who are so scared of going after their dreams they will try to discourage you every step of the way. Why they do this is a mystery. Perhaps, it's because they don't want you to pass them up. Or maybe they feel threatened when you have the courage to go after your dreams. Or maybe it's because other people tend to see your limitations instead of looking for the true power that you actually have inside of you.

I experienced this all too well. It was a cold winter day as I struggled under the hood of a car to position my work light so that I could see the bolts that I was trying to loosen. Even though I was dressed in three layers of clothes, the cold from the poorly heated auto repair shop where I worked seemed to be seeping through me.

I was the new guy on the block in this shop, and I had discovered that because I was paid with a commission for every car that I fixed, outside factors beyond my control were affecting my earning capacity. The mechanics that had been there longer than I had always seemed to get the big "gravy" jobs. These were the jobs that paid at least two or three hours of labor so that the mechanic could get paid for working instead of wasting time like I did taking care of the little jobs. You see, each 15-minute or 30-minute repair job that I did still required me to wait for the dispatcher to give me the work order. I had to go find the car, drive it in, wait for the parts, fix it, test-drive it, and, finally, vacuum the car out as an extra service to the customer.

I knew that I wanted to succeed financially, and on that cold winter morning groping around trying to see under the hood of the car, I felt very far away from living the life that I wanted. This was made strikingly clear to me within the next few minutes.

I noticed that the shop foreman had entered the shop with a big, hot, steaming cup of coffee. I found a mug in my toolbox and went up front to see if I could find the source of this warm beverage. I spied a coffeepot up in the waiting area with enticing spirals of steam wafting out into the air.

I filled up my mug and paused for a moment to wrap my hands around it. I closed my eyes and enjoyed the scent of the fresh brewed coffee while the warmth caressed my fingers. This pleasant moment was interrupted when I heard, "Peter, what are you doing?" I looked up, and the owner of the shop was glaring at me. "That coffee is for *customers* only!" he snarled and then turned and stomped back into his office and shut the door.

I felt horrible. What hurt most was that even though I knew I deserved to be treated better, I didn't have any place else to go. I realized on that cold winter day that I didn't have a plan. I needed a way to be able to create and go after my own financial destiny rather than wait for things to get better by themselves.

I had no idea at this point of the incredible opportunities that would someday come into my life when I finally discovered real estate investing. But I did know that I had to do something. I began my search in earnest on that cold winter day.

Other people continued to discourage me along the way. I'm sure you've either experienced this yourself or will very soon when you decide to really go after living the life of your dreams. When you hear someone telling you that you can't do it, you'll realize that if I could make it starting with nothing, you most certainly can too. I don't care what other people think of you. I know that you can have anything you want in life if you only decide you want it bad enough.

I once heard a quote from the motivational speaker Les Brown that stayed with me. He said, "Don't get mad; don't get even; get ahead!" ■

We once heard a multimillionaire say that there are two doors in life—one marked "freedom" and one marked "security." Most people choose to walk through the door marked security and in so doing lose both.

Can you ever really be secure if you are dependent on someone else for your income? If you have to keep working just to keep your head above water? The only way to find real security in your financial life is to be the one in control of your income. In today's world, you need more than just a job; you need to have income streams that will flow even when you're not working. This is called "passive income." And one stream isn't enough because it can dry up and leave you desperate. You need multiple streams of income to be secure.

According to U.S. Bureau of Labor statistics, out of 100 people who start working at age 25, by age 65:

- 1 percent are wealthy
- 4 percent have adequate capital for retirement
- 3 percent are still working
- 63 percent are dependent on Social Security, friends, relatives, or charity
- 29 percent are dead

Think about it, by age 65 only 5 percent of the population is financially independent. That means that the other 95 percent are either dependent on someone else for money or they're dead. This is the track record of most people in our current system!

Furthermore, if your income streams require you to work full-time just to keep them flowing, then you aren't really free, you're dependent. Independence means you are in control of your own income. You can turn the tap on, as wide as you want, any time you want. And you have the time to enjoy the money you are making.

So building for the future means creating passive income streams that flow to you month in and month out with just a little bit of supervision on your part. That means royalties, real estate, or securities. Royalties are great if you have developed a breakthrough new piece of computer software or if you have written a Pulitzer Prize winning novel. But for the average person, royalties are a little beyond their reach. And securities are great, when the market moves up. But it takes a large pool of liquid capital to earn consistent cash flow of any significant amount in the stock market.

For the average person, there has been, there is, and there will only ever be one real choice: real estate. Real estate has been the common denominator in the success of a huge number of the world's wealthiest people. It's also the simplest and easiest way for average people to create financial freedom for themselves in today's world. Even if you only use it as one part of your overall financial strategy, real estate is one of the most powerful investment vehicles you have at your disposal.

Why Real Estate Is So Powerful

When you think through all the different investment options, you need to consider how each particular vehicle will carry you to your destination. Real estate is a powerful investment vehicle for six specific reasons.

1. Real Estate Lets You Tap into the Power of Upside Leverage

Upside leverage is when a small financial investment earns you magnified rates of return while at the same time shielding you from big losses. When you buy a property using the Purchase Option strategies you'll learn about in Chapter 2, you'll be able to invest with little or nothing down. This use of leverage turns small amounts of starting capital into large cash profits for you. Because you won't be using traditional bank financing for most of your deals, you'll make sure you aren't signing personally on any loans. This will mean that you will hedge your risk in a very intelligent way.

■ David's Story

I remember a real estate deal we did in partnership with one of our students. We found a motivated seller who was moving to Arizona to retire with his wife in the warm and dry climate. He hadn't been able to sell his three-bedroom house because he refused to replace the 20-year-old carpeting throughout the house and to strip off the faded yellow wallpaper that had graced many of the walls for even longer.

We bought the house from the seller on a six-year lease option (a technique you'll learn about in Chapter 2) for $142,000. After we invested $3,000 in the house to repaint and recarpet, the house was immediately worth $155,000. We then sold it on a one-year rent-to-own basis for $165,000. Because we collected $2,400 upfront as a nonrefundable option payment from our buyer, we only had $600 of out-of-pocket expenses in this property.

All totaled, we turned $600 into $23,000 in profit within 12 months. When you plug the numbers into a calculator, you'll find that the rate of return on that $600 was 3,833 percent! That is the power of leverage. It turns ordinary deals into huge money-makers.   ■

2. Real Estate Is One of the Best Tax-Advantaged Investments

The U.S. government gives you all kinds of financial reasons to invest in real estate. For example, when you buy a property for $200,000 and sell it for $300,000, you pay only long-term capital gains tax on it (provided you've held the property for a certain length of time). Long-term capital gains tax is currently only 20 percent. If this were profit from a business you owned, you would have to pay up to 39 percent on the profit *plus* you would have to pay self-employment tax on the profit. Because real estate is tax advantaged, you pay less than half as much in taxes. In this case you make an extra $20,000 in profits from this single tax savings! And we still haven't even talked about things like depreciation, 1031 exchanges, capital gains exclusions on personal residences, and other write-offs the U.S. government gives you. All in all, real estate is one of the last real tax shelters the average person has.

3. Real Estate Investing Operates in an Imperfect Market

You can find real estate bargains as if you were shopping at an outlet store. One of the features of securities like stocks and bonds is that they are sold in a way that at any given point in time most people who buy a specific stock will be paying the same price. Real estate is different. You can have two identical homes on the same block. One might be bought for $175,000, and the other might be purchased by an investor from a motivated seller for $140,000. When you use the negotiating strategies you'll learn in Chapter 3, you'll find that you'll be able to make a huge chunk of your profit the very day you buy your investment property.

One of our students in Ohio, Neil, bought his first investment property for nothing down at 30 percent below market value. He had found a motivated landlord who wanted to dump his rental property and was thrilled when Neil stepped in and took it off of his hands.

We found one of our deals from an ad we were running to get sellers to call us. It turned out the seller was three payments behind and facing foreclosure. We bought the house from her for $40,000 below value. This was a good deal for her because had she gone through foreclosure she would have gotten nothing. By selling to us, she made some money and protected her credit. If the house were a stock, we never would have gotten such a good deal. She could have sold it in 60 seconds and wouldn't have needed us to buy it from her.

Why can you as an investor get such great deals? You can do it because you have specialized knowledge to sell a house for top dollar, knowledge most sellers just don't have. You will acquire exactly this type of specialized knowledge in Chapter 5.

Imperfect markets don't just mean you'll be able to buy properties for bargain prices; it also means that you will often find great deals due to the financing you negotiate with the seller. Remember, in real estate you don't just make money by negotiating a great price; you can also make money by getting great terms when financing the deal.

One of our students negotiated a deal where the seller carried back half the purchase price at 2 percent interest! This meant that the seller got half his money up front, and then he accepted payments over time for the other half of his money. It's called a "Big Money Cash Close," and you'll learn about it in Chapter 2. Financing like this turns many of your properties into monthly cash machines because of the low monthly payments you make on them. Remember, motivated sellers don't care about getting the perfect buyer. All they want is a *real* buyer who can solve their immediate problem.

4. Properties Create Easy Cash Flow

What business do you know where you can advertise for nine days with a small classified ad and some handwritten signs and get 50 potential clients begging you to choose to do business with them? The only one we know of is real estate. When you have an income-producing house or apartment building, you can easily find someone to rent the property. The money that they pay you monthly is a passive stream of income that takes very little work on your part, provided you set up the deal correctly as you'll learn to do in Chapter 5.

■ **Peter's Story**

One of my apartment buildings nets me over $30,000 per year. That money is mine without having to do any work other than look over the monthly statements from the management company and make a few decisions each year. Yes, I had to work hard to put this deal together and to get the property set up correctly, but from that point on it turned into a hands-off deal.   ■

5. Amortization Is a Wealth Builder

This fancy $10 word, *amortization,* means that each month you make a payment to the lender, a portion of that money goes to pay for interest, and another portion goes toward paying off the principal of the loan. For example, with a standard 30-year mortgage, you pay the bank for 30 years, and over time you pay that loan all the way down to zero, when you own the property free and clear. This equity pay down is called the "amortization" of the loan. With real estate, you get to have your tenants pay down your mortgage for you!

■ **David's Story**

"Most investors don't know that you can get the equity pay down when you buy using a lease option simply by filling out the agreement the right way. On a three-bedroom house where we did the paperwork correctly, we realized an extra $6,000 profit just from the amortization alone.   ■

6. The Long-Term Appreciation of the Property Is a Big Money-Maker

Appreciation is probably the biggest long-term money-maker you get from investing in properties. While the real estate market is wavy, with ups and downs, over time this wave is angled up, meaning that properties increase in value over time. According to data collected by the U.S. Census Bureau, the average price of a single family house in the United States has appreciated an average of 6.73 percent each year over the last 35 years. Over the long haul, if you buy intelligently, you can count on your properties increasing in value at a steady pace.

You will have periods where the real estate market will flatten out. You will have times when the market will fall. But when you choose homes in good solid neighborhoods, you know that over time the properties will increase in value.

Imagine you could go back in time just 15 years. Could you find just one property that you would have been willing to pay full price for 15 years ago? You're probably having trouble deciding between several properties which you wanted most! You know, like other people do, that over time real estate appreciates in value.

When you invest in real estate, not only do you get the amortization, and the monthly cash flow, and the tax savings, and the ability to leverage yourself into the property, and the imperfect market which got you a great deal from the start, but you *also* get to ride up the appreciation curve and make even more money.

What Stops Most Investors Cold

So what's stopping most people from investing in real estate? The answer is an ugly four letter word—*fear*. Most people are afraid they don't know enough. Or that they aren't good enough. Or that they aren't talented enough. Most people are stopped cold because they are afraid of taking that next step. Many of them don't even know what that next step is. Right now we are going to reveal to you the one secret of success in real estate investing that will allow you to reach maximum success with a minimum of time, energy, and effort.

The Power of Mentors

In order to be successful in anything you do, you need specialized knowledge. And this learning always comes at a price. If you choose to go it alone and decide to tough out the learning curve with true grit, you'll make it. But you'll have many painful learning experiences along the way. That's because life teaches best through the pain of mistakes. Let's face it. When things are going well not too many of us pay attention to exactly why things are going well. It's only when our train gets temporarily derailed that we step back and take stock.

Now, if we learn best through tough times, the question is: Who do you want to have to experience those tough times, you or your mentor? Just as real estate investing lets you use leverage to buy properties, you can use mentors to leverage your real estate education. That's what we're doing with this book. We're trying to pack all the things we've learned from the hundreds of deals we've been involved with into these 200-plus pages. Hopefully, you will be able to learn from our pain. We've already paid for these lessons we're sharing with you. Let us be your mentors to help you start making money investing in real estate as soon as possible.

Throughout this book, we share private examples with you from our own real-world investing experiences. This way you can use each story as a shortcut to get you to where you want to go faster and easier.

Using a mentor isn't cheating and it isn't a sign of weakness. Using a mentor is a mark of intelligence. It is an indicator of your intelligence and likelihood of success. Remember this, successful people all had mentors who helped them achieve all that they have.

■ Peter's Story

I was at a workshop a long time ago with Robert Allen, one of the founders of creative real estate investing, when he shared with me how he got started investing in real estate. After finishing his MBA, he couldn't find a job. So he turned to real estate. He had the smarts to ask this very successful investor in his city to take him under his wing and show him the ropes. Within ten years, Robert was a multimillionaire. Robert went on to say that if he needed to be successful in any area, whether it be stocks or real estate or writing books, he would hire the best of the best in that field, pay them whatever they asked for, do exactly what they told him to do, and within three years he would be one of the best in that field. I've never forgotten that advice.   ■

■ David's Story

When I give a keynote talk to real estate investor associations around the country, one of the most common questions I get is how did I get started investing in real estate. Most people don't know that Peter was my mentor. We met at a workshop, which is one of the reasons I think everyone who's serious about success should attend at least two high-quality workshops each year—besides all you'll learn, you'll also be able make great contacts. At the time, I was struggling financially and living in the converted attic of a garage in San Diego. I'm tall, about 6′2″, and I remember how there was only one place in the entire attic where I could stand up without banging my head.

Peter and I hit it off right from the start. I admired the way that even though he was so successful in his investing, he was one of the most down-to-earth people I'd ever met. Over the next 12 months, Peter mentored as I began investing. I'll never forget the first appointment we went on together to meet with a motivated seller about buying her house. Her name was Frances, and she was in the beginning stage of foreclosure. We walked into the house and looked around. I was fine making small talk with Frances, although I was shaking inside. When we sat down to negotiate, I kept getting stuck not knowing where to go in the process. Each time I got stuck, I'd look over at Peter with an expression that was a plea for him to step in and help. Each time he'd look back at me and smile, not saying a word. When we left, without buying the house, I should add, I turned to Peter and said, "Thanks for the help! Where were you?" Peter smiled and simply asked me if I was now ready to learn.

I got his point loud and clear. I can be a pretty hardheaded individual who thinks he knows everything, and Peter was showing me that it was up to me to listen and learn. I couldn't go on pretending that I knew it all. I needed to let my ego down and say, "Hey, I don't know how to do this, but I'm willing to learn. You tell me what I need to do and how I need to do it, and I'll do exactly what you say." Over the next three months, I picked up ten properties. That's the power of finding and trusting a mentor. I got to learn all the shortcuts, not through trial and error, but rather by copying someone who had already figured out the success patterns. ■

Six-Figure Freedom

When people get started with their investing, they dream of creating a six-figure annual income stream, but deep down many of them have doubts that they themselves can make it happen.

That's the goal of this book—to give you the starting steps and specific know-how to help you realize that six-figure income. And we want you to do it in a way that creates the lifestyle you want without going out to your property on the weekend to fix the plumbing. We've helped other students of ours do it, and we know you can do it too.

Understand that there are still going to be the naysayers out there, people who say you can't do it in today's market, in today's economy, in today's cosmic layering of celestial occurrences. But you have a choice. You can either buy into what these financially stressed-out individuals are clinging to so hard, or you can let go of your peanuts and go after the future you want and deserve.

The key word for you is now going to be: *until*. You are going to stick with it *until* you succeed. You are going to keep learning from your experiences and those of expert investors *until* you succeed. You are never going to take even a moment to talk with naysayers *until* you succeed. Then you're probably not going to say a word to them; you'll just smile a knowing smile.

We look at buying a property as planting a money seed. You plant the seed, care for it over time, and at some point in the future you harvest your yields. It never ceases to amaze us how sometimes a tiny little money seed can grow into a huge harvest. Here is a quick story about how one such money seed grew.

How I Grew $3,500 into $350,000 with Just Three Deals and How You Can Too!

■ **Peter's Story**

As I was putting down the phone after talking with Bill and Gloria, the owners of a fourplex, my hand was shaking. They had passed my screening and were obviously motivated sellers who wanted to get out of the rental business. By all my calculations, this had the makings of a good deal. I looked there at the bottom of my worksheet and saw that if I did nothing other than buy their property I would net $3,600 at the end of the first year. This would be a 50 percent rate of return on the $7,200 I calculated I would need to buy the property if worse came to worse and I needed to use conventional financing. But first I had to negotiate a contract on the property.

When I met with Bill and Gloria, I learned the property was one older home that had been converted into four separate units. The fourplex had been listed at $89,000 but had been lowered to $79,000 because no one had made any offers on it. This was probably due, at least in part, to the fact that two of the four units were vacant and needed a thorough cleaning and some minor maintenance before they would be nice enough to rent.

It turned out that Bill had inherited the property from his dad who was a part-time investor. Bill and Gloria kept talking about all the bad luck they had had with the property from renting it out to trying to get it sold. They had even sold it once before several years ago for $110,000 and had carried back the financing, that is, the seller had acted like the bank and took payments over time from their buyer rather than a lump sum of cash at the closing.

When their buyer stopped making payments, they had to foreclose. When they got the property back, it was quite dirty and needed several repairs to get it back into rentable condition. I know now that by letting them talk for as long as they wanted about all their reasons for selling, I was helping to close the deal. I wish I could say I did that because I was so smart, but I wasn't. I was just too scared to break in and start asking about the numbers.

They asked me about my background with investing. Because I had thought about what I would say if this came up, I was ready. I looked them in the eye and said, "I don't have much experience besides the one duplex I own. But I'm going to make it as a real estate investor because I am tired of being an auto mechanic." They were either very desperate or saw something about me that convinced them I could turn the property around. Sometimes it happens like that. You meet someone who can see through the surface to your core. I guess they must have liked what they saw.

We agreed on a price of $69,000 with 10 percent down, and they would carry back the balance, $62,100, at 9 percent interest. I knew that the rents from just two of the units would cover this payment and the other fixed costs. I also knew that once I got the other two units fixed and rented, I would be making a positive cash flow.

When I closed on that house, I was able to use three techniques to lower the money I needed to close from $7,500 (my $6,900 down payment plus closing costs) to $3,500. First, we closed on the fourth of the month, which meant at closing I got credited for the lion's share of that month's rent from the two units with tenants. Second, the security deposits that the seller was holding from the tenants transferred to me at the closing. This showed up as a credit to me on the closing statement, effectively reducing the cash I needed at the closing. Third, I negotiated a small repair allowance for some minor repairs that needed to be done.

After the closing I went to work and got the other two units cleaned up and rented. A few years later, I got a call from the seller who wanted to be cashed out of the note early and was willing to take a discount. He had called around and had legitimate offers to pay him $53,000 for the note which, by this time, I'd paid down to $63,000. Again, I wish I could say I was smart enough to have put a first right of refusal in the owner-carry note, a legal clause you'll learn about in Chapter 2, but at this point, I was still new to investing. Bill just called me because he appreciated that I always paid him on time and figured if he was going to give someone a good price on the note it might as well be me.

I sure didn't have $53,000 sitting in my bank account at the time, so I started calling around. One of the people I called was my dad. While I had never borrowed money from my parents before, I figured this case was different. After all, I would be securing the loan with a first mortgage and paying them interest. My parents did end up lending me the money to buy the note. I gave them a first mortgage on the property, and I bumped the interest rate from 9 percent to 10.5 percent. Everyone was happy. The seller got his money, my parents got a solid investment earning a healthy interest rate, and I made $10,000 from the discount in the note.

It wasn't too much longer before I put the fourplex on the market. I decided to use a real estate agent named Keith to sell the property because I knew he had a good reputation in the area. I ended up selling that property for $142,000, which meant that even after paying the commission I netted $80,000. Rather than pocketing the money and having to pay taxes, I decided to use a 1031 exchange to reinvest the money, tax deferred, into another property.

So my $3,500 seed had by this point grown into an $80,000 down payment. I used it to buy an upscale home in the foothills of Denver for $290,000. By this point in my investing, I was already out of the rental business so rather than put a renter in the house, I found a tenant-buyer. He gave me $10,000 in nonrefundable option money and agreed to pay $1,995 per month in rent. This rent covered all my fixed costs on the property. I gave my tenant-buyer the three-year option price of $360,000. Notice how by selling it on a rent-to-own basis, I didn't have to pay any real estate agent. This saved me $17,400.

My tenant-buyer actually bought two years into their three-year term. By this point, my $3,500 money seed was $150,000: $80,000 from the fourplex and another $70,000 from this house.

Again I reinvested the money using a 1031 exchange and bought another property.

This property was an even nicer house in a great neighborhood. Of course, I made sure I bought it from a motivated seller. The seller was in the final stages of a divorce. And if that wasn't reason enough to sell fast, she was also in the early stages of foreclosure! I ended up buying her property for $320,000. After I spent $30,000 for some high-leverage repairs, such as painting the house inside and out, replacing all the carpets, installing a new roof, and cleaning it thoroughly, it was worth at least $375,000. The best part of the deal was that the house was located in an area that had been appreciating at 10 percent to 12 percent for the past two years.

Again, rather than rent it out, I sold it on a rent-to-own basis. My tenant-buyers were a couple with three children and a fourth child due shortly. They gave me $10,000 in option money and paid a monthly rent of $2,100. I gave them a three-year option price of $443,000. As it turns out, one of the tenant-buyer's parents became ill, and they asked me if it would be okay if they were to move. They were so good about helping me find my next tenant-buyer that I refunded almost all their option money. When I did a market analysis of the value of the house, I was thrilled to find out that it was now worth $450,000. When I put my final tenant-buyer into the house, I again collected $10,000 in option money. Only now, the rent was $2,300 per month and their three-year option-to-purchase price was $547,000. When I added the $80,000 profit from the fourplex to the $70,000 profit from the first house to my $197,000 profit from this house, it totaled $347,000. My tiny $3,500 money seed had grown a hundredfold into $347,000.

And that's just one seed. What if you used the ideas in this book and planted three seeds or five seeds this year. Can you imagine how your life would be changed from these seemingly small money seeds you plant and nurture over time?   ■

The Big Picture of Purchase Option Investing

Purchase Option investing is not the competitive jungle of foreclosures; it's not the time-intensive and money-intensive route of rehabbing houses; and it's definitely not the tenants and toilets of traditional landlording.

Purchase Option investing is a simple and systematic approach to buying homes in nice areas with nothing down. It uses a variety of creative financing strategies to get ownership or control of properties with attractive, low-risk terms to you—the buyer. The focus of the Purchase Option System is to keep you in your highest-paying role, that of an investor, not the role of handyman or landlord or loan supplicant.

Many people think that Purchase Option investing is just the five Purchase Option buying strategies we describe in Chapter 2 of this book. It's not. Purchase Option investing is also the negotiating system that allows you, the investor, to get sellers to say, "Yes," to your creative offer, explained in detail in Chapter 3. And it is also a way to systematically lower your risk while investing, explained in Chapter 4. And it is also a system of selling your properties on a rent-to-own basis that allows you to create multiple streams of income without having to be a landlord, explained in Chapter 5.

The one thing all the powerful Purchase Option techniques have in common is maximum profit with minimum risk or effort.

Our Bias in Real Estate Investing

There are many ways to make money by investing in real estate. We want you to understand our bias so that you can take the best ideas in this book and leave behind any you do not like.

We don't like doing rehab projects. As a matter of fact, if the property takes more than a simple paint and carpet cleanup, we typically will either flip, that is, sell, our contract for a quick payment or sell the property as a handyman special. We just don't like getting bogged down in overseeing or doing the involved repair work it takes to rehab properties.

Also, while we still have rental units in our portfolios, we do our best to sell most of the properties we buy to tenant-buyers on a rent-to-own basis so that we have occupants with an ownership mentality not a renter mentality. The difference is huge. Currently, approximately only 10 percent of our properties are traditional rentals. It seems like we have more hassles from these properties than from the other 90 percent combined! So our bias is away from being a landlord and more on being like a banker—receiving monthly payments from well-behaved tenant-buyers. In fact, we're even willing to give up some of the future appreciation to our tenant-buyers just so that we can, for long periods of time, turn our properties into hands-off income streams.

We've seen many other investors get caught in what we call the "Landlord Trap." The Landlord Trap is where a person is so busy managing the properties they have that they don't have the time and energy to go out and acquire more properties. The danger of the Landlord Trap is that even if you are earning a lot of money, you don't have the freedom to enjoy the lifestyle you want. After all, did you get started investing in real estate merely to make money? Or did you start investing in real estate so that you could earn enough money to achieve a certain lifestyle of ease and freedom? We have spent the last several years perfecting the Purchase Option System so that you don't have to get mired down in the day-to-day oversight of rental properties. Instead, you can sidestep the Landlord Trap and create the lifestyle that you want.

Finally, we focus most of our energies on buying homes in the middle to upper-middle segment of the market. These nice homes in good neighborhoods might not spin off as large a cash flow as homes in the lower part of the market, but they appreciate well over time and take a whole lot less work to oversee.

Again, we're sharing our bias with you so that you can understand how we filter our impressions and ideas on investing. You can then make decisions about how you want to invest in real estate for yourself. You'll find that some of our ideas just won't be a fit for you. That's okay. Leave these ideas behind and use the ones that do work for your situation. We find the most fun and profitable part of real estate investing is sitting down and negotiating a deal with a buyer or seller. This is the part that we love, and this is where the Purchase Option System puts most of its focus—on getting you face to face with motivated sellers and hungry tenant-buyers. We like being *investors,* making our money by buying and selling and setting up passive income streams for long-term growth. We know that the more we can keep ourselves in this investor role, the more money we end up making.

■ David's Story

I've only ever done one rehab project where I did most of the work myself. Early on, Peter helped me fix up this three-bedroom, two-bath house in a working-class neighborhood. I'll never forget how we were working side-by-side painting the shelves of the pantry. I was doing my best to paint as neatly as possible. I looked over at Peter and in the time it had taken me to paint one shelf he had finished painting his entire side of the pantry. When I asked him how he did it so fast, he looked over at my work and said, "Because you are trying to be perfect in your painting. The important thing here is speed. We need to turn this property quickly. At your pace, it will take you months to get this property back on the market. This will cost too much in holding costs. If you want to do a rehab, you need to be fast." That project cured me of my fantasy of fixing up houses. I realized that not only didn't I like doing the work, but I wasn't very good at it. On top of all this, it was exhausting!   ■

One of the reasons why the Purchase Option System works so well is that it allows you to create multiple streams of income from your different properties. Because each property is a separate profit generator for you, you have the diversification that helps you weather financial storms. We're never going to tell you to get a second mortgage on your house to buy your first property, then take the equity in that house to leverage your way into your second investment property, and so forth. While that strategy has worked for many investors, we think it's risky. Investing that way is like setting up a line of dominoes (or in this case houses). If you have a problem with one house, you'll risk losing them all. You'll learn in Chapter 4 how to protect the money that you are making and to isolate each of your properties so that at worst you may lose one property, but never your whole portfolio. This is why Purchase Option investing is one of the safest long-term wealth-building strategies around.

■ Peter's Story

I remember back when I was an auto mechanic how I felt financially stressed all the time. For me, the best part about the money you can make in real estate isn't just the ability to buy things. The best part is the freedom it gives you. For the past year, I've been spending time at a local hospice helping out where I can. When you consider that the average patient stay is 10 to 14 days, it helps you get real clear on what is important in life. Everyone I talk with there says the same things: Life is about love; life is about growth; life is about family. I am so thankful for how real estate has provided me the means to focus in on these parts of my life. I know real estate investing can do the same for you.   ■

The Three Main Steps in All Purchase Option Deals

There are three main steps in all Purchase Option deals.

Step 1: Find a motivated seller. A motivated seller is a property owner whose sole aim in life at that moment is to get rid of his or her property. There are many reasons why sellers are motivated to sell, everything from financial problems, relationship breakups, tenant hassles, double payments, you name it. For the moment, what is important is that you understand that when you find and put together deals with motivated sellers, you are helping them win. Remember, for them their property is a problem, whether it's because of debt or distance, and they need your help in fashioning a win-win solution.

Step 2: Meet with that seller and structure a profitable deal. During this step you will learn to ask the questions that help the seller share his real needs with you. You'll use this information to work with the seller in dividing up the negotiating items so that you each come out ahead and feeling good about the deal.

Step 3: Find your end user for the property. Most times you'll sell your property on a rent-to-own basis to a tenant-buyer.

Now it's time to get started by learning five of the major Purchase Option buying strategies. You'll use these strategies to structure money-making deals with your sellers.

Five Purchase Option Buying Strategies

In this chapter, you'll learn all five of the Purchase Option buying strategies. You'll notice that all five of the strategies have the following four things in common:

1. Each of the strategies is designed so that you have none of your own money invested in the property. You're going to learn how to transact deals with no money down from your own pocket. And you'll learn about the best sources of funding to close your deals.

2. Each of the strategies is designed to limit your risks. In the real world, it's not just about the money you make, it's about the money you *keep*.

3. Each of the strategies allows you to have upside leverage. Upside leverage means that for every dollar you put into a deal you will get magnified results. But the best part of upside leverage is that you have at risk only the money and time you put into the deal. Because you'll rarely be signing personally on conventional bank loans, you don't have any negative leverage associated with the traditional ways of buying real estate.

4. Each of these strategies will work best when you're buying from a motivated seller. Great deals come from working with sellers who have a compelling reason to sell—fast.

One of the biggest myths in real estate is the age-old cliché that real estate is all about "location, location, location!" This is true, but it's only half the picture. Real estate is really about "motivation, motivation, motivation!" If you are negotiating with a nonmotivated seller who owns a home in the perfect beachfront location, are you really going to get a great deal on the property? Probably not. What about the seller who owns a home in a decent location, not the plush oceanfront setting of our nonmotivated seller, who is feeling the urgency to sell his home because he is moving in three weeks and his last buyer backed out? You are much more likely to get a good buy on this second home, not because of the location of the property but because of the motivation of the seller.

In our first book, *How to Create Multiple Streams of Income Buying Homes in Nice Areas with Nothing Down,* we shared 21 ways to find motivated sellers. We included the exact scripts you would need to use when you call up For Sale By Owner ads and rental property ads, five ways to network with real estate agents, and how to develop a profitable farm area. One of the most important areas we covered were the seven reasons why motivated sellers sell. When you understand the reasons why motivated sellers want out of their properties, it makes it much easier to find them. Here is a list of these seven reasons.

1. Relocation
2. Divorce and relationship problems
3. Financial difficulties
4. Tenant problems
5. Probate
6. Downsizing to a smaller home
7. Desire for a larger home

Spaced throughout Chapter 2 are many examples of how to find motivated sellers. Some of the techniques will be explicitly presented, and other techniques will be embedded in the case studies of deals that you'll be learning from.

But first, we want you to thoroughly understand five of the most important buying strategies for how to structure deals with motivated sellers. This is the "theory" behind the first half of any Purchase Option transaction—locking up the property under contract. You'll learn the "application" steps of how to do this in Chapter 3 (negotiating) and Chapter 4 (limiting risk). Then you'll learn how to complete the final part of a Purchase Option deal—finding a hungry tenant-buyer for your property—in Chapter 5.

The Four Biggest Barriers to Traditional Investing

Let's start from the beginning. What does it mean to buy an investment property the traditional way? You find a property, pay a substantial down payment, and finance the balance through a mortgage lender. Of course, to buy a property the traditional way, your lender is going to check three things. Do you have a down payment (for most investment properties you'll need 20 percent to 25 percent down)? Do you have good credit? And do you have a steady source of monthly income?

Let's just say you meet all three of these requirements. What do you do now that you've bought this property? If you are investing the traditional way, you find a renter for your property and manage it for the next 30 years until you own it free and clear. Of course, along the way, you deal with the showings, rent collection, maintenance, renter evictions, and all the other hassles of managing rental properties.

Still, in the long run, you will end up building a great deal of long-term equity in your property, both from paying down the loan over the 30 years and also from the appreciation of the property over time. If you did nothing more than buy five to ten properties and then manage them for the next 30 years, you would become a millionaire. It is a sure road to wealth.

Yet when faced with these realities, traditional real estate investing scares many investors away for four main reasons.

Barrier 1: Need for a Large Down Payment

Even if you do have the money for your down payment, if you keep putting 20 percent to 25 percent down on every investment house you buy, pretty soon your pool of liquid capital will dry up. in the lingo of the business, you will become very "property rich, but cash poor."

Barrier 2: High Risk

The more money you have tied up in a deal, the greater your risk is in that transaction. Obviously, if you have $75,000 invested in a property, you can't just walk away from the deal if things don't go well. You are tied to that deal. In investing, the best course of action is to keep your upfront investment as low as possible. If you are able to keep your upfront investment at zero, then your risk is minimized in a very important way.

Barrier 3: Negative Cash Flow

Properties have appreciated in value over 6.7 percent per year in the United States over the last 35 years. While property values have shot up, rental rates just have not kept pace, which means most investors in the first three to seven years of owning a rental property have to deal with negative cash flow.

For homes in the lower income areas, investors can rent them out and create positive cash flows, but then they have to deal with the management headaches associated with investing in these types of homes. In the past, when you wanted to invest in the middle and upper-middle income homes and wanted to leverage your way into the properties, you thought you had little choice but to cover the negative cash flow yourself each month in the early years in order to enjoy the big payoff in the end.

But now, it doesn't have to be that way. In this book, you are going to learn how you can control homes in nice areas and have a breakeven or *positive* cash flow right from the very start. You'll accomplish this by getting above-market rents for your properties by selling them on a rent-to-own basis and by also locking in below-market payments because you're buying intelligently from motivated sellers.

Barrier 4: The Landlord Trap

We've already highlighted this. For every investor who acquires a large number of properties, there is a point at which that investor falls prey to the Landlord Trap. This is the point where the investor is so busy maintaining and managing his or her properties that he or she doesn't have the time to go out and buy more.

As an investor, you make your money by buying and selling properties. When you use your pen to write an agreement to buy or sell a property, you are making a lot of money. But when you fall prey to the Landlord Trap and put down your pen in favor of a hammer or a paintbrush, your income plummets.

Even if you don't do the fix-up and management work yourself, you still have to hire someone else to do it. You will be spending your precious time to oversee the process and to make sure that what you are paying for is getting done right. Your income will take a big hit. Smart investors understand that they make their biggest profits as investors, not as property managers.

Considering all four barriers, it is no wonder that so many people get stuck not knowing how to get started investing in real estate. They know it's a good thing. They have seen many people make their fortunes investing in properties. But in the past, these barriers have made it tough for them to launch their investing business.

Not any longer! It's now time for you to learn how to remove these barriers as you get started buying homes in nice areas with nothing down.

Purchase Option Buying Strategy One: The Lease Option—How to Buy Homes in Nice Areas with Nothing Down

Without question, the single most important of the five Purchase Option buying strategies is the lease option. If you were only able to master one of the five strategies, this one would be the most important. Currently, approximately 50 percent of all the deals we do are lease options. This is the easiest and simplest of the buying strategies. Plus, it is probably the lowest-risk way to get started in real estate investing.

Once you thoroughly understand how the basic structure of this Purchase Option strategy works, we will then explore the other four ways to structure deals. Our goal is to have you learn how to combine the best of the tried-and-true methods of the past with cutting-edge techniques, resulting in a proven success formula.

The Lease Option Simplified

Have you ever seen a rent-to-own store? Did you know that you could walk into that store and buy a brand-new big-screen TV? All you need to do is make nice, easy monthly payments and, in a few years, you will own that TV. Of course, in the long run you will end up paying between two and three *times more* for that TV than if you paid cash up front.

And you know about the latest way of getting a new car—leasing to own. You simply make a small down payment and then each month you make an easy lease payment. At the end of your lease period (usually three or five years), you have the option to buy that car for X dollars more. Or you can simply hand back the keys and go find another car, if you choose. Of course, if you buy the car on these lease-to-own plans, you will end up paying more for it than if you had purchased it for all cash up front.

Why do people pay more for something on a rent-to-own basis? They are paying a premium for the easy financing with which they are then able to own that item. What most people don't know is that you can do the exact same thing with real estate! Just by controlling a property and changing the terms with which you make it available to a new buyer, you instantly increase the value of that property.

You are going to be using the rent-to-own concept, which has been around for many years, in a new way—with real estate. You are going to be a matchmaker, matching up a motivated seller and a hungry tenant-buyer. And by helping both these people get what they want, you are going to get paid handsomely for your efforts.

Remember, your motivated seller is someone who has a compelling reason to get rid of his or her house quickly. Your tenant-buyer is someone who desperately wants to own his or her own home but for one reason or another can't qualify to buy a home in the traditional way right now. Remember the three things you need to buy a home traditionally—a large down payment, good credit, and adequate monthly income? Well, your tenant-buyer is someone who is lacking in one or more of these key areas. Your tenant-buyers figure that while they can't buy right now, down the road, after they clean up their credit or get an increase in salary, they will be able to qualify for a new loan and buy in the traditional way.

Let's walk through a hypothetical example of what we are talking about to make things easy to understand.

Sam Seller is a motivated seller. He was transferred three months ago to a new city. The job is a great career move, with an increase in pay and prestige. The problem for Sam Seller is that he hasn't been able to sell his house yet. He tried listing it with a real estate agent for three months, and he just couldn't sell it. Now he is faced with moving in just three weeks.

His options are either to slash the price of the house for a quick sale, something he is hesitant to do, or he can rent it out until he can find a buyer. But then he would have to either manage the property *long distance* or hire a *property manager* and pay him or her to manage the property—typically 8 percent to 10 percent of the monthly rent—with no guarantee that he won't have a vacancy for several weeks or months at a time.

That's where you come in. As a Purchase Option investor, you are able to help solve Sam Seller's problem. You come in and agree to rent out Sam Seller's house for six years for the amount of his payments. At the same time, you agree upon a price at which you can buy the house at any time you choose over that six-year period. This is called a "lease option" or a "lease purchase" and it is the foundational strategy of the Purchase Option system and the first of the five Purchase Option strategies you are learning in this book.

Take a moment, and look at Figure 2.1, and see exactly what you have done. Sam Seller's payments on the house are $1,300 a month, which includes principle, interest, real estate taxes, and insurance. You will cover this amount so that Sam Seller will have no costs associated with his property over the period in which you control it before you purchase it.

As for the price, to show you how you can pay the seller top dollar and still make money for yourself, you have agreed to pay the seller close to full market value for the property. In this case, the seller was asking $190,000, and you negotiated the price down to $180,000. After all, you tell the seller, he will pay no real estate commission. In Chapter 3, you'll learn exactly how to use this strategy and several others to get the price down without having to wrestle with the seller.

FIGURE 2.1 Your Lease-Option Deal with Sam Seller

You, the Investor		
Motivated Seller		**Hungry Tenant-Buyer**
$ 1,300	**Rent**	
$180,000	**Price**	
6 years	**Term**	
$ 2,000	**Payment**	

Total Profits:

With Purchase Option investing, you can offer the seller a healthy price and still make a large profit for yourself. Obviously, if you are a good negotiator and are able to bring that price down lower, then you will end up making even more money. So you are locking in the price at or below today's value for a long period of time. As that property appreciates, you will capture the future appreciation as one part of your profit in each deal.

If you are in an area with slower appreciation, or even *no* appreciation, you simply negotiate harder on price. Let's face it: If you are talking with a motivated seller in a stagnant market, the seller will have little choice but to be flexible on price. The most attractive feature of the deal is that you only make part of your profit from the difference of the price you lock up the property at and the price you sell it at. Later, you'll learn about hidden profit opportunities, cash flow, and forfeited option payments you keep from your buyers.

What Does It Take in Upfront Money?

Now, if you are like the students we work with across the country, you will probably be able to lock up the property without giving the seller any upfront money. Actually, you will give the seller $1 upfront as "legal consideration" to make your agreement binding.

■ David's Story

Four years ago, we issued a promotional challenge to show all the naysayers out there that you could, in fact, buy property without giving sellers big money up front. We said, "Send us to any city in the United States with a group of beginning investors, and over a three-day period we'll help each of these beginning investors buy or control a minimum of $250,000 worth of real estate using none of their own money." From December 8th through December 10th, we traveled to San Diego. Over the three days we didn't just meet our goal . . . we doubled it! We were able to lock up over $1.5 million dollars worth of real estate with only $37 upfront money!

All totaled, we locked up ten separate properties ranging in value from $60,000 to $500,000. On three of the houses, we gave the seller $10 as "good and valuable consideration" and on the other seven houses we gave them $1. Peter says we were just being frugal. I call it being cheap!

The point is that it doesn't take money to control properties. What it really takes is a motivated seller, a little imagination, patience in structuring the deal, and the know-how to sell the property on the other end.   ■

But let's say in our hypothetical example the seller won't do the deal unless he gets at least $2,000 upfront.

Wait a second, you say. You haven't got $2,000! Just hang in there because in a moment you are going to learn where you are going to find this money. And here's a hint for you—it won't be from your wallet or purse!

Let's get clear on exactly what you and Sam Seller have agreed upon. You have agreed to rent out the property for six years for the amount of the monthly payments of $1,300. You have also agreed on a price of $180,000 at which you can buy the property at any point over the next six years. In essence, you have negotiated a lease with the option to buy.

As for the $2,000 of upfront money, you are going to tell your motivated seller, "Sam Seller, I will give you the $2,000 as soon as I take occupancy of the property or find someone to occupy the property." You'll see in just a moment why it is critical for you to add this part into your agreement because it will be essential in your funding of this deal.

The Best Source of Funding for Your Nothing-Down Deals

Here is the secret to doing nothing-down deals: Nothing down does *not* mean "nothing" to the seller. Nothing down means none of *your* money to the seller. The distinction is critical. Your motivated seller may get money up front—it just won't be your money! The best way to fund any money you need to get into the deal is by using a tenant-buyer's money. In our hypothetical example, your tenant-buyers are the Byers.

The Byers are a young couple who have two children. They have good credit; however, because their current income isn't high enough, they can't qualify for the mortgage on a house this nice, yet. The Byers know that when Mrs. Byers goes back to work (she has been staying home with the children who will both be in school full-time soon) their income will be high enough to qualify for a mortgage to buy a house like this.

You are able to help the Byers by letting them rent to own the house. The Byers will rent out the property from you with an

---

FIGURE 2.2   Your Lease-Option Deal with Your Tenant-Buyers—The Byers

---

You, the Investor

Motivated Seller		Hungry Tenant-Buyer
	$200/month	
$ 1,300	**Rent**	$ 1,500
	$19,900	
$180,000	**Price**	$199,900
6 years	**Term**	2 years
$ 2,000	**Payment**	$ 8,000

Total Profits:

---

option to purchase at a price you have set in advance. Take a close look at Figure 2.2 to see exactly how these numbers fit into place.

In this example, the Byers are going to rent the property from you for two years. (You'll soon learn there is a specific reason you always want a longer term with your motivated seller than with your tenant-buyer.) The current market rent for a house like this in the area is $1,400. But this property isn't just a rental property, it is a rent-to-own property. A rent-to-own property usually commands a premium over the current market rent because of the advantage of the easy financing it offers a future buyer. This means the Byers willingly pay you above-market rent. In this case, they pay you $1,500 a month in rent.

You also agree with the Byers on a price at which they can purchase the property at any point over the next two years. Because you want this to be a win for the Byers too, you set the price at *less* than the house will be worth in two years.

If the house appreciates at just 5 percent per year, then in one year it will be worth $199,500. After two years, the house will be worth $209,475. (We are leaving the money-making effects of compounding out of the equation to keep the concept simple.) You are going to let the Byers have a purchase price of just $199,900.

Because of this value you are giving the Byers, they will pay you 3 percent to 5 percent of the value of the property as an upfront payment (technically called an "option payment"). In this case, you collect $8,000 from the Byers up front as their option payment on the property. This money gets credited toward the purchase price if they decide to buy. If they choose not to buy the house, it is yours to keep for allowing them to lock in their option to purchase and tie up the property for two years. It is *nonrefundable*.

After a year or two, the Byers will be able to get a new loan from their mortgage lender and cash out both you and the motivated seller, Sam Seller. In essence, that's how the system works.

Remember the $2,000 you owe Sam Seller, the motivated seller? Where do you think you are going to get it? That's exactly right! You are going to take the $8,000 cashier's check you collect from the Byers, deposit it, and give $2,000 of it to Sam Seller. What happens to the remaining $6,000? You get to keep it. By the way, as an option payment this money is nontaxable until the year in which your tenant-buyers either exercise or quit their option to purchase.

You might think this is a nothing-down deal, but it's not. It's better than that. This is a nothing-down deal with an extra $6,000 that goes into your pocket.

Let's add up your profits. See Figure 2.3. Each month you are earning $200 in cash flow. Over 24 months, that adds up to $4,800. You are buying the house for $180,000, and the Byers are paying you $199,900 for it. So you make an additional $19,900 from the spread in the sale prices. All totaled, you will earn $24,700 from this Purchase Option deal.

FIGURE 2.3   Adding Up the Profits

You, the Investor

Motivated Seller		Hungry Tenant-Buyer
	$200/month	
$ 1,300	**Rent**	$ 1,500
	$19,900	
$180,000	**Price**	$199,900
6 years	**Term**	2 years
$ 2,000	**Payment**	$ 8,000

Total Profits:
From Cash Flow: 24 months × $200/month = $ 4,800
From Price Spread: +19,900
Your Total Profits: $24,700

The Biggest Difference between Purchase Option Investing and Traditional Investing

Imagine you were buying an investment property the traditional way. You would negotiate a price with a seller, put a large chunk of your cash down, and sign personally on a bank loan for the balance.

Once you closed on this house, you would start to hope. You'd hope that you would be able to find a renter. You'd hope that you would be able to rent it out for more than your monthly payment. You'd hope that you wouldn't have any major repairs to take care of. You'd hope for a lot of things. And then you would wait and see how you would do over time.

The biggest difference between Purchase Option and traditional real estate investing is that you know what you are going to do *before* you move ahead with the deal. What we mean is: With Purchase Option investing you never make a final commitment to a deal with a seller until you have *presold* the house to your tenant-buyer. This way you don't have to worry about how you are going to make those $1,300 a month payments to Sam Seller. You know how you'll do it because you'll have already collected cash in hand for the first month's rent of $1,500 and an option payment of $8,000 from your tenant-buyers, the Byers.

How can you do this? You will use a special "subject to" clause, which states that your agreement with the motivated seller is subject to your finding a qualified resident to occupy the property. In other words, your agreement is subject to your finding a qualified tenant-buyer. If you don't find your tenant-buyer, then you don't move ahead with the deal.

What you do when setting up a Purchase Option deal is to have both halves of the transaction complete before you ever fully commit to the deal. You find your motivated seller and lock up the property. Then you quickly go out and find your tenant-buyer. Then and only then, do you fully commit to moving ahead with the deal.

Here's the exact wording of the clause we use in our lease-option agreement with sellers that makes this possible. We call it "Clause Number Nine" (okay, so we aren't terribly original).

Clause 9: Qualified Resident: Because having a qualified resident to occupy the property is of the utmost importance to all parties, this agreement is subject to Buyer approving a qualified resident to occupy the property.

It seems so obvious to invest this way, but traditional investors don't. They do their best due diligence and then hope. Purchase Option investors don't leave it up to chance. They know that you can only be sure of a deal when you have already found your end buyer for the property who has given you cash in hand to hold the property.

Caution! When you use such a powerful "subject to" clause, you need to be respectful of the seller. You need to let them know right away if you are having any problems finding your tenant-buyers—within two to three weeks. Under no circumstances would you ever want to tie up a seller's property for several months and then tell them that you cannot find your tenant-buyer. That would be both unfair and wrong.

How to Sidestep the Landlord Trap

Unless you have a way to get out of the hassle of the day-to-day management of a property, you are still going to run into the Landlord Trap. Here is how you can safely sidestep the Landlord Trap and escape the hassles of tenants and toilets.

When you are talking with the motivated seller, you will say to him, "Sam Seller, to make this a real win for you, would you like me to take care of the day-to-day maintenance on the property? Why don't I take care of the first $200 of maintenance in any one month? That should take care of 98 percent of the problems. Would that work for you?"

Of course, the seller will be thrilled that you will be taking over the day-to-day upkeep on the property.

"But wait a minute," you say, "how does that get you out of the Landlord Trap?" Next, you go meet with your tenant-buyer. You tell your tenant-buyer, "Mr. Buyer, you're coming into this property as if you are the future owner. And we expect that you would treat the place as if you owned it. Of course, this means that you are going to be responsible for the maintenance on the property. But so that it's a win for you and so that you know that you won't have any major repairs that you are responsible for, let's put a limit on it. Let's see, why don't you take care of the first $200 in any one month and anything above that I'll see that it gets taken care of, okay?"

See how easy it was for you to sidestep the Landlord Trap? If a repair is needed and it costs over $200, who is responsible for the amount over $200? That's right, the seller is responsible. If a repair is needed that is less than $200, who is responsible for it? That's right, your tenant-buyer pays for it. What are you left responsible for? Well, you might have to coordinate some phone calls, but your tenant-buyer will be the one waiting at home for the plumber to come give them a bid. You get to sit in the middle, making money without 90 percent of the hassles of traditional rental real estate.

Of course, you do have other responsibilities. Each month you have to collect a check, deposit a check, and write a check. The beauty of the system is that once you have set up a property correctly and you collect a chunk of money up front, for the most part you have a hands-off residual stream of income that flows to you each and every month. Then at the end of a period of time, you get a large payday when your tenant-buyer gets his own loan on the property, cashing both you and the motivated seller out of the deal.

What Happens If Your Tenant-Buyer Doesn't Buy?

Without question, the biggest fear new Purchase Option investors have is: What happens if my tenant-buyer doesn't exercise the option and buy the property? Remember, the tenant-buyer has the *option* to buy the property, not the obligation to buy.

We can certainly understand the concern. After all, it sure seems that if the tenant-buyer doesn't buy, then we are going to lose out. This just isn't so. Not only are you still in a very secure position, but if your tenant-buyer doesn't buy, you're probably going to make a whole lot *more* money—often twice as much!

Here is exactly why. First, if your tenant-buyer decides not to buy, what happens to their nonrefundable option payment? That's right, you get to keep it. Plus, because the house was a rent-to-own home, you probably have been enjoying a healthy cash flow from the above-market rents they have been paying you. You get to keep the monthly streams of cash flow you have been collecting. Not a bad situation considering the tenant-buyer has been taking care of the property because they had planned to buy it.

Remember that you learned to arrange your lease with the motivated seller for a *longer* period than you do with your tenant-buyer. You will have at least one more year, and usually more, to find a new tenant-buyer and collect another upfront option payment. And because the property has probably appreciated in value, you can get a larger option payment, higher rent, and negotiate a higher sale price!

Let's make this point absolutely clear by going back to our earlier example. You signed a Purchase Option agreement with Sam Seller, your motivated seller, for a maximum term of six years. Your purchase price was $180,000, and your monthly rent was $1,300. You found your tenant-buyers, the Byers, who were paying you $1,500 a month in rent, gave you $8,000 in upfront money as their option payment, and agreed to the $199,900 sale price. Their term was two years. Two years later the Byers decide not to exercise their option; i.e., they decide not to buy the house. What happens now?

You keep the $4,800 from monthly cash flow and the $8,000 option payment. Remember that you have already given $2,000 of the option payment to your motivated seller, Sam Seller, which left you with $6,000. Then you go out and find a second tenant-buyer. See Figure 2.4.

If the property had only appreciated by 5 percent per year for each of the two years of the term, it is now worth $209,475. So, of course, you collect a slightly larger option payment from your second tenant-buyer and you charge a slightly higher monthly rent. Doesn't it make sense that the rent should increase after two years? By the end of this second two-year term, if the house continues to appreciate at just 5 percent it will be worth over $230,000. In this case, you'll set your price with your second tenant-buyer at $219,900.

FIGURE 2.4 What Happens If Your First Tenant-Buyer Doesn't Buy and You Sell to a Second Tenant-Buyer

You, the Investor

Motivated Seller		Hungry Tenant-Buyer
	$200/month	
$ 1,300	**Rent**	$ 1,500
	$39,000	
$180,000	**Price**	$219,900
6 years	**Term**	2 years
$ 2,000	**Payment**	$ 8,000

Total Profits:
From Your First Tenant-Buyer:

From Option Money:	$ 6,000	($8,000 – $2,000 to Seller)
From Cash Flow:	+ 4,800	
Total from First Tenant-Buyer:	$10,800	

From Your Second Tenant-Buyer:

Cash Flow:	$ 4,800
Price Spread:	+39,900
Total Profit:	$55,500

To make sure you have understood the concept, let's say you wanted to find your second tenant-buyer fast. So you advertised the property and didn't raise the rent. You charged only $1,500 a month in rent, which by now was *below* market rent. And you only collected another $8,000 of option money up front from your tenant-buyer. Then you sit back and collect those fat monthly checks from the property.

You get to enjoy a positive cash flow of $200 a month for another two years and ride the appreciation curve up on an asset you do not own, haven't signed personally on a loan for, and have zero maintenance responsibilities for. How's that for a great deal?

And if your second tenant-buyer doesn't buy, you find a third tenant-buyer. By now the house would be priced at over $230,000 and your original sale price is still just $180,000! Again you bump up your rent, you bump up your sale price, and you collect another nonrefundable option payment. See how good it can be when your tenant-buyer decides not to buy?

You might be wondering, what happens if your third tenant-buyer decides not to buy as well? Again, this is still okay for you. Here's why: You have enjoyed a total of six years of positive cash flow and collected and kept over $24,000 of option money (three option payments of $8,000 minus the $2,000 you gave to the motivated seller). You are well ahead of the game. At this point, you have earned $36,400 from the property.

You could tell the owner of the property that you do *not* want to buy the property. Remember that you also had the *option* to purchase the property, not the obligation.

You could simply give the home back to the original owner. In that case, you would have profited by the monthly cash flow and the three option payments. As for Sam Seller, he will put you on his holiday card list for the rest of his life! Why? Well, instead of buying the house for $180,000, you gave him back a property that is worth $255,000 (assuming that 5 percent appreciation rate) that you looked after for the past six years. Do you think Sam Seller is going to mind that you are giving him back $75,000 in equity? Of course not!

Before you do that, though, let us suggest an alternate plan for you. You have a $255,000 house that you can buy for $180,000. Make sure you have a "90-Day Notification Clause" in your option agreement with your tenant-buyer. This clause says that your tenant-buyer has to give you a minimum of 90 days written notice that they want to buy the house. If your third tenant-buyer does not buy, this clause gives you a full three months notice to sell the property to another buyer.

Do you think that even on your worst day you could sell a $255,000 house for more than $180,000? Even if you just sold it for just $215,000, a $40,000 discount in price for a fast sale, you would still make $71,400–$36,400 from your first three tenant-buyers and $35,000 from your quick sale of the property.

So you see, if your tenant-buyer buys, you win. If your tenant-buyer doesn't buy, you win bigger! That's the power of Purchase Option investing. You cash in on the three big benefits of owning property without the risks of traditional real estate investing.

What if the market had taken a downturn and the property had gone down in value? If you had bought the property with bank financing, you would be stuck. But because you controlled the property through a lease option, you just wouldn't exercise your option to purchase. In all likelihood, you would go back to the sellers and renegotiate for more time. If you had made all your payments to the sellers on time, the chances are very good that they will give you that extension. What alternative do they really have? Besides, you would have looked after the house for six years during which time the loan would have paid down a nice bit. If the house continues to generate cash flow, you simply choose to stay in the deal longer. If the cash flow dries up, you turn the property back over to the seller. It's our opinion that you should do everything in your power to remain in the deal so that you can still handle the property for the owner. We feel strongly that this is the right thing to do.

How Lease Options Work in the Real World

Let's go over a couple more examples to show exactly how the lease option method works in the real world. Mark and Trish, two of our students in California, found a motivated seller of a four-bedroom house in an upscale suburban neighborhood. The seller called Mark and Trish after she saw their "I Buy Houses!" sign posted near the side of a road. It turned out that the seller's mother was sick, and the seller was moving in to care for her. The seller just didn't want to get stuck with making payments on their soon-to-be empty $255,000 house. Mark and Trish agreed on a three-year lease option for a price of $235,000, a monthly rent of $1,500, and with $1 paid as option consideration. Yes, Mark and Trish did in fact hand the seller a dollar when they signed up the deal—it's an important formality to make the agreement legally binding.

The neighborhood the property was in had appreciated at over 14 percent for the previous two years. Mark and Trish spent a weekend doing some cleaning and landscape work to the backyard then turned around and sold the house on a rent-to-own basis. They found a tenant-buyer who bought the property from them on a two-year lease option with $15,000 in option money, monthly rent of $1,850, and a purchase price of $295,000. See Figure 2.5. All totaled, they made over $68,000 from this deal.

Another one of our students, Jim, also found a great opportunity. Jim is a soft-spoken architect in Colorado. After a month of frustration over not finding his first deal, Jim met the seller of a vacant condo. The seller was trying to rent the condo, and Jim had called him after seeing his For Rent ad in the local paper.

When they met, they hit it off from the start. The seller was an experienced investor who had struggled to find a renter for the property. It had been vacant for the past two months. The condo was a ground floor unit in an upscale complex and was worth $240,000 to $250,000. Jim and the seller agreed on a three-year lease option with a price of $240,000 and a rent of $1,095. Jim remarked later that when he got home and showed Susan, his wife, the signed deal, she couldn't believe it because he had only met with the seller for an hour.

Jim sold the property to his tenant-buyers, a couple who had just moved to Colorado. Adding up the cash flow, option payment, and remaining profit when his tenant-buyer bought the condo, Jim made $28,000 from this deal.

FIGURE 2.5   Mark and Trish's Three-Year Lease-Option Deal

You, the Investor

Motivated Seller		Hungry Tenant-Buyer
	$350/month	
$ 1,500	**Rent**	$ 1,850
	$60,000	
$235,000	**Price**	$295,000
3 years	**Term**	2 years
$1	**Payment**	$ 15,000

Total Profits:
From Cash Flow: 24 months × $350/month = $ 8,400
From Price Spread: +60,000
Your Total Profits: $68,400

Our final lease option example is a four-year lease option that John, a student of ours in Seattle, Washington, found. Oddly enough, he negotiated most of this deal via e-mail. He found the lead by calling a property advertised in his local newspaper. The seller had just gotten a promotion at her job and had moved closer to her office. Her old house was now about a two-hour drive away! John and the seller went back and forth via e-mail until they reached this deal: a four-year lease option for a price of $180,000.

When John sold the property on a rent-to-own basis, he got 164 inquiries from his ads and handmade signs. He ended up choosing caller number 88. He collected $5,000 option money and sold the property on a two-year rent-to-own basis for a price of $209,980. All totaled, John made over $34,000 of locked-in profits on the deal.

We're hoping, by now, the way the numbers work out on lease option deals are making sense to you. Again, the basic concept is that you are working as that matchmaker to find two halves of a deal. By helping your motivated seller solve his problem, and by helping your tenant-buyers get into a house before they technically get to own it, you are creating great value and being well paid for it. Before we go on to the next Purchase Option strategy, we wanted to share with you one more way to make money from these types of deals.

Find Extra Profit in Every Deal You Do!

There is hidden profit for you in every lease option deal you put together. Most investors miss out on this extra profit simply because they do not have the specialized knowledge contained in this book.

Remember back in Chapter 1 where we talked about why real estate was such a powerful investment? We discussed amortization, or loan pay down, as one of the benefits of owning property. What many investors don't know is that they can reap this benefit provided they know five magic words. We'll get to these words in just a moment. First, we want to make sure you're clear on what this means to you.

Let's say you have a four-year lease option on a house at a $200,000 option price. The loan balance at the time you sign up the deal is $175,000. Hence the seller had $25,000 in equity. This equity is calculated by taking the option price of $200,000 and subtracting the total amount of the money owed against it which, in this case, was $175,000. Why all this fuss over figuring out the seller's equity at the start of the deal? Because when you resell the property to your tenant-buyer in three years, that $175,000 loan will no longer be that high. Depending on how old the loan is and a few other variables, the loan balance will be roughly $170,000. That means there is an extra $5,000 in this deal for someone! It's up to you whether you give this to the seller or keep this money for yourself. It's pretty obvious what *we* think you should do with the extra five grand.

The way that you make sure you get the amortization is by spelling out in your lease-option agreement with the sellers the exact amount of money they will get at the closing. In our above example, the seller is expecting to get his or her $25,000 equity at closing. You simply label this amount as "full payment for seller's equity." In fact, in our one-page residential lease-option agreement we have these five words *preprinted* in our agreement because we want to make sure we remember to write up the deal correctly. It's too easy in the confusion of signing up the deal to forget to calculate the seller's equity at the time of entering into the lease option and as a result forget to clearly contract this as the amount of money you will pay them if you exercise your option. In the above example, at an option price of $200,000 with the current loan balance of $175,000, you would specify that your $200,000 option price is payable as follows: $1 paid cash today, with $25,000 due at closing as full payment for seller's equity. At the closing, the lender gets paid in full and the seller gets $25,000 as full payment for the $30,000 of equity (remember, the loan had been paid down by $5,000). In most lease option deals, simply by doing your paperwork correctly, you'll make an extra $2,000 to $12,000 just from the amortization alone.

We know that you're probably wondering, "What if the seller objects to this?" In our experience, seven out of ten sellers don't care about the amortization. They know what their current equity is, the option price less what they owe, and they expect to get that at closing. Period. The other three out of ten will say something like, "But in four years my loan will have been paid down a few thousand dollars and I'll have more equity than $25,000."

Respond with, "Mr. Seller, of course the loan will be going down. That's one of the reasons we are willing to buy the property. I mean, after all, I am the one who is going to be making the monthly payments for all that time." You'll find most sellers will accept this reasoning. They recognize that if they sell the property, they weren't really expecting to get this money anyway. If you are negotiating with a tough seller, use this as a bargaining chip. Trade it for something else, like a longer term, lower rent, or a lower purchase price. Either way you are still getting a great deal.

■ Peter's Story

One of the houses we picked up on the San Diego Challenge was a three-bedroom, two-bath house. I was there with John Seitz, one of the three students we took with us, and he was writing up the five-year lease option on the house. I stopped him, made one change to the agreement, then let him finish the paperwork. That small change only took 30 seconds but made a huge difference.

Back in the car after we left the sellers John asked me why I had made the change. I asked, "John, do you remember the loan statement they showed us while we were standing in the kitchen?" John replied that he had.

I explained to John that the sellers had a 15-year loan on the property that was already several years old and that this meant that the amortization on the loan was a lot each month. "John, the statement showed that each month they make their $950 house payment they get $325 paid towards principal. Let's forget that this goes up each month and pretend it just stays the same. What's $325 multiplied by the 60 months we have the house under contract?"

John thought for a moment then burst out with the answer, "$19,500! Peter, we just made an extra $20,000 just because we changed a few words in the contract!

■

Purchase Option Buying Strategy Two: Equity Splits—How to "Partner Up" with Your Seller

What do you do when you come across a seller who is motivated to do a lease option with you but is not quite motivated enough to give up on all the future appreciation of the property? This is a perfect scenario in which to try using Strategy Two—the equity split.

An equity split is a way of doing a lease option with the seller of a property. But rather than giving the sellers a set price for their property down the road, you give them a set price *plus* a portion of your profits at the time you resell the property to a tenant-buyer.

Here is an example of how this might work. You find a seller who owns a rental house, and he is open to selling it to you on a two-year lease option. But he's just not motivated enough to give you a longer term. You ask him, "Mr. Seller, if there were a way we could get you your asking price of $180,000 plus a small percentage of the appreciation too in exchange for a bit more time, is this something you might be open to, or maybe not?"

The seller scratches his head and thinks for a moment. You negotiate back and forth for a while, and this is what you agree on: a six-year lease option for a purchase price of $180,000 with a monthly rent to the seller of $1,200. Plus, you also agree to give the seller 50 percent of any amount you resell the property for to your tenant-buyer above the $180,000. This is an equity split.

The seller gets all of the first $180,000, which is your option price, and half the amount you resell it for above this $180,000. Imagine that your tenant-buyer ends up buying it from you for $230,000. The seller gets $180,000 plus half of the $50,000 profit you made for a total payment to the seller of $205,000. You made $25,000 from the resale plus any cash flow from the spread between your tenant-buyer's rent and your rent to the seller.

Now there is no set rule that says you have to do a 50-50 equity split. You can negotiate the deal any way you want. If you want to negotiate a 60-40 equity split or a 75-25 equity split, it is up to what you and the seller can agree on.

Here is a key point: You are only splitting the money from the resale of the property. You get to keep all of the cash flow and all of the option money that is left if the tenant-buyers decide not to exercise their option. After all, you are the one who provided the expertise and effort to find and keep an eye on your tenant-buyers.

One of our mentorship students used an equity split on his very first deal. His name was Matt and he was a pilot for a large commercial airline company. At work, on the company bulletin board, Matt saw a For Sale By Owner flyer for a nice house. It turned out that the seller, who was also a pilot for the same airline, was several payments behind and headed toward foreclosure.

Matt met with him and saw that the seller had a nice home in a good area with a fair amount of equity in the property. Matt also saw that the owner was not going to be able to make up the back payments or continue to pay the lender each month even if he could find the money to cure the default.

Matt and the seller agreed to a four-year lease option with a 70-30 equity split. Matt paid the seller $7,000 up front, which went to the lender to bring the payments current, and he locked in an option price of $242,000—which was substantially *below* the market value for the property. In addition, Matt agreed to split the profits he made from this deal with the seller, with the seller getting 30 percent of anything Matt sold the property for above $242,000 and Matt getting the other 70 percent.

Matt then marketed the property and found his tenant-buyer who gave him a $15,000 option payment and agreed to pay him $2,000 in rent (which gave Matt a $250 per month positive cash flow). Matt's tenant-buyer had an option price of $322,000. It turned out that the seller Matt bought the place from was struggling financially, and Matt ended up buying him out for roughly an additional $20,000. That brought Matt's total investment in the house to $27,000, of which he got $15,000 from his tenant-buyer. So Matt had $12,000 of his cash tied up in this house that was generating at this point over $300 per month of cash flow. Plus, Matt no longer had to do the equity split with the seller! Eventually, Matt's tenant-buyer decided not to buy and Matt just got the house back. At that point, the house was worth over $320,000! Matt bought it for a total of $222,000, $27,000 paid in cash of which $12,000 was Matt's money and $15,000 was his tenant-buyer's money, and the rest was financed by the original owner using a strategy called buying "subject to the existing financing," which you will learn about in just a few pages. He's got close to $100,000 in profit from this one deal alone!

When we last spoke with Matt, he had gone on to do three other deals and was planning to use real estate to allow him to quit flying for a living and pursue his passion—teaching music.

The Hybrid Equity Split

Here is an advanced technique we teach our mentorship students to use to make up to an extra $25,000 or more on every equity split they do. It's called a "hybrid equity split," and we think you'll like this simple yet highly profitable technique and will want to add it to your investment toolbox.

The best way to understand the concept is to walk through an example of a deal we did with the owners of a two-bedroom, two-bath property. The sellers were motivated because the husband had been transferred in his job. When we met with them, we talked through doing an eight-year lease option on the property. Right at the very end they balked, and we pulled out this hybrid equity split idea to sweeten the deal just enough to close it.

The terms of the lease option were as follows: A term of eight years with a monthly rent of $913 and a purchase price of $102,000. The upfront option consideration we paid was $1.

Now, most investors would structure their equity split as follows: They would split with the seller on a 50-50 basis anything they as investors sold the property for over $102,000. For example, if they sold the property on a two-year rent-to-own basis for $120,000, they would give the seller the first $102,000 and split the remaining $18,000 profit 50-50. In other words, they would make $9,000 from the resale plus any cash flow the property generated over the two years.

The way we structured our hybrid equity split was as follows: We did the eight-year lease option as described above and agreed that we would also do an equity split on anything we resold the property for above $127,000. In other words, the first $25,000 in profit would be ours alone, and we would do the equity split on any amount above that.

By the way, why offer 50-50 to a seller when they will often have their needs met and will be thrilled with substantially less? We agreed they would get 12 percent of the amount we resold the property for over $127,000!

How did we get the seller to agree to this? We simply asked the seller, "Mrs. Seller, if there were a way where you would get your full $102,000 we talked about and on top of that you would get a chunk of the future appreciation from the resale of the property is that something we should talk about, or probably not?" (In Chapter 3 of this book, you will learn about the "negative phrasing" we used here.)

Once the seller says that she is in fact interested in talking about that, you simply go on to explain, "Well, I don't know if we could do this, but what if we set a percentage that you would get from the resale of the property? Obviously, we would need to build in a minimum base profit of $25,000 to make this worth our time, but what if we said that you'd get a part of anything we sold the property for down the road over $127,000? What I mean is that you would get all of the first $102,000, that's completely yours, and you would also get, let's say, 10 percent or maybe a little more of any amount we sold it for over $127,000. Is that something we should talk through, or probably not?"

Our seller agreed to this, after negotiating strongly to move the percentage from 10 percent to 12 percent. Notice she just accepted the $25,000 base profit. We then sold the property on a two-year rent-to-own basis with $3,000 nonrefundable option money, a rent of $1,000 per month, and a final price of $120,000.

Our tenant-buyer decided not to buy. When we checked the value of the condo prior to reselling it to a new tenant-buyer, we were thrilled to discover that the condo had jumped in value to $165,000. So we resold to our next tenant-buyer for $189,000 on a two-year rent-to-own basis.

Just remember to build in a base profit for yourself on any equity split deal you do. Even if it's only $10,000 or $15,000 before you split the rest of the money that is *pure* profit for no extra work.

Ultimately, the equity split and the hybrid equity split are both great ways to get the seller to "partner up" with you. When you negotiate these types of deals, the best part is that getting a long term is easy. After all, the longer your term, the more money you will both make and the seller won't have to do any of the work.

Make sure you don't offer an equity split to start off with. Why give away a portion of your profits if you don't have to? Save this new tool to use in those cases where you have a fit but need one last sweetener in the deal to make the seller say yes. As always, make sure you do so "reluctantly" using the Purchase Option negotiating language patterns outlined Chapter 3.

Purchase Option Buying Strategy Three: "Subject to" Purchases—How to Get Long-Term Bank Financing without Ever Talking to a Banker

Our third Purchase Option strategy is to use the existing financing on the property as a way to leverage yourself into the property. You will simply take title and take over making payments on the seller's existing financing without formally assuming the loan. This is called buying a property "subject to the existing financing" or simply "subject to" financing. Before we explain exactly how you'll do this, let's get clear on the five advantages of this buying strategy.

1. Tax Advantages

Because you'll actually own the property, you'll get all the tax benefits of ownership. You'll get all the write-offs like depreciation, property taxes, maintenance, management expenses, advertising costs to rent or sell the property, and the insurance premiums. Used correctly, all of these deductions will let you defer most, if not all, of the taxes you owe on your cash flow from the property.

2. No New Loan Costs

Because you are using the existing financing, you'll save all the costs associated with having to go out and get a brand new bank loan. Remember, when you borrow money from a bank, the monthly interest you pay is only *one* of the expenses. For example, on a $200,000 loan you'll often have to pay expenses such as the following:

- Points (i.e., prepaid interest)
- Loan origination fee
- Appraisal fee
- Loan application fee
- Lender's title insurance policy
- Escrow fee
- Pest inspection and certification fee
- Document preparation fee
- Recording fees
- Courier fees

These expenses could add up to an additional $3,000 to $6,000 just for the privilege of getting bank funding. When you use the existing financing you will save all of this money!

3. No Need to Qualify

Because you won't be formally assuming the existing financing, you won't have to qualify with the bank. Because the loan is already in place, you won't need to spend hours getting together all the pieces for your loan application. There will be no tax returns to gather; no W-2s to sort through. You benefit from all the work your seller did years ago when he or she filled out all the bank's paperwork to get the original mortgage!

And your credit isn't an issue! Because you're going to be using the seller's loan, the bank will never run a credit report on you. This means that no matter what your credit is like, you can still use this buying strategy. And because the loan won't be in your name, it won't appear on your credit report lowering your credit scores if you should ever be applying for a loan on a different property.

4. No Personal Liability on the Financing

Because you won't be assuming the loan—more on this in a moment—and will simply be taking over the seller's payments, you will have no responsibility on the loan to the bank. Of course, you will make sure you make the payment on time every month. Imagine how much easier you'll sleep at night knowing that your assets and your credit are safe from harm should the unthinkable happen.

5. Better Interest Rates

Because many properties you'll buy using this strategy will be owner-occupied, you'll benefit from the great interest rates banks offer to owner occupants. Remember, banks typically lend money to owner occupants at 1 percent to 2 percent lower interest than they do to investors. The reason for this is simple to understand: Banks have determined that the default ratio of nonowner-occupied houses, investor property, is higher than owner-occupied houses. Lower risk for the bank means owner occupants get better interest rates.

■ **David's Story**

There have been houses I've bought using the "subject to" financing technique where I took over the payments on loans with interest rates of 7.5 percent or lower at a time when the best investor loans had an interest rate of 9 percent! The lower rate meant that I made several hundred dollars more in cash flow each month from the same property with no more work.   ■

Now that you see all the good things you get from using this strategy, let us explain exactly what it is and how you'll use it. Imagine you meet with a seller who is two payments behind on his mortgage and heading toward foreclosure. He has a little bit of equity but not a lot. You and the seller agree that he'll deed you the property, you'll make up the back payments, and then take over making the payments each month from there on out. You are *not* going to assume the loan; you are simply going to start sending the seller's lender money each month. You will own the property "subject to" the existing financing. This means you are on the title but your claim to the property comes second to that of any of the loans of record, e.g., the first mortgage.

In essence, what you have done is leverage yourself into the property by leaving the existing financing in place. If the seller's loan is for $100,000, then you are using $100,000 of the bank's money from a loan the seller qualified for and signed personally on to add a new property to your portfolio.

Can you really just take over the payments like this? Absolutely! It's called buying a property "subject to the existing financing," and it is a very powerful Purchase Option strategy. This is a perfectly legal and ethical way to buy property that is commonly used in the industry by expert investors. In fact, in most state Board-of-REALTOR®-

approved contracts there is even a box to check off if you are using "subject to" financing. And if you talk with most experienced real estate attorneys, they will have drafted "subject to" contracts for their clients on many occasions.

This strategy has known pitfalls, which we'll discuss in just a moment, but first we want you to get clear on the concept by re viewing a few examples.

One of our students in Oregon bought a small three-bedroom house in a working class neighborhood using this strategy. The sellers called her classified ad in the newspaper because the husband was having health problems and was unable to work. The couple, therefore, wanted to move closer to the wife's office. The house was worth about $70,000 to $75,000, and the sellers owed $60,000. Our student went back and forth with the sellers and finally agreed to buy the property right then and there with the stipulation that she would start taking over the sellers' payments that month. Normally we recommend that you give yourself at least 30 days before you start taking over the sellers' payments, if possible, to give yourself time to find a tenant-buyer to start making your payments.

The sellers were so thrilled with this deal that they gave our student two bottles of homemade wine as she left their house that day. Our student got the property for $1 subject to the existing $60,000 first mortgage, and she agreed to make that month's mortgage payment even though it took her about three weeks to find a tenant-buyer for the property. The sellers were more than happy to walk away from the property and the $10,000 to $15,000 in equity they had just to be rid of the problem they didn't really want to deal with.

Here's another example of a "subject to" financing deal. We got a call from an ad we were running to attract motivated sellers. This seller, Mary, was two months behind on her payments and headed toward foreclosure. We set up a time to meet with her and drove over to the property. From the outside, the house looked average. The structure looked good, the paint was fair, but there was a lot of "stuff" in the yard that hurt the curb appeal. When we walked into the house, the first thing that hit us was the smell—a strong pet odor permeated the air. It seemed that Mary had the world's largest private zoo!

She had three large dogs, a 19-year-old pigeon, a desert tortoise, and the kicker—a 350-pound pig named "Jodie." Now the pig was a whole lot cleaner and well behaved than the dogs! To make matters worse, she had boxes of "stuff" stacked in every corner and in every hallway. The house was in good structural shape, but between the smell and the crammed feeling, there was no way a retail buyer would ever buy this house as it was.

Strange as it seems, houses that smell can be a good thing. Retail buyers will rarely look past it because it hits them at an emotional level. But you as an investor know that in many cases it is very easy to cure a bad smell simply repainting and recarpeting. That's easy. Remember, we don't do rehab projects because we just don't like them. But we don't mind repainting and recarpeting a house because it's so fast and easy. It just takes two phone calls, very little money, and it *immediately* increases the value of the property. They are what we call leveraged repairs, where for every $1 you spend on the repair you instantly increase the value of the property $3 to $5!

We sat down with Mary and talked through her situation. It turned out that she didn't have enough income to afford the house. At one point we asked what she would do if we didn't buy the house from her. The way we worded this question was, "Mary, just in case we decide that we don't want to buy the house, what is your Plan B? We mean, we want to know what your second option is so that in case we don't want to buy the house at least we can help give you input to make your plan B a little better."

Mary's answer was bleak, "I don't have a Plan B. If you don't buy it, I'll just give it back to the bank." We sat and talked through the financial details of the property with Mary for about an hour. We discovered that she owed $65,000 against the house which if it was cleaned up was worth about $125,000. So she had a big chunk of equity. But if it was sold in a foreclosure sale, the bank would never

---

FIGURE 2.6   Summary of our "Subject to" Financing Transaction with Mary

Value of the House after It Was Cleaned Up:	$125,000
First Mortgage:	<65,000>
Back Payments Owed:	<3,000>
Cost to Paint/Clean/Recarpet:	<2,000>
New Owner Carry 2nd Mortgage:	<15,000>
Total Equity from Start:	40,000
Estimated costs if we immediately retailed house:	
(e.g., real estate commission, holding costs, etc.)	<10,000>
Our Net Profit:	$ 30,000

---

bother to fix it up first. They had no reason to. They would simply force the sale of the property in its current condition without doing any of the cosmetic work. But in its current condition the only one who would buy the property would be an investor, and that would mean that they would pay the absolute minimum they could. This would probably leave Mary not only with a foreclosure on her credit report but with nothing left at all of her equity.

We asked Mary, "What if we were able to step in and buy the property. We would make up the back payments and take over making the payments every month thereafter. We would also be able to give you something for the equity you have. Obviously, as investors, we are going to need to make a profit so we can't pay you top dollar, but what if we gave you $15,000. We would give you $1,000 at the end of each 12 months as an interest-only payment and pay off the $15,000 within five years of us buying the place. Is this something that would work for you, or probably not?" Mary said yes right away. She was thrilled at the prospect of avoiding foreclosure and that she would get something for her equity. See Figure 2.6.

We quickly had the house repainted, recarpeted, and cleaned. We now had a house that was worth $125,000 that we bought for $85,000. We could turn around and sell it to a retail buyer, and after you take into account closing costs and holding costs and any real estate commissions paid to a realtor (buyer's side costs, if needed) we could net about $30,000. Would you like to make more than this $30,000? We did so when we sold the house on a rent-to-own basis as detailed in Figure 2.7.

All totaled, by selling the house on a rent-to-own basis we made an extra $32,260. Plus, we got the tax write-offs for two years, the loan pay down profit of an extra $3,000, and if our tenant-buyer doesn't buy, we now have a house that is worth $145,000 that we can sell to a second tenant-buyer for even more money. As a matter of fact, with all the loan pay down profit and the hands-off cash flow, we wouldn't really care if we never sold this property.

■ **Peter's Story**

I remember this house in Texas we bought subject to the existing financing. The seller had owned it for less than 18 months and had only a few thousand dollars in equity. He was willing to just walk away from the property for a cash payment of roughly $1,000!   ■

The Three Biggest Pitfalls of Buying "Subject to" Financing and How to Sidestep Them

While there are many fine points that you need to be aware of in any real estate deal, buying a property subject to the existing financing has three pitfalls that are so important that we will now cover each of them in turn. We'll also share with you the best ways we've found to sidestep these three known pitfalls so that you can invest with as little risk as possible.

Pitfall 1: The due on sale clause. The single biggest pitfall of buying properties subject to the existing financing is an often-overlooked clause in the seller's loan documents called a "due on sale" clause. This clause is inserted by the seller's lender to protect the lender's interests. It says that if the seller who borrowed money from them ever sells the property, then the lender has the

FIGURE 2.7   Summary of Mary's House Tenant-Buyer Transaction

You, the Investor

Motivated Seller		Hungry Tenant-Buyer
	$140/month	
$ 760	**Rent**	$ 900
	$58,900	
$ 85,000	**Price**	$143,900
Lifetime (we own it)	**Term**	2 years
$ 5,000	**Payment**	$ 4,500

Total Profits:
Cash flow: 24 months × $140/month = $ 3,360
Price Spread: +58,900
Total Profits: $62,260

right to "accelerate" the loan and call due the entire unpaid balance. This sounds many times more scary to investors than it really is, for several reasons.

First, while the bank *can* call the loan due, it doesn't mean that the bank *will* call the loan due. Look at it from the lender's point of view. A person is behind a few months in loan payments. You're wondering if, as the lender, you are going to have to go through the cumbersome process of foreclosing on this person's loan. You're worried if the house will be in good enough condition that when you sell the house in a foreclosure auction you'll get all or even most of your money back. And to top it all off, when you have a loan in default, federal lending guidelines require you to hold an amount of money in reserve to be safe if the loan never gets repaid. That means that if you have a lot of bad loans on your books, you lose out on a lot of interest you could have generated because of the money you are now required to leave in reserve.

And then along comes this check with a note saying that the money is to bring one of your bad loans current. Are you going to cash that check? Of course you are. Does it make good business sense to take a loan that finally is getting paid on time and insist it is still a bad loan in default? Obviously, it doesn't. That said, some lenders will still call the loan due even if it doesn't necessarily make good business sense. In a moment, we'll share with you how to lower the chances that a lender would want to call a loan due.

Remember, most banks have payment processing centers, or outside companies they pay to service their loans, that receive thousands of payments every month. They simply do not have time, nor do they really care, if the name on the check you have sent is different from the person who is the borrower on the loan.

But what would happen if the lender did, in fact, call the loan due, i.e., they did choose to accelerate the loan? The lender would send an official letter to the borrower, who happens to be your seller, notifying the borrower that he is in default of the loan and that the lender is proceeding to call the loan due. In almost all instances, before the lender would ever call the loan due they would give the borrower a warning letter first, asking the borrower to call and explain what is going on. This normally takes 30 to 45 days. If the borrower ignores this warning, the lender will then send an official notice that the borrower is in default and has 30 days to pay off the balance of the loan or to refinance the property. If the borrower doesn't pay off the loan balance or refinance, then the lender will proceed to foreclose on the property which will take at least 90 days or longer in most states. The bottom line is that if the bank does call the loan due, the fastest they can move on it in most states is going to be 120 to 150 days. They can't do it overnight. And because of all the costs to the bank, in almost all instances the lender will work with you to find an alternative solution, such as allow your tenant-buyer to assume the underlying financing, allow you to assume it, or allow you, the investor, time to refinance the property or sell the property to a cash buyer. Remember, if the absolute worst were to happen and the bank did foreclose on the property, because you did *not* sign on the loan, it would not affect your credit or bank account. But realize that foreclosure is a very unlikely thing to happen.

■ David's Story

We got a lead from the owner of a hair salon that one of her customers was behind on her mortgage payments to the bank. (It never ceases to amaze me the things people tell their hair stylists!) She gave us the name and phone number of the owner, Liz. When we talked with Liz, we found out that she and her husband were three mortgage payments behind and were headed for foreclosure. But she didn't want to sell to us because her brother-in-law was a real estate agent, and he was pressuring her to let him list and sell the house for her. Over a month went by and we thought she was not going to call us back, when finally our phone rang.

It turned out that Liz got sick of waiting for her brother-in-law to do anything, and she and her husband were now four months behind in their mortgage payments and in imminent danger of foreclosure. We agreed to make up their back payments (which totaled about $7,500 by the time we closed) and to give them a promissory note for $12,000 for her equity. Notice we kept our out-of-pocket costs down by having the sellers carry back a second mortgage due as a lump-sum payment within 60 months of closing (we'll talk more about "owner-carry" clauses in a short while).

We put a tenant-buyer in the property who gave us $5,000 in option money with an option price of $199,997. This was roughly $40,000 more than our price for the property. The best part about it was that the sellers let us keep their loan in place and buy the property subject to the existing financing. Because Liz and her husband bought the house with a VA loan six years earlier, they had an interest rate of 7.5 percent fixed for 30 years.

About 18 months later, we got a letter from the lender letting us know that they suspected the property had been sold and asking us to call them about formally assuming the loan or refinancing. It happened that I was on vacation during this time, so I didn't get back to them for several weeks. In the meantime, when the lender hadn't heard from us in 30 days, the lender sent an "official" letter that we had 30 days to call them or they would accelerate the loan. I talked with Samantha in the lender's office and explained that we had buyers in the home who had a lease option. I spent about 30 minutes on the phone with Samantha, asking her all kinds of questions and talking through all of our options. We jointly decided that we had four options. Option one was to get our buyers to buy right away and to assume the VA loan. Option two was to simply assume the loan ourselves. Option three was to refinance the property. Option four was to sell the property to a retail buyer. At the time this happened, the house was worth $212,000 to $218,0000 and the loan balance was only $148,000, so we could have easily refinanced the property with nothing down, or we could have retailed the property for a quick cash profit. In the end, I chose to simply assume the loan myself. This cost me $1,140 for the full assumption. While I would have preferred for my tenant-buyers to assume the loan, I was still happy to get long-term financing in place with an interest rate of 7.5 percent. My favorite part is that the loan is paying down $175 each month of principal and this will only get better each year! The bottom line is that if the bank does in fact choose to accelerate the loan you will have time to figure something out in most cases. Just be nice to the bank and make friends with their staff and they will be cooperative.   ■

How to Minimize the Chances of the Bank Choosing to Call the Loan Due

So how do you minimize the risk of the lender calling the loan due? You simply make sure you don't flaunt the fact that you have purchased the property to the lender. Because you never entered into any agreement with the lender, you are under no legal or ethical obligation to tell the lender about your purchase. The most common way an investor flaunts their purchase of the property to the lender is through what we call the "Insurance Trap."

The Insurance Trap happens when you buy a property subject to the existing financing and you go and have the insurance policy switched to name you as the new main insured party. The lender will be listed on that insurance policy as an "additionally insured party" and will get notified of this change. It doesn't take a rocket scientist at the lender's office to figure out that if the main insured has changed, then the property has probably been sold.

There are two ways to handle this. One is to simply leave the first insurance policy in the name of the seller in place and go out and get a second policy naming you as the main insured. Yes, this will mean paying twice for insurance, but the cost is minimal compared to the benefit of getting the property subject to the existing financing. On the first policy the lender remains an "additionally insured party," while on the new policy you don't name the lender at all. The lender's need to have insurance to protect their interest is provided by the original policy; your need to have protection is covered by the second policy; and you, the investor, have never flaunted your purchase to the lender.

The second way to sidestep the Insurance Trap is by using a land trust. A land trust is simply a trust that is created to hold title of a property for the benefit of some "beneficial" party. Any seller may put their property into a land trust without violating the due on sale clause. This is federal law. The seller merely deeds the property you are buying subject to the existing financing into a land trust naming himself as the beneficiary and you, the investor, as the "trustee." Then, in a separate document, the seller assigns the "beneficial interest" of that land trust from himself to you. Now you are both the trustee (who controls the property) and the beneficiary (who gets all the benefits of the property.) For all practical purposes and for tax purposes, you now own the property.

As for the due on sale clause, when you do things this way, the act of the seller deeding the property into the land trust with himself as the beneficiary does *not* violate the due on sale clause. This deed from the seller to you as the trustee of the land trust gets recorded. You help the seller write a quick letter to the lender notifying the lender that the owner has put the property into trust for financial purposes and from here on out all correspondence about the loan should be with the trustee, who just happens to be you, the investor. You give the lender your address in this letter as the trustee and from here on out you will be the lender's contact person on the loan.

In a separate transaction, which can take place ten seconds after the above one, the seller assigns over his beneficial interest in the land trust to you, the investor. While this could trigger the due on sale clause because the property title is essentially being transferred to you, it's very unlikely the bank would ever know about this transaction because this assignment is *never* recorded.

How does this help you with the Insurance Trap? Well, you simply switch the policy from the seller to you as the trustee of the XYZ Property Trust. The lender expects this change and is used to it. Everyone is happy—the bank, the seller, the insurance company, and you. This is our preferred way of doing "subject to existing financing" deals. Once you do one deal this way, you'll realize it really is fairly simple.

We want to be clear here that buying properties subject to the existing financing is a standard way to finance real estate. Ask any experienced real estate agent or attorney and he or she will be quick to tell you that this is an intelligent and ethical way to buy property provided both you and the seller clearly understand the relative risks and benefits of the transaction.

The bottom line with respect to the acceleration clause is that even if you did nothing other than just have the seller deed the property to you and then you started sending in checks without using a land trust or without using a new insurance policy, the chances of the loan getting called due are still pretty small. If you do what we have shared to avoid the Insurance Trap, the odds of the loan getting called due are even smaller. We think this is a manageable risk given the fact that there are so many benefits to buying subject to and given the fact that the downside isn't too great.

Pitfall 2: Accurately identifying all the existing liens. The second pitfall of buying a house subject to the existing financing is to do the deal and then find out that the seller inaccurately disclosed to you all the loans, liens, and title issues with the property. Now, we don't mean to say that the seller will do this intentionally. Although we've both had that happen to us, we find even the best-intentioned sellers merely make mistakes. As an investor, you need to protect yourself from this risk by doing your due diligence. (See Chapter 4 for more information on checking title.)

Pitfall 3: Needing the seller's signature down the road. The third danger you face when you are doing a deal subject to the existing financing is that you may need the seller's signature down the road, but you either won't be able to locate the seller or you will not want to have to convince the seller to cooperate with you years later. For example, imagine you buy the property subject to the existing financing from a motivated seller named Harry. Two years later you resell the property, but there was an excess of $500 in the impound account from the lender. Most times lenders set up an "impound" or "escrow" account where the borrower pays in an amount over the principal and interest payment due on the loan to cover the property taxes or insurance premiums. When you sell the property, at times, there will be an excess in this account that will get refunded back to the owner.

Here you are with a $500 check in your hand made out to Harry, the motivated seller you bought the house from. You could forget about the extra money, which is not our preferred way of handling this situation, or you could track down Harry and ask him to sign over the check to you. Or you could sign the check for Harry and deposit it into your account, provided you have one simple document signed and notarized by Harry that you had him sign at the closing you had with him when you bought the house. That document is called a "Limited Power of Attorney." It gives you the power to sign on Harry's behalf on any document dealing with this one property. See Figure 2.8.

It's called a "limited" power of attorney because it gives you only the authority to sign as if you were the seller in matters regarding this one property, not in other areas of the seller's life. This document is also useful when you need to clear up a title defect or when you need to negotiate with the underlying lender. If all goes well, you'll never need this document. But when you need it, you'll be glad you took care of it up front at the closing. This one little insider's secret will help you make your investing much easier and more profitable.

The Three Best Ways to Find "Subject to" Deals—Fast!

Rarely will you find a seller who is going to sell you his property subject to the existing financing by going to Open Houses. Usually, you will find these types of deals by advertising and getting highly motivated sellers to call you. The two most common types of motivated sellers who will be willing to sell you their property subject to the existing financing are sellers who are behind on their payments and headed toward foreclosure and sellers who have little or no equity.

Here are three of the most cost-effective ways to get these types of motivated sellers to call you. When you use them, we recommend that you direct the calls to a 24-hour voice-mail box with a high-powered 60-second to 90-second outgoing message that gives callers all the benefits of doing a deal with you by just leaving you their name and phone number.

FIGURE 2.8   Sample Limited Power of Attorney Form

LIMITED POWER OF ATTORNEY

BE IT KNOWN, that as principal (the "Principal") I/we, _____

of _____ , have made, constitute

and appoint _____ , as my/our true and lawful attorney-in-fact ("Attorney").
Attorney-in-fact is authorized in Attorney-in-fact's absolute discretion from time to time and at any time with
respect to the following specific and limited purposes only:

Any and all REAL ESTATE matters concerning _____

_____ (Property) including, but not limited to, the following:

In my/our name, and as my act and deed, to transact any acts deemed necessary by Attorney-in-fact concerning loans and liens against Property.

In my/our name, and as my act and deed, to transact any acts deemed necessary by Attorney-in-fact concerning any insurance matters for Property, including, but not limited to, securing appropriate hazard insurance coverage, and negotiating and receiving any insurance claims from any loss on Property.

In connection with the exercise, of the powers herein described, Attorney-in-fact is fully authorized and empowered to perform any other acts or things necessary, appropriate, or incidental thereto, with the same validity and effect as if I/we were personally present, competent, and personally exercised the powers myself. All acts lawfully done by Attorney-in-fact hereunder during any period of my/our disability or mental incompetence shall have the same effect and inure to the benefit of and bind me/us and my/our heirs, devisees, legatees and personal representatives as if I/we were mentally competent and not disabled. The powers herein conferred may be exercised by Attorney-in-fact alone and the signature or act of Attorney-in-fact on my/our behalf may be accepted by third persons as fully authorized by me/us and with the same force and effect as if done under my/our hand and seal and as if I/we were present in person, acting on my/our own behalf and competent. No person who may act in reliance upon the representations of Attorney-in-fact for the scope of authority granted to Attorney in fact shall incur any liability to me/us or to my/our estate as a result of permitting Attorney-in-fact to exercise any power, nor shall any person dealing with Attorney-in-fact be responsible to determine or insure the proper application of funds or property.

My/our mental or physical debility subsequent to my/our execution of the within power-of-Attorney-in-fact shall not revoke said power which shall remain in full force and effect notwithstanding said mental or physical debility.

These presents shall extend to and be obligatory upon the executors, administrator legal representatives and successors, respectively, of the parties hereto.

_____   _____/_____/_____
                    ,Principal

STATE OF _____ COUNTY OF _____ I hereby certify that on
this day, before me, _____ , personally appeared _____ personally known
to me (or proved to me on the basis of satisfactory evidence) to be the person(s) whose name(s) is/are subscribed to
the within instrument and acknowledged to me that he/she/they executed the same in his/her/their authorized
capacity(ies), and that by his/her/their signature(s) on the instrument the person(s) or the entity upon behalf of
which the person(s) acted, executed the instrument.
Witness my hand and official seal in the County and State last aforesaid

This _____ day of _____ , 20_____

_____
Notary Public
My commission expires_____

FIGURE 2.9   Sample Classified Ads to Get Motivated Sellers to Call You

---

"I Buy Houses!"
No Equity, No Problem!
Call 888-555-1212
24 hr. rec. msg.

I'll Buy or Lease Your House
In 7 Days or Less!
Stop foreclosure or double pymts!
888-555-1212 24 hr. msg.

Investor looking to buy houses!
Any area or condition.
No commission or fees!
Call 888-555-1212 rec. msg.

The system we use is a toll-free voice-mail system with nine separate voice-mail boxes. We like the toll-free feature for two reasons. First, you never have to worry about someone not calling you because they are afraid of a toll charge. Second, the system we use captures the caller's phone number on *every* call—even if the caller hangs up! Something about the fact that the caller is dialing a toll-free number means that even if the caller has caller ID blocking, the system *still* captures the number. Also, nine separate boxes (extensions one through nine) allow us to track our ads and mailings better by directing responses to specific extensions. This way we can fine tune our marketing efforts and only spend money in areas that make us money.

The voice-mail system we use is offered through the American Real Estate Investors Association <www.americanreia.com>. We like this system because it comes with all the outgoing messages preprogrammed with professionally scripted messages for motivated sellers to hear. It also has a feature where you can get either pager or e-mail notification that you have a call. This means you can get back to the caller right away so you don't lose out on a great deal. The best part about the system is that the American Real Estate

Investors Association offers it to their members at about one third the cost of what it would normally be if you signed up for a similar service through another company. You can also find voice-mail companies by looking in the Yellow Pages under Voice Mail. Typically it will cost you $7 to $15 per voice-mail box.

1. Place a classified ad. The first way to get the right kinds of sellers to call you is to place a classified ad in your local paper. See Figure 2.9 for three sample classified ads that you can try out.

Where should you place these ads? Insert them in your local paper in either the For Sale section (usually the paper will only allow you to put it here if it is a small paper) or in the Real Estate Wanted section (the most common place to put it).

Call all the local papers in your area:

- Free weeklies mailed out to people's houses like the *Penny Saver* and *Thrifty Nickel*
- Daily newspapers
- Local weekly papers

When you call, get pricing for running an ad. Ask the following questions:

- Who gets your paper?
- How often does it go out?
- When are the submission deadlines?
- What is the circulation?
- Do you charge by the word or the line?
- How much will it cost?
- Do you have any special discounts for small business owners like myself?
- Do you have any volume discounts if I give you repeat business?

- Do you have any discounts because I am a nice person? (We think you get the idea. This is a great place to practice your negotiating skills.)

■ David's Story

"We've been running the same classified ad for the past three years. It costs us about $4,000 per year to run the ad. We consistently pick up at least three houses per year from that ad. And our average profit is over $30,000 per house that we pick up. I'll let you do the math, but I'm fairly certain that spending $4,000 per year to make $90,000 is a good investment of capital.   ■

Donna, a student of ours in northern Ohio, got a response from a classified ad one day from a seller who was struggling to avoid foreclosure. The seller just couldn't keep up the payments on an empty property anymore. Donna came in and bought the property subject to the existing financing for a price of $72,904. Because the property was leveraged to the hilt, the total payments on the first and second mortgage were higher than the market rent. Some people would think this means that an investor would have negative cash flow. Donna solved this problem by agreeing to cover the first mortgage payment of $743 per month. The seller agreed to pay the second mortgage payment of $350 per month. This was the only way the seller could avoid having a foreclosure on his record, and he was a man of integrity who wanted to make sure he fulfilled his obligation to the bank. Donna gets $1,000 per month in rent from her tenant-buyer. When you factor in the spread between Donna's price with the seller and her tenant-buyer, the cash flow she'll make, and the equity pay down from the amortization of the loan, her total profits will be over $50,000. Not a bad deal for her on a house with a market price of $100,000.

FIGURE 2.10   Sample Signs to Attract Calls From Motivated Sellers

2. **Put out neighborhood signs.** The next way to get motivated sellers to call you is to put out small signs around your community. See Figure 2.10.

The signs we use are made out of corrugated plastic and measure 12 inches tall by 18 inches wide. You can simply call a local sign shop and order 100 to 200 signs from them. We also maintain a Web page that lists the best pricing our students have found on signs. For more information simply visit <www.resultsnow.com> and click on Investor Tools. We update this page based on the changing market, and we welcome your input on places to get better deals.

■ **Peter's Story**

One of my favorite students to work with is a man named Martin who lives in Maryland. When Martin got started, he had the most frustrating first four months I've ever seen an investor have. But he simply wouldn't quit. He ended up signing up his first two deals within 48 hours of each other. One was from a postcard he mailed out, and the other was from the "I Buy Houses" signs he put out around his farm area.

The seller of one property couldn't handle the double payments on the property anymore. Martin ended up buying the house subject to the existing mortgage for $1 down. He turned around and sold it on a rent-to-own basis within two weeks. He only made $15,000 on that deal, which isn't a lot of money, but it was his first deal and, as such, it boosted his confidence level. That's the way it typically works: While often the smallest deal you'll ever do, the first deal is the most important. It's the one that lets you know what really is possible if you keep going after your dreams.   ■

3. Mail postcards. The final way to get motivated sellers to call you is to mail postcards to people who are in the initial stages of a foreclosure. At this point in the process, the average seller is behind two to five months in their payments. They are great prospects to approach about stepping in and buying the property, making up the back payments, bringing the loan out of default, and taking title to the property subject to the existing financing.

Mail your postcards (see Figure 2.11) to people who have had Notices of Default filed against them. A "Notice of Default," called slightly different names in different states, is the first step in the foreclosure process. This is the step the lender takes when the owner has missed one or more payments, and this step starts the foreclosure clock ticking. In most states, a borrower has 30 to 60 days to make up the back payments before the lender starts step two of the foreclosure process—filing a "Notice of Sale." You don't want to wait until the Notice of Sale has been filed because at that

---

FIGURE 2.11   A Sample Postcard

I'LL BUY YOUR HOUSE—FAST!

Here's your quick and easy solution:

✔ FAST Closing
✔ INSTANT Debt Relief
✔ FREEDOM From Maintenance Hassles
✔ Guaranteed Written Offer Within 48 Hours
✔ HARD-TO-SELL HOME? No Problem!
✔ NO EQUITY? No Problem!
✔ NO Commissions

24-hour, FREE recorded message
1-888-555-1212
toll-free

---

point the seller may be behind four to eight payments or more. You would much rather catch them early in the process.

The way you get your postcard mailing list is to simply sign up with an information source provider in your area. An information source provider is a company that takes all the public records from the county recorder's office and puts them on a computer database. The company then sells access to that data base in one of three ways: giving you monthly or quarterly updated CD-ROMs containing the information, giving you online access to the information, or selling you a ready-to-go mailing list in a spreadsheet format. In some counties, the public records are available online already. This is rare at the moment, but more and more counties are enabling Web access of their records. So check with your local county recorder's office.

The best way to find an information source provider in your area is to network with other investors in the local real estate investors association (for a listing of these groups, go to <www.american

reia.com>. If you don't have a local group to network with, pull out the Yellow Pages and look under both Information Source Provider and Mailing List Provider. If that doesn't work, call up your county recorder's office and see if they know of a company that has either online access or CD-ROM access to the information. While you have them on the phone, ask them about what services they offer online that you should be aware of. Finally, if all else fails, try Dataquick <www.dataquick.com>, a nationwide information source provider. Typically, Dataquick covers most areas of the United States, but they tend to be a fairly expensive provider, although they generally offer very high-quality service.

Mail your postcards to your list at least three times over the next 60 days. You want the repetition. We recommend postcards on bright yellow cardstock as opposed to a bland white letter for three reasons. First, because a postcard is roughly 30 percent less postage than a letter, you save a lot of money. Second, you don't have to fold, stuff, and seal several hundred envelopes which saves you time. Third, you can use mailing labels and just stick them on the postcard versus direct imprinting the envelopes which takes more time. You don't want to use mailing labels on your letters if you can avoid it because it lowers the number of people who will be willing to open the envelope. With your postcard, it's already "opened" so you don't have to worry about this.

The postcard should direct people to call into your 24-hour voice-mail box. Then you check your messages and follow up with a phone call to the seller to see what his or her situation is and why he or she is selling.

■ **David's Story**

I got a call from Cheryl, who wrote the foreword to this book, asking me what went wrong with her postcard mailing. I asked what she meant by that. She said, "I did exactly what the course materials said to do and sent out a postcard mailing, and I got only two phone calls. What did I do wrong?"

"How many postcards did you send out?" I asked her. "About 75." She had over a 1 percent success rate with her mailing! Any of you who know about direct mail know that a 1 percent response from a cold list is pretty good. And how did it all turn out? Well one of the people who called was just a curiosity seeker. The other caller was a serious lead.

His name was George, and he was a landlord who wanted out. He owned 12 properties scattered throughout Cheryl's hometown. After meeting with him and looking at the properties, Cheryl bought two of them. She bought both houses with nothing down and subject to the existing financing. One of the houses she got for about $15,000 to $18,000 below market value, and on the other house George carried back an $18,000 second mortgage for his equity so that Cheryl could buy it with nothing down. In case you're curious about what magic list Cheryl sent her postcards to, she simply sent them to people who owned "nonowner occupied properties." ■

One Final Benefit You Enjoy When You Get on the Title

One additional benefit you get when you buy the property subject to the existing financing (or with a "big money cash close" or with an "owner carry," both of which are described later) is that you have the ability to offer the property with owner financing when you sell it. If you buy on a lease option you can either rent it, retail it, or sell it on a rent-to-own basis. If you *own* the property as opposed to having the *option* to purchase the property, then in addition to those three exit strategies, you can sell the property with owner financing using either a land contract or a wraparound mortgage. While selling with owner financing is beyond the scope of this book, the key point for you to understand is that when you sell with owner financing, you'll get typically three to five times as much money up front than when you sell on a rent-to-own basis (10 percent to 15 percent down versus 3 percent to 5 percent up front.) Also, you'll typically be able to mark up the monthly payment even higher than you can if you were selling the property on a rent-to-own basis. There are downsides to selling with owner financing. For example, it is much harder to get the property back if your buyer defaults than if you sold on a rent-to-own basis.

■ **David's Story**

A house we bought with two of our students was purchased from a motivated seller subject to the existing financing. The sellers called us in response to an "I Buy Houses" sign. They had an empty house and very little equity in it. We bought it for $1 down. We then turned around and sold it subject to the existing financing for roughly $30,000 more than we paid for it. Why didn't we sell it on a rent-to-own basis? We found that the payments were too far above the market rents. By selling it outright to new buyers with this easy long-term financing in place, they were willing to pay several hundred dollars above the market rent each month. As the owners, they got to write off all the interest they were paying, which saved them over $300 per month on their income taxes. And because we were giving them title, we also collected $25,000 down. The seller we bought it from knew exactly what was going on and was a pleasure to work with. In fact, our students suggested we give the seller a $500 gift that she wasn't expecting just because they felt it was the right thing to do.   ■

As you've learned, "subject to" deals are our favorite method of buying. We do about 25 percent or so of our deals using this strategy. It takes a highly motivated seller to be willing to sell the property to you subject to the existing financing. Still, when it happens, it is a very profitable and low-risk way to go.

Purchase Option Buying Strategy Four:
Big Money Cash Close—How to Pay a Seller
with Borrowed Money

How do you handle a seller who owns a property free and clear, has a strong motivation to sell, but who doesn't want to do a lease option or to carry back all the financing? In other words, these sellers are willing to carry back some of the financing as long as they get a sizable chunk of their equity now.

In these situations, the "big money cash close" is the perfect Purchase Option technique to use. This technique involves getting a new first mortgage secured against the property to get the seller some cash at closing, and then the seller simply carries back a mortgage for the balance of his equity for a period of time.

For example, imagine a $100,000 house. To use this technique you would bring in a new first mortgage of between $30,000 to $50,000 and have the seller carry back the balance as a second mortgage. Because the bank you are going to get the first mortgage from has so much value protecting its money (after all, what banker doesn't like to lend at a 30 percent to 50 percent loan-to-value ratio?), this is a fairly easy mortgage to secure. This strategy is a way for you to get the seller a large chunk of money at closing, but you're borrowing it.

When using this strategy, it is important to note that the sellers will need to be willing to carry a *second* mortgage for the balance of their equity. This is because you will be getting a new first mortgage to give the sellers money at closing. You are still structuring the deal with none of your own money going to the seller. You will have closing costs of approximately 2 percent to 3 percent of your sale price, but your tenant-buyer's option payment should cover this and then some.

If you do use this strategy, you will have to go out and get conventional financing for the new first mortgage. Typically, you can get up to 60 percent of the appraised value of the house or 60 percent of the purchase price, whichever is lower, from the lender on that new first mortgage and still do this with none of your own money down. While this conventional lender will make you jump through hoops to get this money, if you have decent credit and the patience to deal with the lender, this strategy will work well for you. While you will have to give a personal guarantee on this first mortgage, because of the low loan-to-value ratio, this is fairly safe. After all, there is a lot of equity in the property protecting this mortgage. We strongly urge you to make sure that you do *not* sign personally on the owner-carry second mortgage. You'll learn the specific contract clause you'll use to do this later in this chapter.

But what if your credit has holes? Then consider bringing in a partner who can "lend" you his or her credit statement by qualifying for the new first mortgage. Then the two of you can split the profits on the deal.

As with any creative offer you make, the specific language you use is the key factor in getting the seller to say yes. Using the above $100,000 property, the way *not* to phrase your offer is as follows: "Mr. Seller, what if I were to leverage your house with a new first mortgage so I wouldn't have to come up with any of the money from my pocket, and then you just carried back a second mortgage for the rest of your money so I can buy your house using it as the collateral for my loan?" Would this sound attractive to you if you were the seller? Probably not.

Instead, here is exactly how to word your offer, "Mr. Seller, what if I were to bring in new financing and get you $30,000 or so in cash at closing, then you were to carry back a small second for the balance? Obviously, you wouldn't want to have to wait forever for the balance of your money, so we'd put a short-term balloon note of five to seven years on it."

Notice you use the words "bring in new financing" not "put $30,000 down." Technically, if you say you are going to put money down that means you are going to be using *your* money. That's not what you want to do. You'll be using the bank's money instead.

Let's be clear on one critical item. The sellers need to be very clear that their loan will be in second position. You are not trying to pull anything over on them. The reason the language you use is so important is that you need to frame the offer in the sellers' minds the right way from the very beginning. You need to make sure the idea creates a good first impression on the sellers. Later you can go back over the details to make sure the sellers are totally aware of all the advantages and disadvantages of this type of deal.

By using this technique, you are going to be 100 percent financing the property. The critical question on any 100 percent financed property is: Does it cash flow? A property "cash flows" when the income it generates pays at least for all the expenses. Usually, you would use this expression when a property has excess income after expenses, meaning it creates a positive cash flow. If you pay market interest rates for the second the seller is carrying back, it probably won't cash flow. But when sellers carry back seconds, they don't need high interest rates. At least they don't if they are motivated, and if they're not motivated what are you doing wasting your time talking with them?

One of our students recently put together a big money cash close on a $168,000 house. The owners of the property were an elderly couple who were having a hard time selling it. Our student found out that they had sold the property a few months back only to have the sale fall apart at the last minute. The property was vacant, and the couple owned it free and clear. When our student met with the sellers, she offered to bring in new financing and to give the sellers $50,000 cash at closing, with the sellers to carry back the balance as a second mortgage.

They negotiated back and forth, even getting their adult children into the picture, and finally they agreed on our student bringing in a new $88,000 first, with the seller to carry back the other $80,000. After doing the math, our student realized that her total payment, including principle, interest, real estate taxes, and insurance, on the new first would be about $100 below market rent. So she told the sellers that if they wanted her to give them $88,000 at closing rather than the $50,000 they initially discussed, then she couldn't pay any interest on the second but rather would give them the other $80,000 in one lump-sum payment of $80,000 due in full within 60 months of closing.

The seller won because they got more money up front and a quick sale of their house. And our student won because she got a nothing-down house that cash flows from day one. She also negotiated for and got an attached lot thrown in for free that has a value of $35,000! She made sure that the deal for this lot was done in a separate sale from the house for a whopping price of $1. This way she can sell off the lot without having to pay off the $80,000 interest-free loan from the seller.

Here is one final point to consider when doing these types of deals. Where possible, pay the seller in a "lump sum payment of $X due in full within *blank* months of closing." This is a nice way to say *interest-free loan* to you.

If you do need to pay interest to the seller, always talk in terms of an interest-only payment of X dollars *not* in terms of percentage interest rates. If you talk in terms of interest rates, the seller is going to want 8 percent to 15 percent interest. But if you talk in functional terms of dollars they get each month, you can usually agree on a much lower payment. For example, if the seller was to carry back a $100,000 second, offer to pay them $2,000 to $2,500 per year of interest as your way of saying thank you to the seller for being patient waiting for the rest of their money. Notice the way you framed this? Even if the seller negotiates you all the way to $4,000 of annual interest-only payments, you still win—the effective interest rate on your loan is just 4 percent.

One deal we did in partnership with one of the coaches for our mentorship program was a big money cash close. We found a couple who had a house they had been wanting to sell for a while. The sellers had recently made a lot of money when the company the husband had just retired from went public and their stock shot up in value. They were in the process of building a new 10,000 square-foot house in a different state right on a lake with a private dock and all the trimmings. The sellers really wanted to sell their old house and move into the new one before the December holidays. We met with them in early November.

We finally agreed on a purchase price of $175,000, paid as follows: We would bring in a new first mortgage of $87,500 with the sellers agreeing to carry back a second mortgage of $87,500. The sellers were thrilled to make their deadline to get into their brand new house in time for the holidays, and we were thrilled because we got a great house in a good neighborhood with very little money up front. We had to pay only for our closing costs.

When we negotiated with the sellers, we let them know that we had to make sure that the sum of what we were paying on our first mortgage and to them as interest-only payments on the second mortgage wasn't any higher than the market rent for the house. This meant that we would have to be conservative on what we paid them in interest. We went back and forth for a while and finally agreed that we'd pay them $2,000 per year in interest for the first year (effective interest rate of 2.3 percent) with the payment going up by $1,000 every year with a balloon payment for the full $87,500 due at the end of ten years. Because of the great interest rate, this 100-percent financed property will cash flow all the way through year five.

We turned around and sold the property to a tenant-buyer on a three-year rent-to-own basis for a price of $213,000 with $7,000 option money paid. All totaled, we'll have made over $28,000 on this one house.

We just want to give you one final reminder of the key language that makes a big money cash close possible: "What if we were to bring in new financing, giving you X dollars at closing, and you just carried back a small second for the balance." This phrasing works so well, we caution you to not change even a word of it.

Purchase Option Buying Strategy Five: Owner-Carry Financing—How to Turn the Seller into Your Bank

The most well known creative buying strategy is to have the owner carry back all the financing. All the earlier Purchase Option buying strategies have in a sense some form of owner financing involved. Whether it be a lease option or an equity split or a "subject to" financing purchase or a big money cash close, the seller is helping in some way with the financing.

This final explanation of owner-carry financing will outline three more ways to use owner-financing methods to help you leverage your purchase of property in such a way that you can still control your risk.

The first use of owner financing is what most people think of when they hear the expression "owner financing." Sellers own a property free and clear and act as a bank by accepting something down from you, the buyer, and then by taking payments for the rest of their money over time. We call this "straight owner financing."

Here is an example of how you can put together deals with straight owner financing. One of our students responded to a For Sale ad in her local paper. She talked to a nice man on the phone and set up an appointment to see a midpriced home in a quiet suburb. When she met him at the property, she found out that he wasn't actually the seller but was the attorney for the seller who lived out of state. They sat down and talked the purchase over and agreed on our student buying the house with $2,500 down with the owner carrying back a 30-year first mortgage at 8 percent interest. Originally, the attorney told our student she would have to put $10,000 down, but the student used the technique for handling this objection laid out in Chapter 3 of this book. The best part about owner-carried loans like these is that you don't have to pay points or loan origination fees or appraisal fees or any of a number of loan costs. Our student sold the house on a two-year rent-to-own basis for roughly $15,000 more than she bought it for. And the funny thing was that she liked working with this attorney so much that she later hired him to be her family's attorney.

❝ ■ David's Story

I found a seller of a high-end home in San Diego who was selling his 4,000 square-foot house. He had advertised the house For Sale By Owner in our local paper. When I met with the seller, Saul, I liked him from the start. Saul was in his late 70s and was very warm and friendly. As he showed me through the house, which was stunning, I asked him what he did before he retired. "I was a gym teacher." My mouth must have dropped open at this because he quickly explained how he had started buying property back when he was my age. He shared with me how he had kept buying more and more properties—houses, apartment buildings, and office complexes—until he retired from teaching.

Saul and I sat down to do our negotiating, and we spent the next several hours in one of the most enjoyable and challenging negotiations I'd ever been in. I started off by asking Saul all the reasons why he was selling. He explained that he was having trouble with the stairs in the house and the upkeep (it was a large lot) was getting too much. He and his wife had already purchased a smaller house in a retirement community for all cash. When I asked him what other offers he had on the house, he shared that he had gotten a crazy offer from another investor who wanted him to carry all the financing with very little down and at 5 percent interest for seven years. He even showed me the fancy letter the other investor had sent to him in the mail.

I asked him if he was willing to carry back the financing, if he had a serious buyer who was willing to close quickly and not ask him to do all the cosmetic work needed on the house (it needed to be painted and recarpeted). He said if I gave him $100,000 down, he would be willing to carry back the other $495,000 at 5 percent interest only for three years. (Interest-only payments on a loan do not apply to reduce the principal balance owed on the loan. Because you are only paying interest and not adding extra principal in order to pay the loan down over time, loans with interest-only payments have less money owed each month. They tend to be structured to be done in one lump-sum balloon payment down the road.) When I said I had something else in mind, he asked me to write down what I meant. I wrote on a sheet of paper in front of me, "$30,000 to $40,000 down with balance as an owner-carry first mortgage at 5 percent interest only for five to seven years," and slid the paper over to him.

He turned it over, read it for a moment, and then *threw* the offer across the dining room table. I had to work hard to keep from laughing because I knew it was all just a game to Saul. He was just reacting to see if he could shake me up into giving him a better offer. And I also knew that he still wanted to keep talking about putting a deal together.

Eventually, one-and-a-half hours later, and two more thrown offers, we agreed on a price of $595,000 paid as follows: $60,000 down with Saul to carry back a first mortgage of $535,000 at 5 percent interest only with a five-year balloon payment due at that time.

Because of the low interest rate, the house payment was well below the market rent for the house. Also, because it was an owner-carry note, I did it all with no loan application paperwork, no credit check, and no recourse on the loan. The house was so nice I decided to move into it. With about $20,000 to $25,000 worth of cosmetic work, the house had a value of $650,000 to $675,000 at the time I bought it. It was also in an area that was appreciating at 8 percent to 10 percent per year. This appreciation rate meant that two years later, homes on this same street in proper cosmetic condition were selling for $900,000.

The real key to making deals like this work is to have the patience to sit down with the seller and talk the deal through for as long as it takes to come to terms. I used to think that having a face that looks like I'm 18 years old was a disadvantage. After all, who would take me seriously? I've learned to turn this into a great asset. I think that part of the reason Saul gave me such a great deal is that I reminded him of what he was like when he was younger. If I had a face that made me look like I was 90 years old (which I hope to have someday, when I'm 102), I would turn that into an asset and relate to my sellers and buyers in a different way. Saul and I are still friends to this day. Not only did he sell me his house, but he became a great role model for what I could accomplish through investing in real estate.   ■

The second way to structure owner-carry deals is for you to formally assume the sellers' existing financing and have the owners carry back the balance of their equity as a second mortgage. This is probably the least attractive way for you to go as a buyer because you now have all the liability on the loan. Plus, you have to go through all the hoops the lender will set before you in order to qualify for the loan. Still, if the numbers are good enough this is a viable option.

The third way to structure owner-carry deals is to combine the "subject to" financing strategy you learned about earlier with owner financing. What we mean here is that you buy the property subject to the existing financing and the owner carries back a note for their equity. This is much lower risk, plus it will save you money because you won't have to pay a bank to assume the existing loan.

The following example illustrates this technique. Mark and Trish, the same students from an earlier case study, got a call from the "I Buy Houses" ad they were running in their paper. The motivated seller who called had bought a new house and hadn't been able to sell their first house. They were feeling the pressure of the double payments. While they didn't sign up the deal on the spot, Mark and Trish followed up every few weeks and eventually, six months later, the seller sold them the house.

By this point the seller had refinanced out much of his equity with an 80 percent new first mortgage of $280,000. Mark and Trish gave the seller $100 down and bought the house for a price of $350,000 (they agreed to take over the payments on the existing $280,000 mortgage of $2,300 per month with the seller carrying back a $70,000 second mortgage with no interest or monthly payments, with the balance due in full as a lump sum payment within 60 months of closing).

Next, Mark and Trish sold the house on a two-year rent-to-own basis for $400,000. They collected a $24,000 option payment and were getting $3,300 a month in rent! This deal was worth about $65,000 to Mark and Trish.

The Nine Essential Contract Clauses of Any Owner-Carry Financing Deal You Do

The following nine clauses and insider tips apply to any owner-carry deal you do, whether it be a big money cash close, or a straight-owner carry, or any other owner-carry deal. Make sure you go through this list carefully *before* you ever find yourself sitting down face to face with a seller negotiating a deal. Also, come back to this list when you are having your closing documents drawn up on any owner-carry deal. The clauses will help make you lots of money and save you from heartache.

A word of warning: You may not find these clauses racy or exciting, but make sure you study and use them. They will not only make you a lot of money, but they will lower your risk. Talk them through with your attorney. Remember the expression that the "devil is in the details?" Well these clauses are some of *the* most important details in any owner-carry deal you will ever do.

Also, this is a good point to share how important it is for you to create a team of support professionals to help you succeed in investing. Three invaluable members of your investing team are a CPA, an insurance agent, and a real estate attorney. The best way to find these professionals is to network with other successful investors and ask for referrals. When you screen potential professionals, make sure you ask if they have other investors as clients. Ideally, your investing team members would not only have experience working for other investors, but they would also do some real estate investing themselves.

You will tap into your investing team to help get top-level guidance on many of the details that they have spent years mastering. Remember, to be successful as an investor you don't need to know everything, you simply need to know which experts to ask. What follows are the individual contract clauses we have spent years learning to master. You can use this list as a checklist of clauses to put in any owner-carry deal you do.

1. Liquidated damages clause. A liquidated damages clause is critical in minimizing your risk because it lets you contain the cost of walking away from a deal. When you enter into a contract with another party, you both have the right to expect the other party to perform everything that was mutually agreed to in the contract. If one party doesn't do what they agreed to do, the other party may sue for "specific performance." This means that they can ask a court to make the defaulting party live up to the terms in the contract.

When you are buying real estate and you sign an agreement to buy a property, you want to be able to walk away from the deal if after doing your due diligence you discover something is wrong. The way many investors give themselves this freedom is by using all sorts of "subject to" clauses in their agreements with the seller. *Caution:* Do not confuse this with buying a property "subject to" the existing financing. For example, "This agreement is subject to my partner's approval." Or, "This agreement is subject to buyer obtaining satisfactory financing." You get the picture.

If you were a seller and your buyer showed you paperwork with all kinds of these explicit "subject to" clauses, would you feel confident that you had a real buyer? That's where a liquidated damages clause comes into play. It accomplishes the same thing as a "subject to" clause, provided it's used correctly, without arousing seller concerns about your commitment as a buyer.

A liquidated damages clause merely spells out the exact payment one party must make to the other party in a contract should a default occur. When you're buying a property, you use a liquidated damages clause that spells out that if you, as the buyer, default (i.e., don't buy the property), then the seller gets to keep all the money you've paid to the seller so far as "complete liquidated damages." This sounds pretty strong and sellers like that, but remember, you are only giving the seller a token upfront payment. We use a single dollar. Some investors use up to $500. The key is to delay the payment of any serious upfront money until the point that you are done with your due diligence and are sure you want the deal. Preferably also you will have already found your end user for the property before you ever give the seller any serious money, whether you put a tenant-buyer in the property or are selling to a retail buyer for all cash.

Here's what the legalese version of a liquidated damages clause sounds like:

> *In the event of default of Buyer, all money paid to Seller by Buyer shall be retained by the Seller as consideration for the execution of this contract and as agreed liquidated damages and in full settlement of any and all claims for damages.*

2. "... or assigns." Anytime you do an owner-carry deal you want to maintain maximum flexibility. One important component to this flexibility is the ability to assign your interests in the deal over to another party for a quick cash payment. While any contract is always assignable unless there is a clause in the contract limiting or forbidding the assignment of the contract, it still makes sense to clearly put in your agreement the fact that you may assign the contract.

The best way to do this is to preprint in the contract the words, "or assigns," right after the blank where you fill in who the buyer is. The reason you preprint it in the contract is because this is the standard way you will want to set up all your deals where you are the buyer.

If the contract that your seller wants you to use has a "nonassignment" clause, make sure you cross out this clause and have both you and the seller initial the change.

3. First right of refusal. When a seller carries back some of the financing in a deal, there may come a time when the seller is in desperate need of cash and will look to convert that note into money by selling it to a third party for a steep discount. For example, remember that owner-carry deal with Saul where he carried back a note for $535,000? Saul, who is quite wealthy, didn't need the money and was willing to take payments over time. But he is also in his late 70s. What would happen if he were to pass away and the note were to pass on to his heirs. Do you think they'll want to have to wait for years to get their hands on the money? Chances are that Saul's heirs might very well decide to sell that first mortgage at a discount to a third party.

The first right of refusal, which gets written directly into the note itself, says that if they want to sell it at a discount, they have to give you the right to buy it at the same discounted price first. So, in our current example, if they found a third-party investor who was willing to pay them $450,000 for the note, you would get the first chance to buy the note for the same $450,000. That's a quick $85,000 you would make merely for either selling the property and using your buyer's money to pay off the note or, more commonly, by simply refinancing the property to pay off the seller.

Here's the legalese version of what this clause looks like:

In the event that Note Holder ever sells this promissory note, Borrower shall have the first right of refusal to purchase this note under the same terms and conditions at any time.

4. Subordination clause. The single biggest reason to push for owner financing is that you often will get terms that are much better than a bank would ever give you. We've had sellers carry back loans with interest rates of 3 percent (or better). I remember one big money cash close we did with sellers where they carried back a second mortgage in the amount of roughly $65,000 with no interest or payments. How would you like to borrow $65,000 interest free? Sellers are the best banks to borrow from.

That said, you want to maintain your flexibility in a deal, and a subordination clause helps you do this. For example, what if you negotiated a big money cash close where the seller was willing to wait up to seven years to get a lump-sum payment for the second mortgage he was carrying back. What if you wanted to refinance the first mortgage part of the deal (maybe to take advantage of lower interest rates or to pull out some of your equity) without paying off the zero-interest seller-second mortgage?

Ordinarily, you can't do this because in order for your buyer to bring in a new first mortgage all the prior mortgages would need to be paid off. Otherwise the buyer's new mortgage wouldn't be in first position. But a subordination clause says that the old seller you bought the property from agrees to let you keep his second mortgage in second position in the event you bring in new financing. Basically, a subordination clause is like the old seller giving you a free pass to place another loan in front of his loan. Obviously, to be fair to the old seller, you need to make it clear that you will make sure that the loan-to-value ratio for the seller's second mortgage will be at least as good as it was when the he originally carried back the note.

Here's the legalese version of what this clause often looks like:

Note Holder agrees to subordinate this promissory note (and accompanying Deed of Trust/Mortgage) to any future financing Borrower secures against this property providing Borrower maintains the same amount of equity protecting this promissory note by Borrower to Note Holder as existed at the creation of this note. Furthermore, Note Holder agrees to execute any necessary paperwork in a timely fashion to comply with this provision.

5. No personal liability. Two of the scariest words to any investor should be "recourse financing." This is when you have to give a personal guarantee on the loans you are getting. Why is this dangerous? In the real world, things can go wrong; markets can fall. As an investor, you need to insulate your investments from the real risk of losing a property. One of the old ways of buying properties was to buy one property, use the equity in that property to leverage yourself into the next, and so on. Like a line of dominoes, one bad event can cause the loss of all you have worked so hard to build.

Instead, make each property stand alone as one airtight unit. And just like an ocean liner, you can afford to lose one compartment while still maintaining the overall health of your portfolio. This means you never sign personally on loans if you can avoid it, and you don't pledge other properties as collateral other than the single property being purchased.

While banks will *always* make you sign personally on the loan, sellers won't, that is, sellers won't if you're smart enough to make it clear in the loan documents that you are not personally guaranteeing the loan.

Here's the legalese version of what this sounds like:

> *Because the property is the sole security for this promissory note, the Borrower assumes no personal liability whatsoever.*

6. Do business with a corporate shield. Another way to layer in protection for yourself is to operate as a separate entity. This simply means that you form a corporation, either a C-corporation or an S-corporation. Or form a limited liability company (LLC). While you'll have to observe certain formalities, the liability protection of doing business in the name of a corporation is worth the effort. When drafting a note for an owner-carry deal, make sure you don't list your name as the borrower. Instead, list the corporation as the borrower and make sure on the signature line you sign as a corporate officer or manager and not as an individual (e.g., "John Smith, Manager of Action Homes, LLC"). We'll talk more about using corporations and limited liability companies in Chapter 4.

7. Seller guarantees no undisclosed liens. While we recommend a formal title search and buying title insurance for the property to make sure you have found out about all the old liens against the property and are insured to get clear title, there will be times when you might want to protect yourself further from liens against the property that the seller didn't tell you about. This becomes especially important in deals where you are closing quickly and might not purchase title insurance.

We use a clause in our loan agreement with the seller who is carrying back financing that says that the seller has told us about each and every lien against the property (e.g., tax lien, mechanic's lien, etc.). And if the seller was not accurate in his disclosure and a lien surfaces that clouds your claim to the title of the property, then you have the right to pay off the lien directly to the lien holder and for every one dollar you spend on these undisclosed liens you get three dollars off the amount of money you owe the seller. How could a seller not agree to this? After all, if the seller balks at this clause, simply look him in the eye and ask, "Mr. Seller, is there something you're not telling me? I mean, as long as you've told me about all the liens, there won't be a problem, will there? If there is a problem, then we're going to have to sit down and talk this through before I go ahead with the purchase."

Here's the legalese version of the clause:

> *Note Holder has expressly warrants that there are no lien(s) against the property other than those listed in this agreement. Borrower has purchased this property relying on this information. Both parties understand and agree that if this turns out not to be the case (i.e., if there are in fact other lien(s) against the property, either recorded or unrecorded, that existed prior to close of escrow) then this significantly harms the Borrower. In the event any undisclosed lien(s) are later found against the property, then the Borrower may at his or her discretion pay off the undisclosed lien(s) and for every $1 paid by Borrower towards any such lien, Borrower shall be credited with $3 paid on any money owed by Borrower to Note Holder under this agreement.*

8. Automatic renewal or extension of note. Many times when your are structuring owner-carry deals, the seller won't want to have to wait for 30 years to get all of his money. In these cases, using a balloon note works wonders. A balloon note is a note that has a clause saying that all the unpaid balance all becomes due at some future date. For example, we recently bought a four-bedroom house where the seller carried back the financing at 5 percent interest-only payments with a five-year balloon due for the balance of the note. This meant that we paid the seller monthly interest payments, and at some point within five years of closing, we must pay off the balance of the loan (a balloon payment). Typically the balloon payment is made by either reselling or refinancing the property.

Obviously, as an investor the more time you have before that balloon note comes due the more flexibility you have. But there are times when the seller won't give you as much time as you would like. The best way to handle these types of sellers is *indirectly*. Don't argue with them and butt heads; instead, agree to go along with them. Then later in the negotiations simply ask for either a one-time or two-time renewal of the term of the loan, or for an extension if you need it.

Here's the way to ask the seller for this, "Mr. Seller, I'm okay with a balloon note of five years. That should be enough time for me to still conservatively make a profit here. But I would like to have as a worst-case scenario the ability to renew the loan one time. Obviously, I'd have to have paid you on time every month. Does this seem fair to you?"

If the seller won't give you a renewal, ask for the right to extend the balloon note for 24 to 36 months. (Use months here not years; "months" seems much shorter to most sellers.) Even if you only get the seller to agree to a one-time extension of 12 months, that is still one year more on the note than you had before! If worse comes to worse, offer to pay the seller a few thousand dollars to extend the note. If you do use this technique, make sure you spell out that this payment is of principal (i.e., it counts towards the money you would have had to pay the seller anyway and not just interest or a renewal fee). The time to ask and to get it in writing is up front, *not* at the end of the loan.

Here's an example of what the legalese version could look like:

Borrower may renew this note for 2 additional 24-month terms by paying to Note Holder $2,000 of principal on or before 30 days prior to the expiration of this promissory note or any extension thereof.

9. Substitution of collateral. The final clause you should always ask for in your seller-carry deals is called "substitution of collateral." This means the seller gives you the right to free up the property you are buying of the lien that secures the seller's owner-carry mortgage and move that lien over to another property you have. Imagine you are buying a $200,000 house and the seller carries a second mortgage of $50,000 at 7.5 percent interest. You want to sell that house but don't want to lose out on the low interest use of the $50,000. If you have a substitution of collateral clause in your loan agreement with the seller, you can move that low interest second mortgage of $50,000 over and secure it against another property you have that has enough equity in it to be fair to the seller. Again, you don't have to use this clause, but it does give you maximum flexibility.

Here's the legalese version:

> *Note Holder agrees to allow Borrower to substitute any property(ies) in which the Borrower has a total amount of equity equal to or greater than the amount of equity as existed to secure this note at the time this note was created, as collateral for this promissory note and accompanying Deed of Trust. Furthermore, Note Holder agrees to execute in a timely manner any documents necessary for the implementation of this substitution of collateral.*

Five More Quick Owner-Carry Financing Tips Guaranteed to Make You Money

1. Use thank you payments. Many times the only way to make a highly leveraged purchase of a nice house create cash flow from the start is to get the seller to accept below-market interest rates on the money they are carrying. One way that makes this more palatable to a seller is to call these "thank you payments" as opposed to interest payments. Just by labeling the payment this way you de-emphasize the need to get an interest rate. Tell the seller, "Mr. Seller,

I'm even willing to give you a thank you payment of $300 every month as my way of saying I appreciate you being patient while waiting to cash out and get that $100,000 check."

2. Consider adding up your monthly payments into quarterly, semiannual, or annual payments. If the amount of your monthly payment doesn't seem like much, consider offering a larger payment to your seller quarterly, semiannually, or annually. Using our example from above, if $300 per month doesn't sound like much, why not add up the payments and pay your seller annually. Say, "Mr. Seller, I'm even willing to pay you $3,000 to $4,000 every year as an annual thank you payment for your willingness to work with me to make this work for both of us."

3. If you have to make payments, pay *pure* principal. Obviously, as an investor, you would prefer a loan without payments and without interest. That's why whenever possible you'll use the language of paying your seller a lump-sum payment which is due down the road. But if you have to pay the sellers as you go, pay them as principal not interest. What follows is an example of how to word your contract so you are paying pure principal and not interest:

> *Seller to carry back a second mortgage in the amount of $10,000 to be paid by Buyer in 100 monthly equal payments of $100 including principal and interest with the first payment of $100 due within 30 days of closing.*

4. If you have to pay interest, let it accrue. As an investor you need to protect your cash flow. If you are negotiating with sellers who insist on interest, see if you can get them to let the interest accrue to be paid off when you resell the property. This works especially well for properties you are buying far enough below market value that you are going to have the margin to pay for this accumulating interest cost when you resell to your buyer. Make sure you are specific and write up the agreement to be "simple" interest not "compound" interest. This will save you money. Use caution here to make sure there is enough profit down the road to make this possible.

5. Use graduated payments to your seller to protect your cash flow in the early years. See if the seller will accept lower interest payments in the early years with built-in increases of the interest payments in the later years of the note. For example, "Mr. Seller, what if we were able to pay you $300 per month for the first 24 months, and then for the next 24 months we'd pay you $400 per month, and then for the final 24 months you'd get $600 per month?" There are no rules governing this, so be creative.

■ **Peter's Story**
We did one owner-carry financing deal on a four-bedroom house where our interest rate was 3 percent for the first year, and the rate went up each year by 1 percent for the next several years. The seller got a quick sale and higher interest in the later years which we both knew was a strong incentive for us to make sure to turn the property faster.   ■

You now have learned of all five Purchase Option buying strategies. They will form the foundation for the deals you structure. Now, it's time to move forward and talk about how you negotiate and close these deals with sellers.

23 Negotiating Techniques to Get the Best Deal Possible

You've just learned of the five most powerful "nothing-down" strategics. Now you know the kind of deals you are trying to structure with sellers. That said, you are now ready to learn about the specific negotiating techniques you need to get sellers to participate in these deals.

In our first book, we went into detail on the basic five-step system you need to follow when negotiating with sellers. We call this the Instant Offer System. What follows is a summary of those five steps. Then, after the summary, we'll cover 18 more negotiating techniques that will help you fine tune and go beyond the Instant Offer System in order to get sellers to say, "Yes!" to your creative offer.

The Five Steps of the Instant Offer System

The five steps of our Instant Offer System are as follows:

1. Build Rapport with the Seller

If you want to get a great deal on a property, one of the most important requirements is to build an emotional connection with the seller of the property. When you are working with motivated sellers, you need to help them feel comfortable in revealing their situation both with you and with themselves. No matter which of the Purchase Option buying strategies you plan to use, you will always do better if you can work collaboratively *with* the seller rather than combatively *against* them. This means you need to build and maintain a high level of rapport with the seller.

Spend the first five to ten minutes making friends with the sellers. Ask them questions about themselves and find areas of commonality. We all tend to like people who are similar to ourselves. Help the sellers realize all that you have in common.

2. Set an Upfront Agreement

An upfront agreement is an agreement between you and the seller that you will both come to a decision about at the end of your discussion. It is the way that you create a context of getting a decision on the spot from your seller.

In its simplest form, an upfront agreement sounds like the following:

Investor: Mr. Seller, if you end up hating the ideas we talk through tonight, are you okay telling me that you hate them?

Seller: Sure.

Investor: On the other hand, if you feel these ideas are a fit for you, are you okay telling me that too?

Seller: Yes, I am.

Investor: Great, I appreciate that. Now I'll be doing the same thing. If I don't feel it's a good fit for me to buy this property, I'll let you know. And if I do think what we talk through tonight is a fit, I'll let you know. The one thing is that I want to be respectful of your time and my time so at the end I'll let you

know exactly where I stand, either yes it is a fit or no it isn't, and I would appreciate the courtesy from you. Is that fair?
Seller: Yes, that's fair.

3. Build the Seller's Motivation Level for Selling

It's part of human nature that people in tough situations are often in denial. It's your job in Step 3 to help get the seller to open up about why they are really motivated to sell.

4. Talk through the Financial Details of the Deal

After you have discovered the seller's motivation, you move on and get all of the financial details onto the table so you can start working with the seller to create an deal that meets their most important needs and has a fair profit in there for yourself. Done well, this step also helps you lower the seller's expectations of what they will get from the sale so that you can get a good buy on the property.

5. Close the Deal

This is the final step of the Instant Offer System. It's time to close the deal.

The Single Most Important Negotiating Skill

The single most important skill you have as an investor is your ability to connect emotionally with people. This is the skill that will help you get the seller to open up about their real reasons for selling. This ability will help you create trust and rapport with the seller. Master this skill and you'll never really be "negotiating a deal." Rather, you'll be talking over ways of coming up with a win-win solution with the seller. The difference is huge.

■ David's Story

"I often joke with people who attend our workshops that I'll put Peter up against any other investor in his weight division. I laugh and say, "Pound for pound, he's the best investor I've ever seen." And this is true. I've watched sellers literally hug him after they have sold him their home at a great profit for Peter. Why? It's because he is able to emotionally connect with them. He becomes like a trusted friend. And in the end, who are you going to sell to? Some investor who holds you at arms length? Or the investor who connects with you and builds a relationship? The answer is obvious. ■

Many investors use what we like to call the "big stick" method of negotiation. They go in and negotiate with hardball tactics. And for some investors this works. We've found that it isn't a good fit for us and don't recommend it to our students. We just don't feel good going in and beating up the seller. Plus, we have found that this isn't an effective way to get a good deal. Sure, if you're simply negotiating a low-ball cash price for the property this may work— although we still believe there are better ways to get a low cash price. However, when you are looking not just to get a good price on the property, but to also negotiate great terms, then it's essential to negotiate with people in such a way that you maintain your rapport with them. This is one of the biggest distinctions between the Purchase Option negotiating techniques and those used by many other investors.

As a Purchase Option investor you'll learn how to be much more subtle in your negotiating and to do it in such a way that you always maintain rapport with the seller. We'll never ask you to give the seller a "take it or leave it" last offer. Or to fight with the seller over the price. You'll learn how to use simple questions worded with powerful language patterns that do much of the negotiating work for you.

This means that you don't need to have a magnetic personality to persuade sellers to sell to you. You'll follow carefully structured language patterns that will do most of the negotiating work for you. What you'll need to supply is the sincere care for the other person and the willingness not just to listen to them but to really *hear* what they are telling you. When you add these two ingredients to these powerful negotiating tools, you will become unstoppable.

What Really Drives Home Sellers

Answer this question: What really drives people who are selling their home—the lure of making money on the sale *or* the fear of making a mistake? Most people would agree that the average seller is much more strongly motivated by the fear of making a mistake than by the desire to make a profit. What does this have to do with being a great negotiator? Simply this: When people are driven by fear of making a mistake, they try to protect themselves by constantly looking for what's wrong in any negotiation and in any offer. And when people are looking for what's wrong, they tend to do something called "mismatching."

Mismatching is a term that comes out of a school of psychology called Neuro-Linguistic Programming or NLP. What it means to you, the investor, is that when you are negotiating with a seller, that seller will tend to mismatch you. If you tell them it is a great offer, they'll tell you it is a lousy offer. If you say the price is too high, they'll tell you its too low.

Whenever you can anticipate the pattern of interaction with a seller, you can use this knowledge to your benefit. The way you'll do this is to use what we call "negative phrasing." Negative phrasing is the best way to use the seller's own "mismatching" tendencies to your advantage.

The Power of the "Take Away" Close

Another name for negative phrasing is called a "take away" close. Here is an example of what negative phrasing sounds like:

Investor: What else have you tried to sell the property?

Seller: I listed the property with a real estate agent for six months.

Investor: And that worked really well?

Seller: Not really, no. We never found any serious buyers that way.

Investor: Had you thought about just relisting the property with that agent for another six months?

Seller: No, we don't have six months to wait for this to sell. We have already covered the double payments on this house and on our other home for the past four months.

Investor: Well, I guess the good thing is that it's probably not a problem for you to handle the double payments right?

Seller: No, it's starting to become a problem.

Notice the way that you as the investor ask questions you already know the answers to, but you ask them anyway to help draw out the *emotional* response from the seller. For example, when you found out the seller had listed the property with a real estate agent, you asked, "And that worked really well?" You knew it didn't work well or the seller would have already sold the place. But if you didn't use the negative phrasing and said, "Listing the property sure didn't work; the agent must have really bungled this," the seller will usually argue back. Do you really want the seller to argue with you about why selling with a real estate agent is so good for them? Of course not. You want them to vent all their emotional energy about why working with an agent is *not* a real choice for them. The bottom line is that you want the seller to argue for *your* position, and this means giving them the opposite of what you want them to say so that they can have something to mismatch.

Language Patterns of Reluctant Buyers

One of the subtle negotiation applications of this "take away close" approach is for you to become an expert at being a reluctant buyer. Now you have probably heard that you are supposed to be a reluctant buyer when you are negotiating with a seller, but chances are no one has ever shared with you the definite language patterns that reluctant buyers use.

The good thing is that reluctant buyers do in fact use specific language patterns, and you can simply memorize and use these patterns to become a much more effective negotiator. The single biggest language pattern of the reluctant buyer is how they qualify everything they say with phrases like the following:

- I don't know if I could do this, but what if . . .
- My partner might not like this, but what if I could get her to agree . . .
- I might have to talk this through again, but for the moment lets assume this is okay . . .

Notice how the reluctant buyer very seldom makes an unqualified statement of what they could do until very late in the negotiation. Think about it this way. Imagine you and the seller are standing toe to toe facing each other. You each have your hands up in front of you with your palms pressing against the other person's palms. Now imagine you start to push on the seller's palms—hard. What do you think the seller will do? You're right, he'll push back every bit as hard. And so there you are pushing with all your might trying to negotiate harder and harder. After all, you want that deal and you are going to do what ever it takes to get it. So you push harder and harder and pretty soon you and the seller are facing each other red-faced and breathing hard—at an impasse.

Instead, imagine what would happen if while your palms were pushing against each other you were to simply and unexpectedly step back. The seller would fall forward. That is the essence of what you accomplish by understanding how to be a reluctant buyer. By stepping back, you create a space for the seller to fall forward into. In our workshops, we illustrate this by role playing a sample negotiation. Each time the "investor" uses one of the reluctant phrases, he steps back. And because nature abhors a vacuum, when the investor steps back from the deal, the seller steps forward and presses hard to "sell" the investor on buying the property. It's almost funny to watch this happen in the real world, yet it does and knowing how to use it is incredibly powerful.

The other way for you to use what you know about reluctant buyers is to use the negative phrasing you learned earlier. This includes language such as the following:

- You probably wouldn't even consider . . .
- Is that something we should even talk about, or probably not?
- You probably will hate this idea, but what if . . .

Let's listen in on four sample negotiations to hear how an investor could use reluctant buyer techniques through these language patterns. As you read through the following examples, get a sense of the overall *feel* of the conversation in addition to the word-for-word language patterns. Notice how the investor always steps back and qualifies everything he offers. Also, notice what happens when the seller pushes the investor to tell him what he is willing to pay.

Scenario One

Investor: I'm not sure if I could do this, but what if I were able to bring in new financing and get you a chunk of money up front and then you carried back the rest for a while. Is that something that would be worth us talking through or probably not?

Seller: Yes, that is something we should talk about.

Scenario Two

Seller: What are you willing to pay me for the property [pushing for an offer]?

Investor: To be frank, I'm not even sure if I'm going to want to buy the property. I may decide this property just isn't a fit. May I ask you a few questions to see if it might at all be something I'd consider buying?

Seller: Oh, sure go ahead and ask me your questions [much nicer now].

Scenario Three

Investor: You probably couldn't even decide if you wanted to sell me the property today right? You'd probably need three or four weeks to think it over . . .

Seller: No, I wouldn't need three or four weeks to think it over.

Investor: Yeah, but even if we could get all the numbers right where you and I both felt comfortable, which we might not be able to do, you'd probably still not be willing to sell me the property today, right?

Seller: No, if we could agree on the numbers and I felt good about them, I'd be more than happy to agree to sell you the property here today.

Scenario Four

Investor: Well, my partner might hate this idea, but what if I were able to get him to agree to cover your payments for a period of time and to cash you out down the road. That's probably not something you're even willing to talk about, huh? I mean you probably hate that idea . . .

Seller: No, I don't hate that idea. I mean, obviously I'd prefer to just have a cash sale, but, like I told you earlier, that hasn't happened yet and these double payments are killing me. So, you're saying you could cover my whole payment of $1,000 per month?

Investor: Well, I'm not sure we could cover the whole payment, but let's say for the moment we could, is this something we should talk through, or probably not.

Seller: I don't think I could take less than the full payment, but if you could cover that $1,000 per month I'd be open to talking about waiting to get my equity down the road.

There you have four examples of how these language patterns work in a negotiation. While they do take practice to master, they are worth their weight in gold. They will help you turn the situation around and create an experience that is different from what many other investors encounter. Rather than trying to convince sellers to "do the deal" with you, you'll be having the sellers "sell" you on the merits of buying their property.

The Five Keys to Closing the Deal

1. Motivation before Money

An important key to closing the deal is to remember to never talk through any numbers or specifics of price and terms before you have spent time talking through the seller's motivation to sell the property. To get a great deal on a property you need the seller to *feel* motivated. We use the word *feel* intentionally. It's one thing if the seller intellectually knows he is motivated. It is quite another thing for him to feel it in his gut. One is an intellectual response, the other an emotional response. When you can help the seller cut through the layers of denial and get to the emotional core of why this property you are talking with them about buying is such a burden to them, then you *will* get a great buy.

■ David's Story

I remember going with my girlfriend, Heather, to watch her work in the pottery studio. She took out a bag of cold clay and broke off a large lump. She spent the next several minutes working the clay and warming it up. Then she centered it on the wheel and started to throw her piece. As she was working the clay, I thought to myself this is exactly analogous to negotiating with a seller. First, you spend time warming up the situation. You build rapport and get to know the seller. Then, you build the seller's motivation. You help him and you understand his emotional reasons for selling. That's just like kneading the clay over and over. The more time you spend working the clay, the softer and more pliant it becomes. The more time you spend going through the seller's motivation, the more open the seller becomes to your creative offer.

It would be a huge mistake to try to work with a cold lump of clay without warming it up first. You'd probably break your fingers trying. And it is also a costly mistake to negotiate the money part of a real estate deal without warming up the seller first by building their motivation.   ■

■ Peter's Story

Probably the most common compliment we get from investors across the country is on the Instant Offer System. This five-step system for negotiating with sellers took us years to fine tune. Without question, the core step of this system is the "Motivation Step." And it is no coincidence that the Motivation Step comes before the "Money Step." Yes, it will take time to get good at asking the questions that draw out a seller's motivation. But even if you aren't great at it at first, you will always get a better deal if you just remember to ask them why they are selling *before* you move on to talk about the money.

■

We call drawing out the seller's motivation "building" the seller's motivation, a process by which you help guide the seller's thoughts to the emotional core of why they are selling and why a property has grown to be a negative thing for them. You accomplish this "building" primarily through the use of questions, many of which will be the negatively phrased questions such as those you learned earlier in this chapter.

What follows is a list of great questions to use when you are "building" the seller's motivation:

- What were you *really* hoping I could do for you here today?
- What else have you tried in the past to sell the house?
- And that worked really well?
- Why do you think it didn't work out as well as you planned?
- Well, at least it's not a problem for you that you have two payments to cover each month, right?
- What happens if you can't sell? What will you do then?
- When did you want the property handled? Six months, 12 months? I mean, ideally when would you have the property handled?
- What's really the single most important thing you want to get out of this deal?

2. Use *Descriptive* Not Technical Language

Can you imagine the seller's response if you were to say to them, "Mr. Seller, what if we were to lease option your house with an option price of $150,000. We would give you $1 as option consideration, in addition to our commitment to the lease which will be additional option consideration. The term of the lease will be one year with five additional one-year renewals to come up on a rolling basis every 12 months . . . " Have your eyes glazed over yet? Are you a little intimidated by the language? If you feel that way, imagine how the seller will feel: scared and confused.

And a scared and confused seller is *not* going to ask you questions to clarify their understanding or to settle their anxiety. They are simply going to say one word: No!

So make sure you instead speak in descriptive language such as, "Mr. Seller, what if we were to make you a guaranteed monthly payment and then at some point down the road we were to cash you out of the property at the full $150,000 price we talked about a moment ago. Is that something we should talk about, or probably not?"

The funny thing is that what you said in the second example describes in functional terms what you said in technical jargon in the first example. Remember, sellers want to feel comfortable with whatever you offer them. You have got to explain things to them in language that is simple and tells them exactly what they get. Never cloud a discussion by using jargon or fancy language, which usually serves only to bolster your fragile ego at the expense of your bank account.

When given the choice to be a "professional" or to be an ordinary person, be an ordinary person. People don't want to sell their house to a professional. Not only are they afraid that the professional might be so sharp as to take advantage of them, they also find it difficult to build an emotional connection with a professional. Instead, be a person, an ordinary individual. Most beginning investors fall into the trap of putting on their professional persona almost like a suit of armor. They feel that this armor will protect them from the discomfort of a seller saying no to them and from the anxiety of looking like they don't know what they are doing. Little do they know that this armor that protects them also keeps the seller at a distance. It is almost impossible to have an emotional connection with the seller if you hold them far away by being too professional. And as you already know, the single most important key to being an effective negotiator on a property is to build an emotional connection with the seller.

Here's how we handle this issue when it comes up with a seller.

Seller: What company are you with?

Investor: Company? I'm not with some big nationwide company. My company is small, just me. Did you only want to sell to a huge corporation, because if that's the case I want to be respectful of your time and my time? (Notice the negative phrasing subtly used here.)

Seller: No, no. I just wanted to know if you were with a company or by yourself. Actually, I'm glad you're not a huge company; I find them a bit intimidating. Can you tell me what your program is?

Investor: Program? I don't really have a program. I mean, I meet with property owners and talk with them. If I can buy their house in a way that is a fit for them and I can conservatively make a profit, then I buy the property. If not, then I don't. Did I need to have a program to talk with you about buying your house?

Seller: No, no. It's just that the last investor I talked with had this canned program he kept trying to push on me. Where do we go from here?

Investor: May I ask you a few questions to see if this is a property that I would even want to buy? (And you're off and running.)

Many real estate investors mistakenly believe that projecting a professional image gives them credibility in the eyes of a seller. We'll talk more about this later in this chapter as we explain how important playing dumb in a negotiation can be. But for now, understand that credibility doesn't come from being the "expert." Credibility is a state of mind. When you believe in yourself, the seller will too. Putting on your professional "armor" and trying to force fit a program on a seller is not the way to go. In order to be successful investing, you need to take a small risk—letting your real self come through. While we realize you do risk the seller saying no to you, we guarantee that you will dramatically increase your chances of getting a yes.

3. Get the Seller to Agree to Say Yes *before* You Ever Make Your Offer

Wouldn't it be nice to be able to only make offers to sellers you *know* will say yes? Imagine you had a hidden device that would make a small beep if the seller were going to say no and beeped twice if the seller were going to say yes.

> "I'll pay you $340,000 for the house—(Beep!)—I mean $342,000—(Beep! Beep!) what do you say?"

Obviously, that would be an extremely powerful advantage to have in any negotiation. Until electronics manufacturers come out with a device such as this, you're going to have to use your own ingenuity. And you are going to do it by using the two most powerful words in any negotiation: *what if*.

What if is such a powerful phrase because it commits you to nothing and commits the other side to everything. For example, imagine you are negotiating a lease option on a nice three-bedroom house. You've done most of your negotiating, and you're in the final stages of closing the deal. Rather than making an "offer" such as, "Mr. Seller, I'll pay you X dollars for your house," instead ask a "what if" question.

> "Mr. Seller, I don't know if I could do this, but what if I were able to pay you X dollars for your house, is that something that would work for you or probably not?"

Notice the subtle difference between these two ways of making your offer. When you make a formal offer, you have given all control over the deal to the other party. You've made an offer; they get to say yes or no. When you qualify your offer using the "what if" phrasing you aren't really making a formal offer. Yet once the seller agrees to your "what if" offer, the seller has committed himself to saying yes! This is your way of never making an offer until the seller has agreed to accept it. Think of it in the following way.

Imagine you, the investor, are a baseball pitcher. As the pitcher, you are totally in control until the moment you throw the ball. Once you release the ball, who is in control then? The batter. The seller is the batter who is waiting for you to pitch the baseball (the "offer"). Once you as the pitcher have thrown the ball, i.e., made your offer, you have given all control over the next step to the batter, i.e., seller. The batter can either choose to swing or not. You can only wait and hope.

Wouldn't it be nice to be able to fake throw the pitch to see if the seller was going to swing before you ever released your offer? Yes, we know that is not allowed in baseball, but it *is* allowed in investing! That's exactly what using "what if" phrasing does for you. It commits the seller to swing at your offer before you ever officially make it. Only when the seller says yes to your "what if" offer, do you actually make it. If the seller says no to your "what if" offer, you simply move on to another "what if" offer until you find one that the seller says yes to. Then, you see if you can put a deal together based on this acceptable "what if."

We've watched hundreds of investors negotiate deals and find that almost all of them, except the most successful ones, chase the deal in the closing stages of the negotiation. This means that they give the final power to say yes or no to a deal over to the seller. These investors leave the negotiating table knowing that they've missed out on thousands of dollars in profits, but they do not know what they could have done differently. Put the power of these two seemingly innocent words—"what if"—to work making you money.

4. Make the Offer Their Idea

Have you ever heard the expression, "The cook always loves his own cooking best?" Well, the same thing is true in real estate. If you can give ownership of the offer to the seller, the seller will be much more committed to that specific offer. And this means you'll have a deal that will stay closed.

It's easier than you might think to make the offer the seller's idea. Here's exactly how you do it:

> Investor: I don't know if we could do this, but what if we were able to pay you the $1,800 per month, and at some point during the next five years completely cash you out of the property at the full $245,000 price we talked through earlier. Is this something that would work for you or probably not?
>
> Seller: I think that would work for me.
>
> Investor: You *think* that would work for you or you *know* that will work for you?
>
> Seller: I know that will work for me.
>
> Investor: Oh, okay. So if I'm hearing you right, you want me to make you monthly payments of $1,800 per month and to cash you out at some point within the next five years at the full $245,000 price. Did I get that right?
>
> Seller: Yes, you got that right.

See how you, the investor, were able to make it the seller's idea? And we all know, we generally value our own ideas more than other people's ideas. Notice also how you still continue to use your knowledge about the reluctant buyer right until the very end and the agreement is finalized on paper.

You can even play out one more powerful technique here at the end to make sure the deal closes—higher authority.

> Investor: Now, Mr. Seller, I want to make sure that before I ask my partner to go along with this deal that you're sure this is a fit for you and you want to move forward. So you're absolutely sure that you feel this is a win-win deal? Okay, in that case let's put what we've just agreed to down on paper.

And now, you get to pull out your agreement and finish up the detail work. It's this detail work that is the subject of our final key to closing the deal.

5. Use the "Two Chair" Close to Lock Up the Deal

How would you cope with this situation? You had a seller agree to your spoken "what if" offer, you pull out your agreement, you fill it in with the seller, and then at the very end just before he signs on the dotted line he gets cold feet. He starts to say things like, "What if the roof comes crashing in; are you going to pay for that?" Or, "What if the housing market collapses and I have to foreclose on the property and it's only worth 50 percent of its earlier value?" Or, "What if my neighbor's daughter's aunt's psychic tells me this isn't a good deal?" Your deal is being "what if'd" to death?

Here is an effective tactic to close the deal when you are at this point. It is the simplest strategy we employ. It's called the "two chair close."

Of course, you remember that childhood game called musical chairs where you and your friends would dance around a circle of chairs that was just one short of the number of people circling around. When the music stopped, you would all scramble for a chair and the one left standing without a chair would be eliminated. You would remove a chair, start the music, and begin the next round. Well, the "two chair" close resembles this game.

At the end of any negotiation, the two parties involved always play out two roles, the reluctant role and the eager role. The reluctant role is played out by the party who starts to question the deal and who is beginning to talk themselves out of the deal. He or she is afraid of making a bad decision and starts to get scared. The eager role is played by the party who wants the deal to stay closed and who tries to talk the reluctant party into sticking to the deal. At the closing stages, the eager party in essence tries to sell the reluctant party on all the benefits of the deal.

Knowing that at the end of your negotiation there are these two empty chairs, one marked "reluctant party" and one marked "eager party," which chair do you want the seller to sit in? Of course, you want them to sit in the "eager party" chair. The only way to make sure they sit in the eager chair at the close of the deal is to beat them to the reluctant chair. You do this by introducing doubt and concern at the very end to force the seller into the eager role of selling you on the deal.

Let's walk through an example of how this works in the real world. Imagine you have just gotten the seller to agree to a five-year lease option on their house at a fair price and fair monthly rent. You know you can make money on the deal and want to make sure it stays closed. You have written up the deal with the seller, signed the agreement yourself, and now turn the agreement to the seller and hand him the pen. Here is what you do next:

> Investor: Let's see, my name goes down here as buyer. Your name goes down here as seller (hand them the pen). I noticed in the living room a bit of water stain on the ceiling, have you fixed that leak yet?
>
> Seller: Oh sure, we fixed that several months ago.
>
> Investor: Oh, okay . . . (let the seller continue to read for three to five seconds) How about the neighbors? They don't throw any loud parties do they?
>
> Seller: No, no they don't. They're great (continues to read for three to five seconds).

Investor: What about the water pressure in the house? Is it stable, or does it drop radically when two people use the bathroom at the same time?

We think you get the idea. The longer the seller takes to sign their name, the more potential negatives you bring up. In essence, you are gently introducing doubt in the seller's mind about you staying in the deal. This sparks a fear of loss in the seller, and he or she immediately sits in that eager chair and pushes for the deal to close. Does this work in every instance? Of course not. Still, it is the most effective close we have ever used to make sure the deal stays closed.

Four More Secrets to Phrasing Your Offer So the Seller Says, "Yes"

1. Flush Out the Seller's *Real* Deadline to Sell

Obviously, if you know when the seller needs to sell, you have an advantage in the negotiation. The thing is that many sellers won't openly share this crucial piece of information with you. That is, they won't *unless* you know how to ask for it in the right way.

Here's how we recommend you ask for this information. We call it the "Go Long" technique:

Investor: Mr. Seller, when did you want the property handled by? Six months, 12 months? Ideally, when would you have the property handled?

Seller: I can't wait that long; I'm moving in five weeks! Ideally, I would have had the place handled yesterday!

This question is an offshoot of the "take away" phrasing you learned earlier. In essence, you are saying to the seller, "You don't need a quick solution right? You could wait for six months or even 12 months and it wouldn't be any skin off your back, right?" A motivated seller is obviously going to stand up here and say they need a much quicker solution than that.

Most motivated sellers are under the 60-day timer. They have less than two months to sell or lease their property before it causes a major problem for them. The closer they come to their true deadline, the more motivated they become. Always make sure you flush out why this deadline is so important to the seller. This is yet another way you are building their motivation.

> Investor: When did you want the property handled, six months? Twelve months? Ideally when would you have it handled?
>
> Seller: No, not that long. I want it handled in the next two weeks.
>
> Investor: Oh, in the next two weeks. I'm a little confused. Why is it important to you to have the property handled in the next two weeks?
>
> Seller: Because I live about eight hours drive to this place, and I took two weeks off of work to clean it up and sell it.
>
> Investor: Oh, but at least it's no big deal if you need to take more time off work and to drive down here for another week or two right?
>
> Seller: Yes, it *is* a big deal. I'm going to get this place sold in the next two weeks no matter what!

See how you not only flushed out the seller's timeline, but you also got the seller to emotionally feel his sense of urgency and motivation. The more you do this, the better your deal will get. And finding out the seller's "real" deadline to sell is an important part of the equation.

2. Get Agreement on the Concept, *Then* Pin Down the Details

Always do your best to get the seller to agree to a broad, vague offer that outlines a general concept, and work from that concept to a progressively finer picture of all the details.

> Investor: I want to make sure I heard what you just told me right. So what you're really saying is that you want me to take on the responsibility of the property so you don't have to be a landlord ever again, and you just get a guaranteed monthly payment. Did I get that right?"
>
> Seller: Yes, you heard me right.
>
> Investor: Okay. Hmm. Well, I don't know if I could do this, Mr. Seller, but what if I could give you a guaranteed monthly payment for a period of time and take care of the day-to-day maintenance, and then at some point down the road I were to cash you out of the property. Is this something we should spend any time talking about, or probably not?
>
> Seller: Yes, we should talk about it. I mean it's not my first choice, but like I told you earlier I don't have time to be a landlord anymore. What specifically did you have in mind?

See how you got the seller to agree on the general concept of you making him a guaranteed monthly payment for a period of time and then cashing him out down the road. This descriptive statement could be describing a lease option, a subject to purchase, or even an owner-carry deal. When you get the seller to agree to the concept, *then* and *only then* do you move to pin down the deal to specific numbers. If you include all the numbers in your trial "what if" offer, there is too much information that the seller might object to. Far better to introduce fewer variables into the negotiating equation to help you determine where you need to spend time working with the seller, where the seller is unwilling to go, and where the seller is happy to go.

Investor: So if we were to make you monthly payments for say five or six years and then cash you out at the $245,000 price we were talking about earlier, is this something we should even bother to talk through, or maybe not?

Seller: Well, I don't know about five or six years, but yes it's something we should talk about.

Investor: Oh, you tell me. What's the longest period of time you'd be willing to go knowing that I may very well cash you out earlier if I can sell at a profit earlier, and knowing that the longer you give me the more willing I am to get closer to that $245,000 price?

Seller: Well, I might be willing to go as long as three or four years.

Investor: Oh, four or five years is the most you'd be willing to go? (You just used the Range Technique which you'll learn about in a moment.)

Seller: Yeah, I guess I could go as long as five years.

3. Ask Them Why They Think the Deal Is a Fit

One powerful way to build the other side's motivation to do the deal is to simply ask them why they said yes to something.

Continuing on with the earlier negotiation:

Investor: So if we were able to make you monthly payments for at most five years and then cash you out at $240,000 or $245,000, which I'm not sure we could do, but if we could do that, would it work for you, or probably not?

Seller: Yes, that would work for me.

Investor: Oh, okay. Tell me, why do you feel this is a fit for you?

Seller: Because at least I don't have to be a landlord ever again. Yes, I could make more money each month if I rented it out myself, but then I'd have to deal with tenants. Plus, I get the tax deduction from staying on title. It may not be ideal, but it sure sounds good to me after the last few months having to do that eviction and then clean up this place.

Notice that when you asked the seller why he felt it was a fit for him, you put the seller on the spot to justify his yes decision. This taps into the power of consistency which says that people will go to great lengths to make sure they and other people perceive them to be acting consistently with their past actions. When sellers are rationalizing their yes decision, they are publicly affirming their decision to do the deal. This, in turn, makes it even more important for them to remain consistent and finalize the deal. See how you are layering in another level toward closing a profitable deal.

4. Play Dumb

In any negotiation, there are two payoffs, a psychological pay-off and a financial payoff. Rarely can you have both. Which one do you want? Do you want to be the expert and use all kinds of fancy real estate terminology to impress the seller and feel really good about yourself—the psychological payoff—or are you willing to let the seller feel he is smarter than you are and feel in control in the exchange in order for you to make a fair profit—the financial payoff?

We don't know about you, but we're sure willing to pay the seller in psychological dollars any day of the week as long as we're trading for real dollars in return.

Imagine you were the seller. If you were being totally honest, would you rather sell to an investor whom you felt was smarter than you, or would you rather sell to an investor you *knew* you were smarter than? We won't ask you to shout your answer to the world, but if you are like most people, you probably would rather sell to an investor who was dumber than you. Why? If the investor were smarter than you, you would have to worry about getting taken advantage of. But if you feel smarter than the investor, this puts you at ease and helps you feel confident. Aren't you, or any seller for that matter, more likely to make a decision to move forward with a deal if you are relaxed and feeling good about yourself? Of course you are more willing to say yes to the deal.

How, as an investor, do you play dumb? You move the conversation along by asking questions. You let the seller tell you the facts and figures. And you *never, ever* try to impress the seller with displays of fancy terminology and general "know-it-all-ness." If you do need to inject a fact, use language like, *"I was talking with this real estate broker, and he told me that it's customary for the seller to pay for the title insurance policy at closing."*

Two final ways to "play dumb." First, talk slow and pause a lot. Most beginning investors who meet with sellers are nervous, and being nervous they tend to race ahead with their pace of speech, losing the seller from the start. The seller won't ask you to slow down, he'll simply be confused and shut down. Don't let this happen to you. Instead, pace yourself. Take frequent pauses for a deep breath. Ask a friend to go with you on an appointment or two to see if from the outside they notice you going so fast that you lose the seller, or if your pacing is slow enough to help the seller feel comfortable.

Second, make sure you do *all* math slowly and step by step. Look at the following example:

Investor: Let's see here, you had the property listed at $200,000 for a few months. What percent would the real estate agent have gotten there?

Seller: 6 percent.

Investor: Oh, so let's see, 6 percent of $100,000 is $6,000. So if you had a price of $200,000, the real estate agent commission would have been $6,000 plus $6,000. That's $12,000 in commission. Did I get that right?

Seller: Yes.

Investor: Okay, so $200,000 minus the $12,000 would have meant you would have gotten $188,000, if you got a full-priced offer with the real estate agent. Did I do the math right? Sometimes I get the numbers mixed up.

This may seem unnecessary to you, especially if you are a whiz with math, but we have observed that most sellers get real nervous when you talk about numbers. Maybe they are remembering back to elementary school and having to perform math on the blackboard in front of the whole class—and making a mistake. Or maybe they just aren't good with numbers. The best way to make them feel comfortable is to talk them through the numbers very slowly. Don't bring in a fancy calculator. If the seller offers to lend you a calculator say, "Great, but I'm not too good with these things. Can you help me out and figure this out with me?" Then walk them through exactly what to punch in the calculator, and let them give you all the answers. Can you see how much better this will make the seller feel?

This is a very different approach from most investors who walk into the living room with their fancy reverse logic, turbo-charged calculators that they use to whip out amortization charts right before the seller's eyes. Remember, these investors are making themselves look good at the expense of the seller. It is a thousand times more important for the seller to feel smart than it is for you, that is, if your real goal is to make money. So play dumb!

Not only will it make the sellers feel more comfortable, but it will also get the sellers to be more willing to help you in the negotiation. This, in turn, will raise the sellers' self-esteem to give them a feeling of being in control, making them more likely to decide to sell to you. It will also involve the sellers in the whole negotiation process as collaborators rather than as competitors.

Three Surefire Techniques to Get the Best Price

When it comes to price, many investors have trouble getting the seller to come down in a way that still keeps both parties feeling good about the negotiation. Remember, to get sellers to participate in the financing, which is the key common denominator in all Purchase Option deals, you need to maintain rapport throughout the entire negotiation.

Bully tactics of banging the seller over the head with all the repairs you will need to do, the high cost of closing, and the general lack of appeal of their home might work if you were negotiating an all-cash offer, but it is not the best way to get the seller to be flexible on terms. Here are three surefire techniques that you can use to soften the seller up with respect to their asking price for the property. They work best when you use these three techniques in turn, one right after the other. We'll give you an example of what they sound like in a negotiation, then we'll go back through each of the three techniques giving you insider tips to make them more effective for you.

Investor: What was it you were asking for the property again?

Seller: I'm asking $350,000 for the property.

Investor: Oh, and what did you *realistically* expect to get for it? (Technique #1)

Seller: Realistically, I think I'll get at least $335,000 to $340,000.

Investor: Okay, so you realistically expect to get around $330,000 to $335,000, or so . . . (Technique #2) Okay, that makes sense to me. Hmm. If a real estate agent came in here right now with a serious buyer who was willing to give you that full $330,000, or so, you'd probably turn that down huh? (Technique #3)

Seller: No, at this point I'd probably take it just to be done with it.

Investor: Sure, I understand. Let's see, 6 percent of $330,000 is . . . Hang on a second, it's been a long day for me: 6 percent of $100,000 is $6,000, so 6 percent of $300,000 is $18,000; . . . and then 6 percent of $30,000 is hmm . . . (Notice you're playing dumb again and doing the math very slowly.)

Seller: That's $1,800.

Investor: Oh, thanks. Let's see, $18,000 plus $1,800 is just about $20,000 of commission. Okay, so bottom line you'd be getting $310,000 out of it. Okay, that makes sense.

Did you notice how comfortable it felt to take the seller's asking price of $350,000 and turn it into $310,000? You didn't have to kick, club, or scream. You simply used these three techniques in turn to get the seller's price $40,000 lower. Let's go through each technique in the order that you will be using them.

Best Price Technique One: "What Did You *Realistically* Expect to Get?"

Look at the seller with that insider glint in your eye that says, "Hey, come on now. We both know that you might be asking $350,000 for the property, but you don't really expect to get that much do you?" This question will usually get the price down by 3 percent to 10 percent.

What happens if the seller doesn't come down at all? At this point you don't fight with him or her about it. You haven't lost anything by asking, and you still have two more techniques to use.

Best Price Technique Two: The Range Technique

Turn whatever the lowest number the seller gives to you about the price into a range with their number as the high end of the range. If the seller doesn't object, he has just accepted the low end of the range as the new point from which you will negotiate. In our example above, we asked the seller, "So you realistically expect to get around $330,000 to $335,000, or so? " This is a question, but not one you want to have the seller answer. You simply state the question, nodding your head up and down, yes, then move on to your next question a few seconds later. Because you don't want the seller to object, you just don't give them much time in which to voice their objection.

It's important here to nod your head up and down and give out all the nonverbal cues that you are agreeing with the seller even though you are subtly changing their answer in a way that fits for you.

As for the range to use, this will depend on your local real estate market. If you are in a slow market, be aggressive in your choice of opening ranges. If you are investing in a hot market, use a smaller opening range.

If the seller does object to your range and says something like, "No, not $330,000 to $340,000 but $335,000 to $340,000," you respond as follows: "Oh, $333,000 to $335,000. Okay." Notice you have just shrunk the range you use in response to the seller's objection. This lets you test the water and find out where the seller's real limits are. You can shrink your range two or three times until you find the point that the seller is comfortable with.

Best Price Technique Three: Introduce a Fictitious Buyer through a Real Estate Agent to Help Knock 3 Percent to 6 Percent Off the Price

This one is self-evident. If the seller would accept an offer through a real estate agent, he would have to pay the commission to the real estate agent. So, in essence, he is saying the price would be lower by 3 percent to 6 percent to cover the commission. Some sellers will point out that they would be willing to pay for a buyer's agent commission but not for a listing commission. In this case, they are saying that they are willing to knock 3 percent off the purchase price.

Two key points with this technique are for you to use the negative phrasing as shown in the example and to make sure you do the math slowly to ensure the seller feels comfortable with the final answer.

So when you've used these three techniques to talk the seller's price from $350,000 down to $310,000, does this make $310,000 the final price? No, it simply means that $310,000 is the starting point of what the seller wants. If you are writing notes on a scratch pad in front of the seller, do not write any number down *until* you get to this number. Then when you write this number down, you are legitimizing it as the "top dollar" price. Depending on the terms you negotiate, you may go ahead and give the seller this top dollar price, or you might feel that you still need to negotiate this lower. At the very least, you have just learned how to simply and easily get the price down by at least 8 percent to 10 percent or more from the original asking price.

The Four Most Common Seller Objections and How to Handle Them

Seller Objection One: *What's Your Program?*

While this might not seem like an objection, it is a subtle one. What the seller is really saying is, "Come on, Mr. Investor, tell me what you can offer me so I can make a snap decision if I should spend any time with you or not."

Here's exactly how you should answer this question:

> Program? I don't have a program. I guess my program is to meet with property owners and talk with them. If I can buy their property in a way they feel is a fit and I feel I can turn a profit on it then I buy it. If not, then I don't buy it. Do I need to have a fancy program to buy this property?

See how you are reframing the negotiation in a way that the seller knows you are there to listen to their needs and to see if you can both meet their needs and make a profit too. This will go a long way to getting the seller to work *with* you rather than against you in the negotiation.

Seller Objection Two: *Are You a Real Estate Agent?*

Again, this one might not sound like an objection, but in most cases it is. This objection typically comes when you call up the seller on the telephone. You see, most sellers who are selling For Sale By Owner get flooded by calls from agents looking to list the property. These sellers quickly learn the only defense to these calls is to quickly screen out the calls from agents from the calls from direct buyers. Sellers think in these concrete terms. Callers are labeled either "buyers" or "agents." Most sellers simply don't have other categories for people who call about their property. You need to make sure you end up in the buyer category.

We are not saying that real estate agents aren't providing a great service out there. They overwhelmingly are. It's just a perception that many sellers have. Remember, real estate agents are a great resource for any serious investor to tap into. That's why, in our first book, we detailed how you can effectively work with real estate agents to your mutual benefit. As an investor, you need to make sure you don't get sorted into this "out" basket along with the agents. The single most effective way to respond to this objection is to simply answer as follows:

Seller: Are you a real estate agent?

Investor: No, do I need to be? (Said timidly as if you were afraid the seller were not going to sell to you unless you were an agent.)

Seller: No, no you don't have to be. It's just that I keep getting all these calls from real estate agents trying to get a listing on this house, and I'm getting a bit tired of it, that's all.

This response instantly reframes the seller's label of you and puts you in the preferred category of "buyer." What if you are a real estate agent? You answer the seller's question as follows:

Investor (who in this case has a real estate license): Actually, I am an agent, but I was interested in maybe buying this property as an investment. You probably would never even consider an offer from an investor, even if it was an attractive offer, would you?

Again, you need to quickly get out of the agent category and get the seller to perceive you as a buyer.

Seller Objection Three: The Attorney Objection

This objection tends to be the one investors dread the most. They know that many attorneys will kill any deal that is creative and nonstandard. If you negotiated a Purchase Option deal and the seller takes the paperwork to their attorney, many attorneys will kill the deal simply because they aren't real familiar with nonstandard real estate transactions.

Here is the most effective way we have found to deal with the attorney objection. This response comes in three steps:

Step One. Validate the seller's choice to have their attorney check things over and match their need to do their due diligence.

Seller: I'll need to run this by my attorney.
Investor: Of course you will. That makes good sense. (This validates their need to talk with their attorney.) I also need to

do my due diligence. I have to check on the property values and to double-check to make sure you are on title and all that. (This matches their need with your need to be prudent and do their due diligence.)

Step Two. Pace their attorney's reaction so you program the seller to say yes even if their attorney says no.

Investor: But before you spend the $400 to 500 to have your attorney check this over (you are pointing out that it won't be free to get their attorney's opinion—it will have a hefty price tag), I want to make sure that you're spending your money well. I can guarantee you that your attorney is not going to like the fact that you are agreeing to the price up front at today's value and not charging us a future value. He's going to kick and scream and maybe even throw a few books across the room. (You are walking them through how their attorney might react. Of course, no real attorney will ever react quite so strongly. So it won't be as big of a deal if their attorney has a strong statement or two about the deal.) Now, you understand that we need to be able to have the option to buy at the price we agreed on because as investors we have to make a profit or we can't do the deal. Now, if when your attorney has a fit about this, which he will, you're not going to want to move forward with this deal, then I want to save you the $400 or $500 that your attorney is going to charge you, and we can just cancel this agreement right now. What should we do? Should we cancel this deal right now or should we keep moving forward?

Seller: Oh no, let's keep moving forward with this. I just would feel better to have my attorney take a look at the paperwork when we're done, that's all.

In the example above, we were talking about a lease option deal. If we were talking about buying the property subject to the existing financing you might instead say, "You're attorney is going to hate the fact that we're leaving your loan in place for a while. But you understand that one of the reasons we're willing to make up the four back payments and take over the monthly payment is because of the low interest rate loan you have in place. If we had to bring in our own loan, we would not get such a good interest rate plus we'd have about $4,000 in loan costs. That would kill the deal for us."

Step Three. Sign up the deal *subject to* their attorney's review.

The final thing you need to do is to sign up the deal "subject to" their attorney's review. Here is how the clause should read:

> *This agreement is subject to seller's attorney's review. In the event that seller's attorney wants to cancel this agreement, seller's attorney may cancel this agreement by giving written notice to* _____ . *In event that written notice to cancel is not given by 5* PM *on* _____ *then this agreement shall remain in full force and effect.*

Notice that you make this clause read that the seller has decided to accept the offer and must take a definite step within a limited period of time to cancel the deal. This dramatically increases the odds that you have a deal because *inaction* on their part results in a permanent deal.

■ **David's Story**

The way I feel about it is that if the seller isn't willing to sign up the deal with the right to cancel after talking with their attorney, then they probably don't want to do the deal. I would rather know this up front before I invest any more of my time with them. I let them give me notice by faxing me a short letter. This makes them feel more comfortable that it won't be too hard for them to cancel if they want to, but it still requires that they do it in writing.   ■

Seller Objection Four: The Seller Wants a Large Down Payment

Nothing will ruin your day faster than sellers who insist that you need to pay them a down payment. Now, some sellers won't budge from this, and there is nothing you can do. Typically, these sellers just aren't motivated to sell quickly. But most motivated sellers are willing to take a lot less money up front than they initially ask for.

Here are two ways to handle this objection. The first is used when you are negotiating a lease option.

Seller: I'm willing to do this five-year lease option, but I'm going to need a down payment of $10,000 to do it.

Investor: I understand that you need some money up front so that you can feel secure in this deal. That seems reasonable to me. If you were just renting out this property, what would you collect as a security deposit?

Seller: I'd collect at least $1,400 as a last month's rent.

Investor: Oh, that much. Well, if I could talk my partner into it, what if I were to give you $2,800 up front. That's a full month's rent plus a hefty security deposit.

Seller: I'd need more than that.

Investor: Oh. Well, again my partner might kill me for offering this much, but what if we gave you $3,400 up front. That's a full month's rent and a $2,000 security deposit. I know that's not ideal for you but I'm bending as far as I can. Would you be willing to bend a little here too?

Seller: Sure, I guess that would be okay with me.

Your response reframed the seller's request for down payment into them sharing with you their need to feel secure in the deal. From here, it was just a short hop to talking about a security deposit. Remember, if you are talking with the seller about down payments you can only lose. Convention says that down payments by investors are between 10 percent to 20 percent. You need to shift the conversation to security deposits where convention says you only need to give the seller ½ to 1½ percent up front. This is why we stress that you need to control how you label the various parts in the negotiation.

Use the second way when you are negotiating any other type of owner-carry deal.

Seller: I'm willing to carry back the financing as long as you give me 10 percent down which is $20,000.

Investor: I understand your need to get a healthy chunk of money up front to make sure you feel secure in the deal. But to be frank, silly as it seems, I can actually buy four or five houses with the same $20,000. I'm willing to give you a chunk of money up front to show you I mean business and so you can feel secure, but I need to be making a smart investment myself. You understand that, don't you? I want to be fair here, but I need to be fair to myself too.

Seller: Yeah, I understand. Look, if you are willing to give me the full $200,000 price we were talking about earlier with $10,000 down we have a deal.

Investor: Oh, so basically as long as I agree to get close to your $200,000 price you're okay with getting $5,000 to $10,000 up front. (Notice you just used the range technique—twice—once on the $200,000 price and once on the $10,000 down payment. See how easy this is?)

Seller: I couldn't do $5,000 down; I might go as low as $8,000 down, if you agree to the $200,000 price.

Investor: Oh, so if I agree to the full $200,000 price you'd be open to $6,000 to $8,000 up front.

Seller: I didn't say $6,000; I said $8,000.

Investor: Oh, $7,000 to $8,000. Okay.

Seller: I guess I could live with $7,000, but I couldn't take any less.

See how you used what you are learning in this book to get the down payment from 10 percent all the way down to 3.5 percent? If you find the right tenant-buyer, you will probably get most, if not all, of this money back from your tenant-buyer's option payment!

One of our students, Cheryl, was negotiating on a small house with a seller who said he would be willing to carry back the financing. He said he would carry a first mortgage as long as she came in with $10,000 down. Cheryl responded that she certainly understood his need to get a down payment so he would feel secure in the deal. But to be frank, with that same $10,000 she could go out and buy three or four houses and make a much better rate of return on her money. The seller said he understood that and came back and said he would need at least $2,500 down!

Cheryl kept her cool and remembered to play the reluctant buyer. And she calmly accepted his offer of buying the property for $155,000—with $2,500 down and the owner carrying back the balance as a first mortgage with interest of 4.72 percent.

Cheryl later resold the property on a rent-to-own basis and made a nice cash flow from the spread between her payments and the rent for the place. She also sold it for $22,000 more than she paid for it. And the final part to the deal was that she also collected $5,000 option money from her tenant-buyer up front, so this was really a nothing-down deal for her.

So there you have the four most common seller objections and how to handle them. Remember that most seller objections are just their way of saying they feel a bit uncomfortable. Use this as a signal to slow things down, go back over things, and make sure you are continually building your level of rapport with the seller. If the seller feels comfortable with you, then you will have a much better chance of picking up the deal. Most seller objections melt away when sellers feel a sense of emotional connection with you, the investor. So learn to build this connection.

Negotiating Wrap Up

You've just learned 23 specific techniques to help you get the best deal possible. Remember, all of these techniques work best when you are able to establish an emotional connection with the seller.

Also, it takes practice to put these new techniques into action. Repetition is the best way for you to internalize these negotiating attitudes and language patterns. The payoff is worth the time and effort to master these strategies. Over the years, our students have used them to buy, sell, and lease option over $100 million worth of real estate. They will work for you too.

14 Lessons to Lower Your Risk

So far, we have focused on making money by investing in real estate. While we have worked hard to help share with you ways to make money by investing in real estate, we want to make sure you also learn intelligent ways to hedge your risk to avoid losing money while investing in real estate. There is an old expression that says it's not about the money you make, but it's about the money you keep. We agree. We've seen people make millions of dollars through investing in real estate in amazingly short periods of time, only to lose it all even faster. We want to share with you 14 of the most important lessons we've learned over the years to help you create safeguards in your investing.

Lesson 1: Always Build an Escape Hatch into Every Deal You Do

One of the most important safety steps you can take to protect yourself in any real estate deal is to always leave yourself a painless "out" so you can walk away from the property if it turns out the deal isn't as good as it looked on paper. Ask any seasoned real estate investor what's the most important consideration they make before they enter into an agreement and they will answer, "To make sure I know what my exit strategy is if I have to get out in a hurry."

Think about a pressure cooker. You turn it on and let the steam build up. Without the safety valve that lets the pressurized steam escape, it might explode. In real estate investing, we call a safety valve an "escape clause."

There are two types of escape clauses you need to learn to use. The first is called a "subject to" clause. This type of clause says that the agreement is "subject to" some other event happening. And if this event doesn't happen, or if it doesn't happen at the level you wanted it to happen, you may cancel the agreement. Here are several subject to clauses you can choose from:

When Buying

This agreement is subject to Buyer's partner's approval.

This agreement is subject to Buyer obtaining satisfactory financing in the amount of $_____ with an interest rate not to exceed ___ %.

This agreement is subject to Buyer's inspection and approval in writing of the property.

When Selling

This agreement is subject to Seller's satisfactory review of Buyer's loan application and credit history.

This agreement is subject to Seller's attorney's approval.

This agreement is subject to Seller closing on purchase of their new home on 123 Smith St. by January 15, 20__.

Notice that a "subject to" clause can be used when buying or selling. It's important to note that you don't need to flood your agreements with "subject to" clauses. One or two properly worded "subject to" clauses are all you need. You wouldn't want to put five or ten of them in your agreement because the more of them you have in your agreement, the more the other party in the deal *feels* like you aren't really committed to the deal. This can be unsettling for the other party and cause a deal to unravel.

The second way to create an escape hatch in your deals is through the use of a "liquidated damages" clause. A liquidated damages clause, as discussed earlier, says that in the event that you default on the terms of the deal and back out, you have an agreed upon amount of money that is the full settlement cost you are responsible for. Here is an example of a liquidated damages clause we use in every purchase contract with a seller when we are *buying* a house:

> *In event that Buyer should default on any provision in this agreement, then any money paid to Seller by Buyer shall be retained by Seller as full and complete liquidated damages and agreed upon settlement in full.*

This sure sounds like tough language that any seller would love to have in the contract when they are selling to a buyer. And it would be, if it weren't for one essential item: When you are buying a property, you are never going to give the seller a significant chunk of money up front until you are done with all of your due diligence on the deal (see Lesson 3: Do It with Nothing Down). If you do it as we teach our students to do it, you will only be giving the seller a single dollar, or in some cases $10, as upfront money. That's a pretty low cost for you to be able to walk away from a deal.

When we're buying a house, our standard purchase agreement does not include any obvious escape clauses but instead contains a liquidated damages clause. We don't want to load up on "subject to" clauses that might make the seller balk at signing.

"

■ David's Story

I've probably locked up three houses under contract for every one I've gone ahead and bought. I constantly urge my students to make this their mantra: "When in doubt, sign it up!" They can always give it back to the seller. I look at it this way. When you go fishing and you get a bite on your line, you don't stick your head under the water to see how big the fish is. You reel it in. And if it turns out to be too small, or a type of fish that isn't very tasty, you simply release it. The same thing applies to real estate investing. When a seller nibbles, you need to reel him in and sign the deal up. This commits him to the deal but leaves you an out. Then you quickly do your due diligence and decide if it's a keeper or a releaser.   ■

Once you understand you are using good contracts with properly drafted escape clauses, it allows you to get out there and lock up property under contract very quickly. Most investors think that they need to do all their due diligence and research *before* they sign up a deal. This is totally backwards. What happens if you spend several hours doing your due diligence on a deal and then the seller says no? You've just wasted your valuable time.

Instead, you should sign up the deal as quickly as possible, making sure you have a good escape clause in your contract, and then and only then should you complete your due diligence on the deal. Why worry about the due diligence details of a deal that a seller hasn't agreed to? The only reason some investors ignore this rule is fear. They're afraid of getting stuck in a deal that causes them to lose money. You won't let this happen because you'll only use contracts that give you an out—somewhere—and at an acceptable price. The bottom line is that as a shrewd real estate investor, you are going to always make sure you know how to ethically walk away from the deal if your research shows it isn't profitable enough.

We need to again emphasize that when you use powerful "subject to" or liquidated damages clauses in your agreements with buyers and sellers, you have an ethical responsibility to do your due diligence very quickly and let the other party know if any problems arise. In most cases it should take you only seven to ten days at the most to complete your preliminary due diligence. If you notice a potential problem, this is your chance to either renegotiate the deal or to advise the other party that you may choose not to move forward. This is treating the other party fairly. Still, be fair to yourself too by conserving your time and only doing your due diligence on deals you have under contract.

Lesson 2: Do Your Due Diligence So You Don't Get Burned

Doing your due diligence means doing all your checking, inspecting, and number crunching to make sure a deal really is profitable for you. As you have already learned, we believe in signing deals—fast—with a "subject to" or liquidated damages clause and then and only then doing your due diligence. Remember, doing due diligence on a property you do not have under contract is like doing extra-credit homework for a class you aren't even enrolled in. It might be fun, but it isn't going to get you a higher grade.

Here are the seven steps for you to follow when you do your due diligence on a property. (See Figure 4 1 for a checklist.)

Step One: Check the Comps

Property values are determined for single family houses by what other similar, or comparable, houses in that area have sold for in the recent past. For example, a four-bedroom, two-bath, 2,100 square foot house is probably worth what other comparable houses have sold for in the same area. Obviously, for two properties to be comparable they need to be of similar square footage, with the same number of bedrooms and bathrooms of similar construction type

FIGURE 4.1   Seven-Step Due-Diligence Checklist

Step One: Check the Comps (Sales Comparables)

Comp #1 _____ # Bed _____ # Bath _____ Sq. Ft _____
Sale Date _____ Sale Price _____ Features _____
❏ Sale within 3 months   ❏ within 6 months   ❏ Same # Bedrooms   ❏ Sq Ft within 20%
Property determined to be <u>similar construction and similar location</u> to subject property by:
❏ Info from owner of subject property ❏ Info from real estate agent
❏ Personal visit by investor to exterior of comparable property on (date) _____
❏ Other: _____

Comp #2 _____ # Bed _____ # Bath _____ Sq. Ft _____
Sale Date _____ Sale Price _____ Features _____
❏ Sale within 3 months   ❏ within 6 months   ❏ Same # Bedrooms   ❏ Sq Ft within 20%
Property determined to be <u>similar construction and similar location</u> to subject property by:
❏ Info from owner of subject property ❏ Info from real estate agent
❏ Personal visit by investor to exterior of comparable property on (date) _____
❏ Other: _____

Comp #3 _____ # Bed _____ # Bath _____ Sq. Ft _____
Sale Date _____ Sale Price _____ Features _____
❏ Sale within 3 months   ❏ within 6 months   ❏ Same # Bedrooms   ❏ Sq Ft within 20%
Property determined to be <u>similar construction and similar location</u> to subject property by:
❏ Info from owner of subject property ❏ Info from real estate agent
❏ Personal visit by investor to exterior of comparable property on (date) _____
❏ Other: _____

Comp #4 _____ # Bed _____ # Bath _____ Sq. Ft _____
Sale Date _____ Sale Price _____ Features _____
❏ Sale within 3 months   ❏ within 6 months   ❏ Same # Bedrooms   ❏ Sq Ft within 20%
Property determined to be <u>similar construction and similar location</u> to subject property by:
❏ Info from owner of subject property ❏ Info from real estate agent
❏ Personal visit by investor to exterior of comparable property on (date) _____
❏ Other: _____

Comp #5 _____ # Bed _____ # Bath _____ Sq. Ft _____
Sale Date _____ Sale Price _____ Features _____
❏ Sale within 3 months   ❏ within 6 months   ❏ Same # Bedrooms   ❏ Sq Ft within 20%
Property determined to be <u>similar construction and similar location</u> to subject property by:
❏ Info from owner of subject property ❏ Info from real estate agent
❏ Personal visit by investor to exterior of comparable property on (date) _____
❏ Other: _____

FIGURE 4.1   Seven-Step Due-Diligence Checklist (Continued)

Step Two: Check the Market Rents

	Address	# Bedrooms	# Baths	Rents For?
Rental Comp #1	_____	_____	_____	_____
Rental Comp #2	_____	_____	_____	_____
Rental Comp #3	_____	_____	_____	_____
Rental Comp #4	_____	_____	_____	_____
Rental Comp #5	_____	_____	_____	_____

Step Three: Check the Title

- ❏ Who owns the property?
- ❏ Liens?
- ❏ Judgments?
- ❏ Current Loan Status, Terms, Balance?
- ❏ Taxes Current?
- ❏ If Home Owners Assoc. How Much Are Fees? Are They Current?
- ❏ Pending Bankruptcy of Seller?
- ❏ Personal Liens Against Seller Not Yet Recorded Against Property?
- ❏ Mechanics Liens?
- ❏ Accurate Legal Description of Property?
- ❏ LETTER FOR LETTER Double Check of Name and Spelling On Your Paperwork?

Step Four: Inspect the Property

- ❏ Professional Inspection?
- ❏ Thorough Personal Inspection

Step Five: Check out the Neighborhood

Step Six: Run the Numbers

Step Seven: Have a Trusted Advisor Run the Numbers

---

and condition, etc. One often overlooked determinant of value is the actual area the property is in. If your property is located in Clarksville and the house across the street is in Adamsville, then the two properties may not really be comparable, especially if Clarksville homes have a much better school district for its residents to enjoy compared to schools available to Adamsville residents.

All of this is a simplification of the process of determining value. It takes time to learn how to value a home and it is a skill you will learn over time. In the beginning, if you sign up a deal, latch on to a good real estate agent in the area who can help you determine its value. As a fall back you can always hire a professional appraiser for the first house or two you buy. This step is to just make sure that the property really is a good buy at the price and terms you have agreed to with the seller.

Four Ways to Find Sales Comparables for Free
1. Network with a local real estate agent and ask them for a market analysis of the property.
2. Go online to <www.realestate.yahoo.com>, <www.home gain.com>, <www.byowner.com>, <www.homepricecheck .com>.
3. Go online and use one of the major search engines to find other sites such as those above. Also, check to see if your county government's Web site has access to recent sales information. Try checking your county recorder's office or county clerk's Web sites.
4. Start to keep your own file of sales comparables for your farm area and become an expert in that area. Visit several open houses in that area and talk to the listing agent about home values and recent sales in the neighborhood. You can even bring along your property information and ask the agents you meet to give you their opinion of what your property is worth. Most agents have a good sense of values in the areas they specialize in.

Step Two: Check the Market Rents

A rent survey is an analysis of what similar properties to the one you have under contract are renting for. Real estate, like many other things in the world, is valued by what other people, known as the market, are willing to pay in order to use the property. This is the market rent value of the property. While you might not be able to determine exactly to the dollar just what this value is, you'll almost always be able to determine a range of rents that properties similar to your property are renting for.

Finding the rental range is important because, in most cases, once you start looking for a tenant-buyer, the clock is ticking. Asking too much rent can cause you to waste your time showing the property and your money paying for ads. In addition, you'll want to snare that perfect tenant-buyer by having your property rent at the right level beginning with your first showing. A good rent survey will allow you to fill your properties more quickly, which means that you won't ever have to walk away from the profits that are yours simply because you were asking far too much rent. Also, if you've agreed to pay too high of a monthly payment to your seller, then the rent survey will allow you to have the information you need to go back and renegotiate the payment with the seller.

The easiest and most direct way to do a rent survey is to simply walk down the street and start knocking on doors. Note: If you aren't comfortable doing a rent survey for a property because of the neighborhood it is in, then you shouldn't buy a property in that area. This gives you a chance to look closely at the neighborhood as you walk through it. Ask the people who you meet the following question, "Hi, I was thinking of renting in this neighborhood, do you by chance know how much other people are paying in rent for a ___ bedroom house (or condo/townhouse) around here?" Notice that you ask them if they know what *other* people are paying in rent. We've found this is a less intrusive question than asking them what *they* are paying in rent.

How do I know that I've gotten valid information? If you've talked directly with the person who is paying rent, then you've gotten good data. If you're talking with a teenager who makes a guess, then we wouldn't count on it. A response like, "Oh I don't know, maybe $1,200 a month for a three-bedroom" should be given much less weight than, "We pay $1,500 for our three-bedroom and the Walkers pay $1,400 for a two-bedroom." By getting several people's input, you are able to compare all the responses you have gathered.

Another way to do a rent survey fast is to check your local paper's For Rent classifieds and see what things are being advertised for in that area. Also, you can call up a few rental agencies and ask them what a similar property in that area will rent for. The key to determining the market rent for an area is to get answers from several different sources so you can compare answers and determine the real rent range.

The Five Most Common Mistakes Made When Doing a Rent Survey

1. Not doing the rent survey. You wouldn't think that a professional investor would ever skip this important step, but it's done all the time with some pretty severe consequences.

2. Taking the seller's word for how much you can rent the property out for. Yes, the seller is your friend. And you still need to accurately verify any information the seller shares with you.

3. Going on "ballpark" estimates provided by real estate agents. While most real estate agents are good sources for property sales values, they are usually a poor source for rental values.

4. Not getting at least five rental comparables. You need at least five comparables to get an accurate and reliable indication of rental value.

5. Ignoring the *real* market rent experts—your prospective tenants. You can verify the information from your rent survey when you are showing the property to prospective tenant-buyers. Any of the people who come to the showing for the house who don't fill out an application are a great source of feedback as to the rental value of that house. After

all, they are probably looking at several different homes in that same area.

■ **Peter's Story**

We once did a rent survey for a two-bedroom duplex. We found that rents ranged from a low of $325 to a high of $975 for almost identical properties. We also found out that most of the properties in this neighborhood were renting between $700 and $800 a month. We knew that we could get *at least* $700 per month and probably $800 each month. With this information we *knew* we had a great deal on the duplex and went ahead with the purchase with a sense of confidence.   ■

Step Three: Check the Title

Does the seller you are buying from really own the property? Are they the sole owners or are there other people on title you need to get signatures from? These are questions you can only answer by checking the title to the property.

To do this, you'll need to get a title report, which is as easy as calling up a local title company and asking them to do a "title report" on the property for you. In some parts of the country this is called an "Ownership and Encumbrance Report" or "O and E Report" or even a "Preliminary Title Report." This is your first look at the title. The cost will range from free to $200. You will get a closer look at the title later when you order your title insurance policy for the property.

NOTE: We recommend that unless you are a seasoned investor who is willing to take a calculated risk that you spend the money and buy title insurance. This will mean that the title insurance company you are working with will do an exhaustive title check on the property. The key thing to remember is that you need to go through all the "exclusions" to the title insurance policy very carefully because this is where you'll find out about things like the IRS tax lien or the judgement from a lawsuit, etc. We don't always buy title insurance ourselves. If we are getting the property for nothing down, then we'll do a title search but usually not buy title insurance. We figure if the seller lied to us about the liens on the property and our title search missed it, if worse comes to worse, we'll walk away from the deal. On deals where the seller carries back a mortgage for part or all of the money we owe them, we also are more frugal with when we decide to buy or not buy title insurance. In every promissory note we use with a seller who is carrying back financing, we always use the "Undisclosed Lien Clause" discussed in Chapter 2 of this book. If we have to put any serious money in the deal and the owner is not carrying back a large note, then we *always* buy title insurance. Again, we want to reiterate that if you are not an experienced investor who understands the risks involved, we recommend you buy title insurance. It's worth the peace of mind it will give you.

How to get a free title report. Over the years we've worked with a number of different title companies from the large nationwide companies, such as Chicago Title and Stewart Title, to the smaller regional or local companies. We tend to give all of our title business in one area to one company because when we are a good customers of theirs, they give us perks—like *free* title reports. For example, in San Diego we work mostly with one company. They have done a great job for us. Even though we don't always buy title insurance when we are buying a property, our buyer always needs it when they bring in new financing to cash us out of the deal. Because our buyer doesn't care who we use for the title insurance, we give a large chunk of our business to our favorite company.

We have a good relationship with our sales representative at our favorite company, and whenever we need a title search done, she'll get it for us for free. And she will make sure to include things like sales comparable data so we can check the price we have for the property. In fact, when she switched title companies, we went with her, and she still takes care of us. This is why it is so important to build good relationships with other people in the real estate world. It's a win-win relationship. She gets continuing business, and we get free title reports.

Also, ask the sellers to see a copy of their title insurance policy. While this is a bit out of date, it will be a good way for you to check on the chain of title for the property for the time preceding your sellers' purchase of the property.

Checklist for examining title to the property. Here is a long list of questions to ask when examining the title to a piece of real estate:

- Who exactly is on title to the property?
- Does your seller really have the authority to sell the property to you?
- Do you need any other signatures?
- Did you get the spelling of the seller's name to match letter for letter exactly how it appears on the deed?

■ David's Story

We were setting up the escrow paperwork on a three-bedroom house we had in San Diego when I got a call from the escrow officer informing me that the deed that was in escrow was faulty because the sellers had signed with only their middle initials when they used their full middle name on their deed when they bought the house. Now because I had a good relationship with the sellers (because I always pay early each month), they simply signed a new deed. But I learned a lesson. I now go over every name on every document with a magnifying glass and triple check that it is *letter for letter* how it appears on their deed.   ■

- What liens or judgements are recorded against the property?

■ **David's Story**

I signed up a house in Victorville, California, subject to the existing first mortgage of $110,000. The seller said the house was worth $125,000 and that he was moving to San Diego. Once I had the signed deal, I started doing my due diligence. I found out the house was really only worth $115,000. Still, this wasn't too bad because it was only a dollar down to buy the house. But then I got the title report on the property. It seemed the seller forgot to tell me about the $20,000 second mortgage against the property. That meant that there were $130,000 of loans against this $115,000 house. In some cases such as this, it makes sense to move forward with the deal and negotiate a discount with the mortgage holders. In this case, it wasn't worth it. I simply canceled my agreement with the seller and wished him the best of luck. Sometimes walking away from a deal is the best solution.   ■

- Have you confirmed the loan balance on all loans with the respective lenders?

    You'll need to get an Authorization to Release Information form signed or to do a three-way call with the seller on the phone to the lender. Or, many times you can even call the lender's toll-free hotline and punch in the seller's Social Security number and loan number and hear an up-to-the-minute description of the seller's loan and its current balance.
- Are the property taxes paid? When is the next installment due and for how much?
- Is there a Home Owners Association (HOA)? If yes, are all the fees current?

- Get the seller's Social Security number and permission to both do a credit check and to run a search for them in the public records for judgments, pending bankruptcy, or any other item that might attach to the house or affect your purchase of the property.
- Any recent work on the house?

  Remember, in most states, contractors have up to 90 days to place a mechanic's lien against the property. If yes, are there signed releases from the contractors stating that they have been paid? If not, are there at least receipts proving that the work has been paid for?
- Do you have an actual copy of all promissory notes and deeds of trust?

  This is especially important if you are taking title to the property subject to the existing financing.

All that said, the single most important thing to triple check when you review the title report is *who* owns the property. It will be a rare case when a seller is trying to fraudulently sell you a house he or she does not own. What is more common is that they forget to mention that someone else is on title with them, for example, their son or daughter. Or maybe you live in a community property state and their spouse has an equitable claim to the property even if he or she is not on the deed recorded at the county recorder's office. If you live in a community property state such as California, make sure you talk with a good real estate attorney who can explain to you how this affects title to the property. When meeting with a seller in a community property state, make sure you ask the seller if they are married. If they are married, get the spouse to either sign all of the paperwork or have the spouse quitclaim their interest in the property to the seller you are dealing with in order to make sure that when you are buying the property you are buying *all* of the property, not just a half interest.

The most common mistake when looking at the title report is to forget to check the exact wording of the title. You want to make sure that the names on all the closing paperwork reflect the *letter* for *letter* spelling exactly as it is on the deed. If the seller on your closing paperwork is "Paul Smith" but it appears "Paul Nathan Smith" on the actual deed, then you will have problems with the title down the road. Make sure you get the names and spelling accurate, even if you have to get the seller to re-sign several documents.

You should also use the title report to make sure you get the exact legal description to the property for your agreements. The legal description is *not* the street address for the property. It is the official way to describe the exact property. An example of how the legal description looks is, "Lot 4, Block 5 Monument Creek Village, Section One, as recorded in document 32884 of County Recorder's Office in Jakes County . . ." The easiest way to get this is to copy it from the deed that gave your seller title. It's very important to get this legal description accurate.

■ **Peter's Story**

I hope that by reading this book you won't make some of the same mistakes that I have over the years. Getting all of your due diligence done before you put substantial money into a property is an important lesson to learn. I had been looking at purchasing an 18-unit apartment building in the Capitol Hill area of Denver. The owner had mismanaged the property, and out of 18 units only 3 of them were occupied. I had run through the numbers and felt that the property was easily worth about $265,000, once all the units were rented.

The real estate agent let me know that the owner was ready to make a deal and was open to any offers. I met with the agent from "Crown Realty" and wrote up an offer of $195,000. I couldn't help but think about all of the money I'd be making on this deal as I sat with the agent at a table in a fast food restaurant putting the final touches on the deal. He said, "I need $15,000 as an earnest money deposit because this is such a good deal. We need to let the owner know that you are serious about buying."

I wrote out the check and made it payable to "Crown Financial" at the agent's request. I was unsure about handing over that much money, but then I reasoned that it was only going to go into the escrow account—I thought—and I would be able to get it back in the event the property didn't check out when I did the inspection.

As it turned out, the seller was an aggressive investor who provided a legal description to the agent that didn't include the parking lot. When I was told that I'd need to pay another $35,000 for the parking lot, which I thought was included, I decided to throw in the towel. "Let's unwind this deal," I said to the agent. "I won't approve the inspection. Just give me my earnest money back, and I'll go and buy a property from someone who's willing to play fair."

Unfortunately, the agent wasn't playing fair either. "I can't give you your $15,000 back," he said. "I spent it to pay my taxes." It turns out the agent had diverted the money into his own shell company, which he had cleverly named Crown Financial so as to sound like the company that he worked for, which was Crown Realty. Obviously this was illegal for him to do. It was fraud. But if I had followed the simple rule about due diligence that you've learned in this book, I wouldn't have put substantial money into a property before I had completed my due diligence. If I had offered, instead, to give the agent a promissory note, due upon removal of all contingencies, I wouldn't have had to go home that night and explain things to Joanna, my wife.

I can still remember the conversation. "Oh, hi, Peter. How did your day go?" she asked. "Not so good," I responded. "We lost $15,000 dollars today."

I did end up getting my money back. It took me almost two years before I was able to get the state real estate commission to pay me out of a recovery fund. I could have avoided all that worry and frustration if I had just followed some of the simple rules you're learning in this book. ∎

Step Four: Inspect the Property

Obviously, before you go through with your purchase of the property, you are going to want to take a close look at it. How close of a look will depend on the type of Purchase Option deal you have put together with the seller. For example, if you have a five-year lease option with the seller where they are responsible for any maintenance over $200 in any month, then you might not feel the need to spend $300 to $500 for a professional inspection. If you are buying the property using a big money cash close, you will definitely want to hire a reputable, professional property inspector to go through the entire property.

We've bought houses from sellers and done just a walkthrough inspection ourselves, and we've bought other properties and paid for a professional inspection. The real question is: How much money are you putting in, either your money or borrowed money? If a seller lies to you and fails to disclose that there are $6,000 in needed repairs, with many Purchase Option deals you could either get the seller to do the repairs or, if the seller refuses to do the repairs, you could choose to cancel the agreement, or you could choose to pay for the repairs yourself and get a credit on any money owed to the seller that you put into the repairs. In the agreements we use, we have clauses in them that give us these options. But because you can never count on the seller doing these repairs, if you ever put serious money into any deal, always hire a professional inspector. (If you want to learn more about property inspections, a good book is, *The Home Buyer's Inspection Guide* by Boroson and Austin from John Wiley and Sons, Inc. 1993.)

Step Five: Check Out the Neighborhood

Next you are going to take a close look at the neighborhood the property is located in. Because homes are usually valued by what similar houses in that same location sell for, you want to make sure that the other properties will help your property grow in value.

Here is a list of good questions to ask:

- Is the area in demand?
- What is the average time a house for sale in this area sits on the market before it sells?
- On average, what percent of the asking price do most houses in this area sell for?
- Is this an area you feel safe in? How about after dark? Are you willing to spend time at the property showing it?
- What is the average rate of appreciation for similar properties in this area?
- Are most homes in this neighborhood owner-occupied (this is best) or rentals?
- Are there any new building projects or business developments in the area that will affect the value of the property?

Where can you find answers to these questions?

- Experienced real estate agents in the area
- Local chambers of commerce
- Experienced property appraisers in the area
- Experienced property managers in the area
- Local planning commissions
- Local departments of transportation
- Local residents

Step Six: Run the Numbers

Taking into account all that you have learned about the property and the area, go back and run your numbers again. Does the deal have enough profit to make it worth the time, effort, and risk?

Step Seven: Have an Outside Party Run the Numbers One Last Time

Human nature being what it is, by closing time you will be so close to the deal that it will be worthwhile to have a trusted outsider go over your financial projections for this deal. If you are doing the deal with little or nothing down and no personal liability for the loan, then you may decide to skip this step. After all, your exposure is very low. On the other hand, if you are giving the seller $8,000 to deed you the property subject to the existing financing, you will probably want to have someone go over the deal with you. Often times they will question assumptions that you didn't even know you were making.

Lesson 3: Do It with Nothing Down

The more money you have at stake, the more you have to lose. This is true of any investment. The good news is that the less money you have in a deal the less risk you have. If you can keep your upfront investment in a deal at zero, then you have lowered your effective risk in a significant way.

Imagine you bought a house the traditional way—you put 20 percent down and got a bank loan for the balance. If that house were a $250,000 house and things started to go wrong, could you walk away from your $50,000 down payment without it hurting?

Now imagine the opposite. You bought a house on a five-year lease option with no money down. Then, two weeks later you find that the house was built with absolutely no permits whatsoever and wasn't built to code. What are you going to do? You will walk from the deal. You may have *time* at stake that you will lose, but you won't lose *principal*.

We once heard that Warren Buffet, arguably the single best stock investor of all time, said that the single most important rule of investing was to never lose principal. That advice has stayed with us through the years.

Promise yourself that you will never give the seller of any property any significant money without giving yourself at least 72 hours to do your due diligence. Ideally, you wouldn't give the seller any of your own money—ever. And if that doesn't work, you will give yourself enough time to make sure the deal is good enough to warrant you putting some of your own cash in. If a seller ever pushes you to give them money faster than in 72 hours—*don't*! Give them a promissory note that you'll convert to cash upon removal of all contingencies. Or, go to a title or escrow company and deposit the earnest money for the seller subject to your due diligence. Just don't hand the seller cash without having taken the time to do your checking.

Could this cause you to lose out on a good deal? Yes, but remember the name of the game is to keep the money you make and to never lose principal.

■ Peter's Story

One of the best deals I've ever found for nothing down was a 24-unit apartment building. The owner was an elderly woman living out of state who was very upset with the costs of paying property management firms to take care of the property.

I spoke with the owner's daughter, Barbara, who had authority to make decisions about the property. I listened quietly as Barbara explained that now the heating system was broken and how the property management company wasn't able to give them any estimates beyond "we'll bill you for whatever it costs."

I asked Barbara why they didn't just sell the property. She responded that they would like to, but if they did sell it for the $450,000 that it was worth they'd end up paying over $100,000 in taxes due to both the capital gains tax and also because they would have to recapture the depreciation they had written off over the years.

Barbara agreed to fax me the rent rolls and a list of all the property expenses from the past two years. I looked over the expenses and realized that Barbara and her mom had been making an average of $2,000 a month over the past two years from this property. I knew that if I could put together a deal that got Barbara more than $2,000 a month, I would have a good shot at getting the property.

When I saw that the property management firm had been charging Barbara almost $1,000 a month for management and leasing fees, I saw a possible solution. I proposed to "master lease" the apartment building for a net payment of $3,000 a month. I would collect all the rents and other revenue generated from the property and be responsible for paying all of the bills. I also negotiated an option to buy the building for $450,000. This is what it was worth at that time, based upon the current rents and expenses. This "master lease option" is almost exactly the same as a lease option on a single-family house.

In putting together the paperwork to complete the deal, Barbara's lawyer suggested that we structure it so that my option could not be exercised until Barbara's mom passed away. She was almost 90. The attorney explained that this would save the family over $100,000 in taxes because the taxable basis for the property would "step up" to full market value upon the mother's death, leaving no capital gain at all!

I agreed to have my option limited in this way in exchange for two things. First, Barbara agreed to carry back the financing if I couldn't find a commercial lender when the time came for me to buy. Second, she agreed to allow me to make my payment of $3,000 on the 15th of each month.

I took over the property on October 1st, and by October 15th I had collected all of the rents. I used some of this money I had collected from the tenants to pay Barbara the $3,000. Just like you learned to do, I did my rent surveys and realized that other one-bedroom apartments in the area were renting for as much as $425 a month. Because we had long-term renters who were paying as little as $300 a month, I figured it was time for a rent increase. I've found that one of the best times for a rent increase is when you buy or take over a property. The tenants are expecting it. Don't disappoint them. As leases expired, we sent out new ones with increases along with a nice letter offering them free carpet cleaning if they stayed.

Each month, out of the eight tenants we sent a rent increase to, four or five would move out because they were used to the low rents. We painted, cleaned carpets, and rented to new tenants who were willing to pay the market rate to live in a nice building. Over time we increased the cash flow of the building by several thousand dollars per month.

Because the value of an income property like this is tied into the income that it creates, each time I raised the rents, reduced the expenses, or improved the property using the cash flow from the property, the value went up.

When the time came for me to exercise my option to purchase, I called several mortgage brokers to see what kind of a loan I could get. I knew that Barbara had agreed to carry back the financing if I needed her to, but I really wanted to get her paid off at this point, if possible. I figured that if she got all of her money up front, she wouldn't care too much that the value of the apartment building had increased so much over the past four years.

I explained to Scott, the mortgage broker, that I hadn't put anything down on the property and wanted to get new financing of $450,000 without putting any of my money into the property. Scott said he could find a loan that would meet that criteria but only up to 60 percent of the value of the property. If the loan needed to be larger than 60 percent of the value, Scott told me I'd have to put some of my money in to cover the amount over the 60 percent.

I held my breath as I opened the appraiser's report. Right on the front page it said: $875,000! Not only did this mean that I could get the loan without putting any of my money into the property, it also meant that this nothing-down deal had $425,000 in equity, plus a large positive cash flow of several thousand dollars each month. Not too bad a return for a nothing-down deal. People still tell me that they don't think nothing down will work. Let's let them keep on thinking that way. It means less competition for you and me when we're out there buying properties creatively. ∎

Lesson 4: Never Commit to a Deal unless You Have Found Both Buyer and Seller

If you follow this rule, you will never be a motivated seller. Before you give your final commitment on any deal with a seller, make sure you have *presold* the property to the end buyer. Now, your end buyer could be a retail buyer, a tenant-buyer, another investor, or even a qualified renter. The key is to have both halves of the deal sealed before you are ever fully committed to the deal.

How do you know when your seller is committed? When you have a binding contract in place with him. How do you know when you have an end buyer lined up for the property? When you have collected a cashier's check for a nonrefundable deposit from your buyer. Promises on a contract are good enough from your seller, but they are *not* good enough from your end buyer. Make sure your end buyer has a financial commitment in the deal.

Lesson 5: Avoid Recourse Debt Like the Plague

Recourse debt is borrowed money which you have personally signed for and guaranteed. This means that if you can't pay the loan back for any reason, the lender can come after you and all your assets for any deficiency! They can also ruin your credit. While banks will always want a personal guarantee, most sellers won't require this. Make sure you insert a clause in every promissory note you ever use that states that you have no personal liability just as you learned in Chapter 2.

■ **David's Story**

The old-school nothing-down techniques called for you to buy a property using borrowed money like a home equity line of credit. Then you would leverage this property to finance the conventional purchase of your next house. This is called "pyramiding" your debt. The danger is that these loans are probably all conventional loans you had to sign on personally. If something goes wrong, you won't just lose a single house, you'll lose everything, including your good credit. Purchase Option investing does away with the need to put so much at risk. You are still using extreme leverage, but you are only using "upside" leverage.   ■

Lesson 6: Pass the Maintenance onto Your Buyer and Seller

If something breaks and needs fixing in a house you either own outright or control with a lease option, who do you want to be responsible for organizing the repair and paying for it? Obviously, anyone other than you!

Let's take the case of you lease optioning a house from a motivated seller. If you had bought the house outright and it needed an $800 repair, what would it cost you? $800. But because you set up your contract as you learned to do in Chapter 2, how much of the $800 repair will you have to pay? If you asked the seller, he would say that you are responsible for the first $200. But you passed on this amount to your tenant-buyer. In this way, you won't have to pay for any of the repair. Wouldn't you like to have this kind of "home warranty" on every house you buy?

Now, let's take the case of you buying the house from the motivated seller outright. In this case, you are responsible for repairs, but how do you get someone else to take care of them? You pass on *all* maintenance responsibility to your tenant-buyer. Now there will be some cases where you will have a legal responsibility as a property owner and lessor (the landlord who is renting out a property) to make sure the property meets minimum standards of habitability, but most tenant-buyers will be more than willing to take over *all* of the repairs as part of their option to purchase the property.

By doing all of this, you are buffering yourself from having to perform or pay for any of the repairs the house needs. This lets you maintain your role as a passive investor rather than a sweat-drenched landlord. The difference will be one that you'll enjoy.

Lesson 7: Quickly Record Your Agreement

Have you been wondering what keeps your motivated seller from backing out of your agreement and selling the property to another investor? The simplest protection you have is to record your agreement with the seller (whether it be a lease option agreement or a purchase agreement) against the property.

What do we mean by "recording" your agreement? Every county has a public office called the county recorder's office, or county clerks office, where all the official records for property ownership are kept. Once upon a time, these records were all in paper form, but with modern technology they are usually on microfiche or computer databases.

For a small fee, anyone can go to their county recorder's office and have a document recorded against a specific property. There are three main requirements of having a document recorded:

1. Notarized signatures of the parties
2. The property's legal address needs to be on the document (in some counties the "Tax Parcel" number will work)
3. The names of the parties

When you record a document, you are giving the world "constructive knowledge," which is just a fancy way of saying that anyone who is dealing with that property has been given reasonable notice of all publicly recorded documents with respect to that specific property. When you record your agreement, you are placing a cloud on the title of the property which will protect your interests in it.

When you record your lease-option agreement or purchase agreement, you are telling the world *all* the details of your deal with the seller. You may not want to do that. Instead, you can record a document called a "Memorandum of Agreement" or "Memorandum of Option" (see Figure 4.2), which simply tells the world that you and the seller have entered into an agreement concerning that property and that any interested party should contact you at your address and phone number. Notice that the Memorandum of Agreement or Memorandum of Option does not spill the beans as to what your purchase/option price is or other critical terms of your deal.

So which should you record? Your complete agreement or a Memorandum of Agreement? In a perfect world, you should record a Memorandum of Agreement. But, if you are pressed for time and won't be able to get a Memorandum of Option signed and notarized for several weeks, then just record your actual agreement. With a house, you're probably fine because most potential tenant-buyers won't check the title to see what your terms and price were. If you are ever buying an apartment building, however, always use a Memorandum of Agreement because your buyer will most likely be much more sophisticated and will probably look up all the recorded documents with respect to the property.

Lesson 8: If You're Going to Have a Delayed Closing, Escrow Your Closing Documents Up Front

A delayed closing is any closing that doesn't happen within 60 days to 90 days of the day the deal was signed up. For example, if you have lease optioned a house from a seller, you might not exercise your option for several years. In these cases, it makes sense to

---

FIGURE 4.2   Sample Memorandum of Option

RECORDING REQUESTED BY:

WHEN RECORDED MAIL AND UNLESS OTHERWISE
SHOWN BELOW, MAIL TAX STATEMENTS TO:

SPACE ABOVE THIS LINE FOR RECORDER'S USE

Memorandum of Option

Be the world hereby apprised that I/we _____ (Optionor) have granted

to _____ (Optionee) an exclusive option to purchase the

following legally described property:

<<PropertyLegal>>.

Anyone dealing in and with the subject property should contact optionee at: _____

_____

Regarding the terms of option to purchase and the parties' respective rights thereunder.
IN WITNESS WHEREOF, the parties have signed this agreement.

Dated _____

STATE OF _____)

COUNTY OF _____) **S.S.**   _____

On _____ before me,   **Optionor**   **Date**

_____ ,

personally appeared_____

_____ ,

personally known to me (or proved to me on the basis of
satisfactory evidence) to be the person(s) whose name(s)
is/are subscribed to the within instrument and
acknowledged to me that he/she/they executed the same
in his/her/their authorized capacity(ies) and that by his/
her/their signature(s) on the instrument the person(s), or
the entity upon behalf of which the person(s) acted,
executed the instrument.

WITNESS my hand and official seal.
Signature_____
MAIL TAX STATEMENTS AS DIRECTED ABOVE

MY COMMISSION EXPIRES:

set up an escrow for all of the needed closing documents. You do this because you don't want a seller getting cold feet after you collect payments for several years. Remember, in many cases, the property has significantly gone up in value.

An escrow agent is simply a neutral third party who holds all the needed paperwork and processes the transaction according to mutually agreed upon written instructions from all parties. In some states, escrow companies perform this role; in other states, title companies do. And in still other states, attorneys perform most escrow functions.

Here is a list of the most essential documents you will want to have signed and placed into escrow on any lease-option transaction you do:

- Signed Purchase Agreement spelling out the exact terms and conditions of the eventual sale. This agreement clarifies the terms of sale if you the investor do in fact exercise your option.
- Signed Escrow Instructions.
- Signed Deed from the seller to you, the investor. This is the document that transfers title to you.
- Signed Quitclaim Deed from you to the seller. In case you don't exercise your option, this document is used to "erase" your recorded option.

By having the above documents held in escrow, when you go to the closing, you already have all the needed documents signed and notarized by the seller to consummate the transaction.

■ **Peter's Story**
We have found that at the closing which happens a few years after we have signed up a deal on a lease option, we actually use freshly signed documents. But we have also found that it is much easier to

get the seller to sign documents if they are duplicates of ones they already signed before.   ■

Lesson 9: If You're Buying on a Lease Option, Record a Performance Deed of Trust or Mortgage

Remember how you recorded your option or Memorandum of Option. Well, that put a cloud on the title. An option, however; is a contract and *not* an interest in real estate. In plain language, what that means is that a recorded option protects your interest like a 7 out of 10. A 9 out of 10 is to have the seller execute a deed of trust or mortgage in your favor to secure your interest. A 10 out of 10 would be having the seller actually *deed* the property to you putting you or your company on title. This is one reason why buying subject to the existing financing is almost always better than buying with a lease option.

What exactly is a deed of trust or mortgage? For our purposes, they are functionally the same thing so we'll only talk about deeds of trust. (In some states they use a mortgage to perform essentially the same role.) A deed of trust is a "security" document used typically when you borrow money from a bank to buy a house. The bank makes you sign two documents: a promissory note (your IOU to the bank) and a deed of trust (the security instrument to make sure you pay). Think about it this way.

Have you ever seen the movie, *The Godfather*? Whenever someone would borrow money from Don Corleone, the Godfather, the borrower would promise to pay the money back. This promise is like a promissory note or IOU. The big guy standing behind Don Corleone with the mean look on his face is the guy who makes sure the borrower pays. He is like a deed of trust. If the borrower doesn't pay, he steps in and makes sure they do.

A deed of trust is the document that says that if the borrower doesn't pay the bank, the bank takes back the property through foreclosure. Typically, the deed of trust secures a promissory note, but not in this case. In this case, you are going to have the seller sign a deed of trust that secures "the seller's specific performance of the lease option agreement."

Why go to all of this trouble? Because a deed of trust *is* an interest in real estate, and it gives you many more rights than those you have with just an option. While not every seller will agree to give you one, you should always try to get one. This is something you should talk over with a very sharp real estate attorney in your hometown. While the consultation will cost you some money, a good attorney's input will be worth many times more than their fee.

Lesson 10: Remember to Recommit the Seller to the Deal

It seems a part of human nature that once a seller has made the decision to sell you the property that they start to worry. And if left unchecked, that worry will lead to doubt, and that doubt will lead to the seller trying to back out of the deal. This is sometimes called "seller's remorse," the kissin' cousin of "buyer's remorse."

But you are going to handle things differently. You are going to anticipate that the seller is scared of making a mistake and will need some gentle reassurance. The way you are going to do that is by holding a follow-up meeting with the seller. Your follow-up meeting between you and the seller is your chance to both reassure the seller about the deal and to position yourself to renegotiate the deal if needed.

This meeting should take place within 48 hours of signing up the deal. As you are leaving with the deal in hand on your first visit with the seller, simply say, "Mr. Seller, when is a good time for us to get together tomorrow or at the latest the day after tomorrow? I am going to want your input as to the nicest selling features of this house and the area that will let me know how to best market the property to my future buyer."

See how easy it was to set up this meeting. Bring a clipboard to the meeting and do three things: First, have the seller help you list the top selling features of the house and area (while you could probably do this yourself, it makes sense to get the seller involved in the process and feel like a part of your team). Second, go through the property closely to see what work needs to be done to have the house show well. Many times, the seller will offer to fix and clean things at this point. Let them! Third, place your Rent to Own sign or For Sale sign in the front yard. There is something so powerful about the seller making that little step to allow you to put out your sign. It is the seller making a public statement to the world that they are committed to the deal.

One Final Question to Ask to Make Sure Your Seller Doesn't Get Cold Feet

Many times the reason sellers get cold feet is that they don't see all the effort you are putting in. This isn't a question of truth but a question of perception. If the seller doesn't perceive that you are committed to the deal, they will feel unsettled. Here is the simplest question we know to settle the seller down:

"Mr. Seller, would you be okay if I went ahead and started to spend money on my advertising for this property?"

Can you imagine any sellers saying they don't want you to pay for advertising? Of course not. You bring this up because you want *them* to know that you are going to invest in doing this deal, and this is the most tactful way to let them know. You will need to get your advertising going right away anyway, but this question gives you the credit for it in the mind of the sellers.

By following all the lessons above, you significantly hedge against the possibility of the seller ever backing out! Because you've put so much effort into finding and closing the deal, take these extra steps to make sure the deal stays closed.

■ David's Story

I must admit I have been guilty of not following this advice. One five-bedroom house I had signed up as a five-year lease option cost me $75,000! I signed up the deal on a Monday night and didn't call the seller back for five days. In that period, the seller's imagination got going and the seller panicked and backed out of the deal. He did end up paying me $2,500 to back out, but two years later that house I had locked up as an option to purchase at $250,000 was worth $325,000! That was a painful mistake. Remember, sellers are just like you and I are. They sometimes get scared and need reassurance.   ■

Lesson 11: Use Corporations and Trusts to Keep Your Wealth Safe

Wherever possible, you never want to do business in your own name. Always operate from within the shelter of a properly maintained entity that gives you liability protection. The simplest way to do this in your real estate investing is to form a limited liability company, or LLC, or corporation.

An LLC or corporation that you control is the front layer of protection in your financial armor. In order to be effective, it needs to be properly drafted and maintained. There is a great series of books on forming and running your own LLC or corporation by attorney Anthony Mancuso available from Nolo Press.

To get real liability protection out of any corporation, you need to really treat it as a separate entity from you personally. This means everything from not commingling funds, to having annual board of directors meetings, to updating decisions in the corporate minutes. This might sound complicated, but it isn't. Running an LLC or corporation is a simple process when you learn how and a necessity in today's sue-happy world.

If corporations are the front layer of your financial armor, then land trusts are the second layer of defense. As we stated earlier in Chapter 2, a land trust is simply a trust that is created to hold title of a property for the benefit of some beneficial party. The reason a land trust is a smart way to title the properties you decide to hang onto long term is that it can help you keep a low financial profile. This is important because the first thing any opposing attorneys are going to do if someone comes to them asking them to sue you on a contingency fee basis is to search the public records to see what kind of assets you own. If your name shows up as the owner of 32 properties, you can bet that lawyer is going to take the case! But for you, because you were smart and titled your properties in land trusts, your name won't be on the public record. For all practical purposes, you'll own the property, but you just won't be the owner of record. A "trustee" will own the property on behalf of the trust in which you own all of the "beneficial interest."

If all this stuff about LLCs and trusts sounds complicated, it isn't. If you don't have many assets yet, then get started with your investing now. After you have made money from your first deal, set aside a little of it to invest in some good legal help in setting up your legal bulwarks. If, however, you are starting off and you do own a lot of assets, then it will be worth every penny to hire good professionals to get your legal ramparts structured and set up from the start.

Lesson 12: Always Maintain Adequate Insurance to Cover Property Damage and Lawsuits

One of the best resources you can have in your team of financial advisors is a top-notch insurance agent. Your agent will be able to help you make sure you have the right amount of insurance to cover your exposures. Your agent will need to review the policies on each property you own or control to make sure you are covered.

> ■ **David's Story**
> My insurance agent Eric is an incredible resource. Not only has he helped me make sure I have the right coverage, but he is always willing to answer my questions regarding insurance. He has also given me great referrals to other professionals that he has worked with in other areas. All in all, he is a trusted member of my financial team. ■

Also, make sure you talk through an "umbrella liability policy" with your agent. The cost for $1 million worth of coverage is cheap. If you have significant assets, then $1 million of coverage won't be enough. Your agent will help you determine if $5 million or $10 million of coverage or more will be appropriate for your needs.

One final word with insurance. It doesn't make sense to buy insurance on price. You need to make sure the underwriter is going to be there for the long term. You can check with either Moody's (212-553-0377) looking for ratings of AAA or AA-1, or you can check with Standard & Poor's (212-208-1527) looking for a rating of AAA or AA+. Can you imagine the consequences of saving a few bucks, having a major claim, and finding your insurance company has declared bankruptcy! It happens. So be intelligent about the insurance company you use, and do your homework.

Lesson 13: Disclose! Disclose! Disclose!

When in doubt about whether or not to tell the other party in a real estate deal about something you think might bring up later liability, *disclose it.* Do it in writing, do it up front, and get the other party to sign that they have received the disclosure.

Lesson 14: Do Business with Integrity

Some of what we just covered can seem a bit scary. But really it's not. We just want you to be prepared for the worst cases so that your life of real estate investing will be filled with pleasant surprises.

In the end, the simplest way to lower your risk is to treat other people you do business with fairly and ethically. If you always do what you say you are going to do, that integrity will be your best protection against things going wrong in a deal. If you treat other people fairly and ethically, they will more often than not treat you the same way. Ultimately, this is the best advice for staying safe in your real estate investing.

Now, it's time for you to learn how to find your tenant-buyer.

Selling Your Properties for Top Dollar

If buying right helps you to create equity, then selling right helps you convert your equity into cash. In this chapter, you are going to learn the real-world tactics that will help you make the maximum profit from your real estate investment properties with the least amount of work.

With Purchase Option investing, you have the choice of selling right away for cash or selling for a larger profit paid over time. We'll discuss both of these choices and give you a format for making the right decision. The real benefit of selling real estate by using these Purchase Option strategies is that you get to choose how much money you make and when you make it.

The typical way you'll sell a house using the Purchase Option strategies is to sell it on a rent-to-own basis, which means you are going to sell the house on a lease option. A key point that you are going to learn is that when you *sell* a house on a rent-to-own basis, you will approach things very differently from when you *buy* a home on a lease option. You'll learn about important contract differences and negotiating attitudes when selling and buying. But first, we want you to see the real beauty of selling on a rent-to-own basis.

How to Get the Best Deal from Both Buyers and Renters without the Traditional Downsides

Buyers are great. When you sell outright to a traditional buyer, you are going to get a lot of cash because the buyer is bringing in new financing to cash you out. Furthermore, because the buyer has bought the property, you never have to deal with it again. The buyer will take care of the house, and you get it out of your hands completely.

But there are downsides to selling, and the biggest one is that once you sell a house, you never make any more money from it. If the house goes up in value, you don't get any of that appreciation. When the loan gets paid down, you don't get any of that amortization. When you sell the house, you have to pay a chunk of your profits in taxes. You can, under specific circumstances, use a 1031 exchange to defer these taxes, but that is outside the scope of this book.

■ David's Story

I think that some of my biggest regrets in real estate involve the properties I've sold. When I watch them go up in value over the years and know that I took my money and sold out, I feel a bit disappointed. Sure, I made money, but I liked how that property used to be like a money tree for me, growing into ever-increasing profits and cash flow. Like most investors, I have had problem properties that I am glad I sold. But there were other trouble-free properties where I got greedy and took the quick cash profit and lost out on an even larger long-term gain. I think every investor needs to find the right balance for themselves as to short-term needs for quick cash and long-term needs for net worth. This is a very personal decision, and I urge investors to be careful to not sell too quickly but to hold a portion of their properties for at least a short while to help earn more money for them long term.   ■

The benefits of having a renter in one of your properties are great. Your renter pays your monthly payment for you. Your renter also gives you monthly cash flow from the excess rent they pay you above what you have to pay to your lender. With a renter you also make money from the loan pay down as you pay your lender every month. You get all the tax advantages of owning the property. And finally, one of the biggest benefits that a renter gives you, you get to capture *all* the appreciation of the property.

With all of these powerful benefits, you'd think that every property owner would turn into a landlord. But for all the above benefits, renters bring with them some pretty big headaches too. First of all, not every renter pays the rent on time. Some never pay at all. Having to deal with collecting rents, doing evictions, and finding new tenants is expensive in terms of time and money. Next, being a landlord means you will be responsible for maintaining the property. Those late-night phone calls from renters with a leaky faucet or a furnace that went out can drive you crazy. It can be a huge drain on your time and a strain on your emotions. Having a renter often means an undercurrent of worry in your daily life. Somewhere in the back of your mind, you worry if your renters are taking care of your property or if they are throwing a huge destructive party. The bottom line is that when you have a renter, you pay for the benefits you get.

■ Peter's Story

It was 2 AM and I was dead tired. Because I had gotten several months behind in my bookkeeping, I'd decided to stay and work in the office until I had reconciled my books to see how I was doing financially. I had a sense that things weren't going well, but I didn't really know for sure.

What I discovered was hard to believe. I double-checked my figures to make sure and realized that the costs associated with managing all of my properties had gotten out of control and that I was losing money.

Several years earlier, I had made the decision to find other people to help take care of the maintenance and repair of my properties. I knew that as long as it was me that was fixing doorknobs and unplugging toilets I would never be able to live the life that I wanted, spending quality time with my family.

So I had hired, trained, and fired over time until I found 15 employees who were all happily making money by helping me oversee my properties. What annoyed me was that while I was no longer fixing or painting things myself, I found that my goal of freeing up my time had eluded me. I was now feeling more stressed than ever because my employees were constantly paging me with various questions like, "What should I do now? It looks like that employee you fired last week took your airless paint spraying equipment."

On top of that, it seemed like I was trying to take care of one pressing deadline after another. Payroll, quarterly reports, negotiating and buying parts and materials, and dealing with less-than-dependable employees left me with very little time to be with my family. On top of all of this, I no longer had any time to go out and look for more properties to buy. I had fallen into the Landlord Trap, and at 2 AM it felt like the trap was pressing me in from all sides.

I was at a breaking point. I knew that I didn't want to be doing the maintenance and upkeep on my properties myself, yet I realized hiring other people to do the work didn't seem to be the right solution either. The thing that hurt the most was that I knew that my relationship with my family was suffering.

I decided at 2 AM that I would find a way, some way, to escape this trap that I had fallen into. I didn't know how I would do it yet. I just knew that there had to be a better way. ■

When you sell your property on a rent-to-own basis, you don't get a buyer and you don't get a renter. You get a tenant-buyer. A tenant-buyer gives you all of the best parts of a buyer, such as a large chunk of money up front, called an "option payment," an owner mentality to treat the property well, and a hands-off feeling for you, the investor. And you get these benefits without giving up all of the appreciation. Also, because not all tenant-buyers end up buying, you might very well get the chance to sell the property a second or even third time to new tenant-buyers for even more money!

When you sell your property on a rent-to-own basis, you also get the best parts of a renter like monthly cash flow, loan amortization, and all the tax benefits. You get these benefits without having to be a landlord. (Note: To get the tax benefits from a property, you must own it. If you control it with a lease option, then your seller, the person you lease it from, not you, will get the tax benefits from the property.)

How to Turn Your Properties into Hands-Off Money-Makers

When you are selling your property on a rent-to-own basis, you simply find someone who is agreeing to rent out the house for a period of time—typically one to three years—with a set option price at which they can purchase the property at any point in time over the lease. For the privilege of tying in their purchase price, they will pay you a nonrefundable option payment of 3 percent to 5 percent of the value of the property.

Because they have given you a chunk of money up front and because they are coming into the house with the intention of buying it, your typical tenant-buyers will treat the house much kinder than the typical renter. This lets you, the investor, relax and collect a check each month, pay your lender, or seller if you lease-optioned the house yourself, and just spend or invest the excess cash flow. If something breaks, your tenant-buyer is responsible for not only paying for the repair but also for calling up and getting the repair person to come over to fix the problem.

We typically set up our tenant-buyers to pay for *all* the maintenance responsibilities. After all, if they had purchased the house, then they would be paying for all the repairs anyway. If we have lease-optioned the house ourselves from a motivated seller and we have agreed on a $200 a month maintenance cap with our sellers (which is standard for us), then we might step in and save the tenant-buyers some money on a big repair. For example, if there is a plumbing problem and it will cost $800 to fix, our tenant-buyers expect to have to pay for it all. Because our motivated seller expects to pay any amount over $200, we tell our seller that we'll see that the first $400 gets taken care of, saving them $200. This makes our seller happy. Then we turn to our tenant-buyer and say that because they have been so good in the house we are going to see that they only have to pay for the first $400 of the cost of the repair. This saves our tenant-buyer $400. See how we get to be the hero to both our seller and our tenant-buyer?

■ David's Story

I sold a three-bedroom, 1½ bath house to a tenant-buyer named Rhonda. This was the first house Rhonda had ever bought. She came in as my tenant-buyer after giving me $4,500 on this $140,000 house, which we had purchased for just under $100,000. I called her up because I was changing the address that I wanted her to mail her rent checks to when she told me about her first visit to Home Depot. It turned out that she had never been there before and during the past weekend she and her family went there and bought new curtains, paint, and other touches for the house. I remember thinking how much I liked tenant-buyers. I have yet to have a renter fix up one of my properties. I *have* had several other tenant-buyers fix up my properties and pay for the upgrades without ever asking me for a dime. On another house I had, the tenant-buyer did a $10,000 repair to the septic system without asking me for any money. There is a world of difference between a renter and a tenant-buyer.   ■

Why Tenant-Buyers Mean Cash Flow

One of the biggest benefits you get by selling one of your properties on a rent-to-own basis is cash flow. For example, we had one three-bedroom property that was bringing us an $81 per month cash flow. Do you get excited over an $81 cash flow?

Hard as it is to believe, many people don't salivate over an extra $81 each month. Perhaps, the fact that we *do* in fact get excited over $81 extra each month tells you a little bit about how cheap we can be! But, hey, that's a good quality in a real estate investor—someone who knows the value of a dollar—or the value of $81. But before you skip down to the next section, consider this. Our tenant-buyer for that property also paid us a $7,000 nonrefundable option payment. For a time it looked like that tenant-buyer was *not* going to actually exercise his option to purchase. Let's look at what this would have done for our cash flow.

We already had $81 per month for 24 months. This totaled $1,944 in cash flow over the two years. See how that small monthly cash flow adds up. But wait, it gets even better. If you add in the $7,000 option money you get to keep along with the $1,944 of cash flow, you get a total of $8,944. When you divide this by the 24-month period we are talking about, you get $372.66 of cash flow each month. Do you get excited over this monthly cash flow? Remember that this is money that you got mostly *up front*. And you didn't have to deal with the maintenance of the property. Now do you see why a sale on a rent-to-own basis means more cash flow? And wait until we share with you later in this chapter about "rent credits" to boost your cash flow by a few hundred dollars more each month.

■ **David's Story**

We were involved with a house in Idaho with one of our students, and our second tenant-buyer gave us $3,000 as a nonrefundable option payment. Two months later he moved out of the property. It took us about three weeks to find a new tenant-buyer. Because of the option money we collected up front, our cash flow on the house was approximately $1,000 per month!   ■

The Right *Attitude* to Take with Your Tenant-Buyers

With sellers, you have learned it's effective to be clumsy and to play dumb. When *you* are the seller you make a 180-degree turn and take a controlling role. The analogy to think of is that of a parent. The best investors are like great parents—they are kind but very firm on what they expect their children to do. They clearly set expectations, define boundaries, and lay out consequences for behavior. The operative word is *consistency*. If you let your kids stay up until 10 PM and their bedtime is 9 PM then forever after they want their bedtime to be 10 PM or later. If you allow your tenant-buyer to pay late without incurring a late fee, then they will repeatedly pay you late. Firm, consistent, and nice are the traits of the best investors. Remember, this is a business relationship and needs to be treated as such.

The Three Magic Words to Find Your Tenant-Buyer

Finding a tenant-buyer is fairly straightforward when you know the three magic words that grab their attention and clearly communicate what is in it for them. These words go bold and centered in your signs and at the start of any of the classified ads you run. These words are: Rent to Own.

Don't change them. Don't use "lease with option to buy." Don't use "lease option." "Rent to Own" works, don't change it.

When someone sees your Rent to Own classified ad, they instantly know what it means. And what is more important, they know that they may want it.

See Figure 5.1 for an example of our standard Rent to Own ad. We place this ad in the For Sale section of the newspaper. Note: Some larger city newspapers have a separate Rent to Own section of the paper, e.g., *San Diego Union Tribune.* If your paper does have a special Rent to Own section, then that is where you should run your ad. The reason you place the ad in the For Sale section and not in the For Rent section is that you are looking for someone with a buyer mentality *not* a renter mentality. Plus, you want them to have enough money to give you up front as an option payment. In most cases we only run our ad on Saturday and Sunday to save money. These days give you the biggest bang for your buck. Check out the costs of your local paper. You might be able to run your ad all week at a very reasonable price.

The Single Best Way to Find Your Tenant-Buyer

Without question, the single best way in getting great leads on a tenant-buyer for your property is the use of signs. Dollar for dollar, signs are the cheapest and fastest ways to get a flood of interested people calling you up. Used in conjunction with your classified advertising, signs generate the final flow of leads that will help you fill your properties fast.

We use two kinds of signs. For the front yard and corner lot of the street the house is on, we use a professionally made Rent to Own sign. These are fairly inexpensive (they'll cost you about $30 to $50 each) and can be created by any local sign shop in your area. Figure 5.2 has an example of this type of sign.

Also, you can attach a weather-proof envelope to the sign in the yard containing copies of a flyer about the property stapled to a rent-to-own application with a fax number on the bottom. Each time you go to the property to show it to prospective buyers, you

FIGURE 5.1   A Standard Rent to Own Ad

Rent to Own! Spacious 3 Bed, 2 Ba house. 30% Rent Credit. Great schools. $1,495/mo. 888-555-1212. 24 hr. rec. msg.

can replenish this stock of stapled flyers and rental applications. Note: We don't recommend you put any pricing on these sheets other than the starting rent amount. We feel strongly that the only time to talk pricing with prospective tenant-buyers is after they have gone through the house and have told you they love it. We'll cover more on this later in this chapter.

In addition to these professional signs, we encourage you to consider flooding the area with your own handmade signs. These signs are incredibly cheap and effective. Go to your local office supply store or drug store and buy a stack of bright poster board. Cut it in half and with a thick black marker handmake your signs. See Figure 5.3 for a sample of what they should look like. One key point here is that you should take only 30 seconds to 60 seconds to make each sign. Don't be an artist here. Quick, fast, and easy is the key.

One of the reasons these handmade signs work so well is that they catch people's eyes. After all, when you are hunting through your farm area looking for a deal on a house, which attracts your attention more, a real estate agent's sign or a small, handwritten For Sale By Owner sign? Of course, the handmade sign does. You see that and think, "If they can't even afford a *real* sign, they must really need to sell. This may be a great bargain!" You are simply using this psychology in your favor. Furthermore, you are less likely to get in trouble with your city's authorities for handmade signs because city enforcement officials are less likely to fine you because they may think this is a one-time occurrence rather than a full-time business. Now, we have to caution you that there are probably city ordinances about the use of any signs. We can't tell you to use these signs. We

FIGURE 5.2   Professional Rent to Own Signs for the Front Yard and the Corner Lot of the Street the House Is On

Rent to Own

**3 bed, 2 bath House
For Details Please Take a Flyer**

Call 888-333-1212 ext. 6

Rent to Own!

**[space to write in info on house
e.g., 3 Bed, 2 Ba, 1,900 sf, etc.]**

Call 888-333-1212 ext. 6
24-Hour Recorded Message

are simply letting you know that they have worked for other investors, and you should investigate the policy and rules in your area and make your own independent decision whether to use them or not. How is that for a disclaimer!

FIGURE 5.3   Handmade Rent to Own Signs to Put Out around the
Neighborhood near the House

Rent to Own!

3 bed, 2 bath House
Call 888-333-1212 ext. 6
24-Hr. Msg.

The Three Keys to Finding Your Tenant-Buyer

1. Use a 24-Hour Recorded Message

You have probably noticed in the sample classified ads and
signs that we directed all calls these advertisements generated to a
24-hour recorded message. This sounds fancy but is really just a
voice-mail box that we rent. We talked about this earlier in the book
in Chapter 2 where we discussed getting motivated sellers to call
you. Now you are using another voice-mail box to screen your buyers. The system we told you about in Chapter 2 has nine voice-mail
boxes. We use four of them in our advertising for motivated sellers
and five boxes for our tenant-buyer searches. We set up each property with it's own separate voice-mail box. This way we can tailor
our voice-mail message to that specific property.

When you put out your Rent to Own ads and signs the problem
won't be too few calls, the problem will be too many. In most areas
of the country, when you advertise your property on a rent-to-own
basis, you will get between 20 and 40 calls per week on the property. Can you imagine the hassles of having all these calls come in

on your cell phone? Remember, the reason you are investing in real estate is to create a lifestyle of freedom and security. Don't sacrifice this and put yourself on call at all hours of the day and night. Instead, direct all calls to your 24-hour recorded message.

This recorded message will have on it a scripted message 60 to 90 seconds long. Here is an example of this script that we used on a home we were selling on a rent-to-own basis:

> Hello, here's your chance to quickly and easily rent to own your next home. There are no banks to qualify with. You don't even need perfect credit. This program was designed so that anyone can quickly and easily get in their own home right now. We even have a down payment assistance program.
>
> Just one of the properties we have available is a beautiful three-bedroom, three-bath, 3,500 square-foot home nestled in the quiet community of Green Mountain Falls. This house has a large sun room, a fireplace, hot tub, stunning mountain views, and a large covered deck.
>
> The rent for this home starts at $1,495 and depending which program you choose, up to $400 of each rent payment will be credited towards your purchase of this home!
>
> Here's what you can do to help us help you. After the tone, leave your name, phone number, and the upfront payment you have to work with. Obviously, the larger the upfront payment you have to work with, the more likely we are to choose you to buy this home. We'll get back to you as soon as possible to arrange to show you the house. Remember, leave your name, telephone number, and the amount of upfront payment you have to work with, and we'll call you back just as soon as possible.
>
> Thank you for calling and have a great day.

This scripted message does three things.

First, it introduces the caller to the benefits of the rent-to-own program: "Your chance to quickly and easily rent-to-own your next

home. There are no banks to qualify with. You don't even need perfect credit. This program was designed so that anyone can quickly
and easily get their own home right now. We even have a down payment assistance program."

Next, it gives the four or five nicest features of the property:
"Beautiful three-bedroom, three-bath, 3,500 square-foot home nes-
tled in the quiet community of Green Mountain Falls. This house
has a large sun room, a fireplace, hot tub, stunning mountain views,
and a large covered deck."

Finally, it qualifies the caller as to how much upfront money
they have to work with: "Here's what you can do to help us help you.
After the tone, leave your name, phone number, and the upfront
payment you have to work with. Obviously, the larger the upfront
payment you have to work with the more likely we are to choose you
to buy this home." By qualifying the caller this way, you can save
time and know who you need to call back first, and who can wait.
You simply pick and choose those in whom you want to invest your
time and call to set up a time to show them the property.

One of our students, Gary, whom you will be reading about in
Chapter 6, sent us a letter about his experience using recorded
voice-mail messages. He wrote, "So far we have been the "lessor" using the rent-to-own concept four times. The first two times we had
not yet been to your three-hour lecture, and it took us four to five
weeks to find suitable tenant-buyers. The last two times we used the
24-hour recorded-message voice-mail and were able to lease-option
both properties to suitable tenant-buyers in less than one week. The
ad came out in the newspaper on Sunday and by Thursday both
properties were rented." Voice-mail works wonders for saving you
time and effort. Try it.

2. Create Competition for Your Property

When you are buying a property, you want to be the only person talking with the seller about the potential sale of the home. If

you accomplish this, you know that your price will go down and the terms will be in your favor. When you are selling, the exact opposite principle applies: If you can create competition for the property, you will drive the price up, and will be able to set the terms.

To create competition, you need two or more people who both want the property and who both know that they are in competition with each other for the property. It is not enough to have two people who both want to buy the property. In order to create competition, both parties must in fact *know* that they are in competition with other.

So exactly how do you make this happen? You create a situation where you place *all* your potential buyers in direct competition with each other. Here is how to do this.

Use group showings to create competition. From now on, never show the property to just one party. Always have two or more people meet you at the property at the same time. Not only is this the best use of your time, but, more importantly, it creates immediate competition for your property.

■ **David's Story**
I remember one group showing I had for a three-bedroom, two-bath ranch-style home. Seven couples were there. At one point, a woman walked up and said she thought the house would be perfect for her goddaughter. I said great, have your goddaughter come in and fill out an application. She told me that her goddaughter was in the hospital recovering from minor surgery. I looked around at all the people in the house and said that it might mean she would miss out on the house. About 20 minutes later, while I was still at the house, I got a call on my cell phone. It was the goddaughter calling me from her hospital bed! She gave me her application right over the phone. That would have never have happened if there were not other people in the house creating a feeling of competition.   ■

To set up a group showing, simply call back the people who responded to your Rent to Own ad and set up a time for them to meet you at the property. The group showing part comes from the fact that you will set up the exact same time with each of the people!

Here is an example of how you should control that conversation:

> Ring, Ring.
>
> Potential Buyer: Hello?
>
> Investor: Hi, is John there?
>
> Potential Buyer: This is John.
>
> Investor: John, you called me about a rent-to-own home I have in Parker. Sounds like I caught you in the middle of something.
>
> Potential Buyer: No, no you didn't.
>
> Investor: Okay, where are you living now?
>
> Potential Buyer: In a house over off Sutter street.
>
> Investor: How much are you paying in rent there?
>
> Potential Buyer: We pay $1,350 for a three-bedroom place.
>
> Investor: Okay, and how many people will be living with you?
>
> Potential Buyer: Just me and my wife, Sarah, and our daughter.
>
> Investor: Great, and how much money did you have to work with as an upfront payment? Roughly.
>
> Potential Buyer: We could come up with $8,000.
>
> Investor: Oh, $8,000 to $9,000, okay. (You remember the range technique you learned when buying? You just used it here!) I'm looking at my schedule right now to see when I am available to have you and your wife come over and take a look at the house and for me to meet you both. Let's see, the best time for me would be Wednesday at 6:15 PM. Does that work for you?
>
> Potential Buyer: Yeah, that would be great.

You then give them directions to the property and say c more thing:

Investor: Okay, John, I will meet you and your wife at the house on Wednesday at 6:15 PM sharp. I need to let you know that I am one of those people to whom time is very important, and I promise I will be there right on time. I need you to make sure you're also there right on time, okay?

Potential Buyer: Sure, we'll be there right on time.

This final statement helps establish the right tone with your buyer—you are a nice person who is a stickler for the rules. Now you are ready to call your next potential buyer back. You go through the above script with them. When it comes time to set up an appointment to meet them at the property, guess what day and time you are going to choose? That's right, Wednesday at 6:15 PM. You go through your list of people who called into your voice-mail from your advertising and get as many of them as possible to come to the house at the same time. The more people the better. Remember, not everyone will show up. So don't be upset if only six or seven out of ten people actually make it to the property (and about three of them will still be late).

A final note on setting these appointments to show the property: *Never, ever* call it a "showing." If you call it a showing, no one will show up. They figure if it's a showing, no one will miss them if they don't make it. Instead, set a "definite appointment" with each potential tenant-buyer. It's just that all of the definite appointments will be for the exact same time.

If anyone asks you if other people will be there, which seldom happens, just tell them the truth. "Of course, other people will be there. I have been flooded with calls from people who want to rent to own this house, and I just don't have the time to show it to everyone unless I get several people to meet me there at the same time. Now, you have directions to the property and will be there right at 6:15 PM?"

Safety into the Deal for Yourself

There are two ways that you build safety into the deal for yourself with respect to your tenant-buyer. First and foremost is the
financial commitment you require from your tenant-buyer. Second
is through the intelligent use of contracts and disclosure forms.
Let's look at each of these in turn.

The single biggest safety net you have is the cash you collect
up front from your tenant-buyer. The average rental property
owner collects one month's rent and one month's security deposit
before giving leasehold control of the property over to their renter.
If the market rent is $1,500, the landlord collects $3,000 up front.

As a Purchase Option investor, you are going to collect three to
four *times* as much money up front. In our earlier example, you are
collecting $10,000 of upfront payment and a first month's rent of
$1,600 for a grand total of $11,600 cash before you ever give your
tenant-buyer leasehold possession of the property. Can you see why
they are geared to treat the property so much nicer? Plus, they have
the responsibility of handling all the maintenance. This means they
are much more likely to take care of the property over time. Not to
mention that they plan to eventually purchase the property.

There is nothing in real estate that money can't fix. And when
you have enough money to work with, the standard hassles of owning a property are smoothed out. Your tenant-buyer's option payment will go a long way to buffering you from the bumps of owning
an income property. As we mentioned earlier, of course, you'll
check their past rental history. Of course, you'll verify their current
job and income. Of course, you'll run their credit. But the single
biggest factor influencing which tenant-buyer to choose is the
amount of money they give you up front.

The second way that you build security into the relationship
you have with your tenant-buyer is through the intelligent use of
contracts. You want to do all you can to make sure the relationship
between you and the tenant-buyer is a landlord/tenant relationship

not a seller/buyer relationship. You may think this contradicts what we have been talking about all along about not being a landlord, but if there is any surface contradiction, you'll soon see why it's worth living with.

When you sell a property and carry back the financing, how do you get a buyer who isn't paying you your monthly payments out of the property? What is the fancy name of this process? If you said *foreclosure* you are right on the money. And how long does it take for this process to happen, worst case, in most areas of the country? Let's assume your buyer really wanted to fight you on this and did all kinds of nasty things like declaring bankruptcy, hiring a high-priced lawyer, etc. In most areas of the country, your buyer could drag the process out well over six months to a year, during which it would probably cost you several thousand dollars in attorney and court fees. During all that time, you'd be getting no payments, and they would be living in your property rent free. It makes us mad just thinking about it. Note: In some states, you would have to do a quiet title action, rather than foreclose, to extinguish the tenant-buyer's claim to the title, if a judge deems he or she is a buyer and not a renter.

Now, when you rent out a property of yours and you don't get your monthly payments from the renter, what process do you go through to get them out of the property? If you said *eviction* you were correct. And as you know, in most areas of the country, even with the renter fighting you every step of the way, an eviction only takes 45 to 60 days at the very most.

All that said, if you had to pick one of the two ways to remove a nonperforming occupant of your property, foreclosure or eviction, which process would you want to go through with your tenant-buyer? Of course, you'd want the eviction process. Not only is it faster, but it is *much* cheaper and less stressful to go through. This means you need to clearly establish a landlord/tenant relationship with your tenant-buyer.

How to Make Sure Your Tenant-Buyer Is a Renter *Not* a Buyer

First, make sure you separate out both halves of the transaction with your tenant-buyer. The first transaction is the lease; the second transaction is the option to purchase. Use a separate lease and a separate option agreement with your tenant-buyer. Now, when you are *buying* on a lease option, you do not want to separate your lease and option but tie them in together. The opposite is true when you are *selling*, where you will use a "prolandlord" lease with all kinds of tough language in it to protect you. Also, your option agreement with your tenant-buyer will clearly spell out how your tenant has the option to purchase, not the obligation. An option is not an interest in real estate. It is merely a contract and as such the optionee, your tenant-buyer, has no claims to the title of your property. You use a stand-alone lease so that if you ever go into court to evict, you can show the judge a simple lease agreement without any option language in it to muddy the waters.

It's not enough to just say your tenant-buyer is a "tenant." All the elements in your actual relationship, or at least as many as possible, must support that claim. What do landlords always collect from their tenants? A security deposit. At one time, we didn't have our tenant-buyers pay us any security deposit; we called all the money they gave us up front "nonrefundable option consideration." After all, who wants to collect a security deposit that you have to give back if they don't exercise their option when you can just call it all option money and keep it? Well, this is another lesson we learned the hard way so that you don't have to (you're welcome). If you don't collect any security deposit, it looks to a judge like you don't have a tenant. And if they aren't tenants, your tenant-buyers must therefore be buyers. You can't evict buyers; you have to foreclose them from the property. Are you willing to make an intelligent compromise on this one yet?

What we do now is collect as much money up front from our tenant-buyer as possible and label most of it "nonrefundable option consideration" and a small part of it "security deposit." If our tenant-buyer doesn't buy, we have to give them their security deposit back, according to the laws of the state in which we are investing. In our example of choosing John and Sarah as our tenant-buyers, they gave us a first month's rent of $1,595 and $10,000 upfront money. We take that $10,000 and break it into two chunks. Chunk one is their security deposit of $800. We use half a month's rent as our standard security deposit amount. Chunk two is their $9,200 nonrefundable option payment.

Have you noticed how we never called the tenant-buyer's upfront payment a "down payment?" That's because buyers give down payments. Tenant-buyers give option payments. Also, in all of our paperwork with our tenant-buyer we *never* call them a "buyer" or a "tenant-buyer." They are simply a "tenant." In explaining all this to you we do use the word *tenant-buyer*, but in all of our lease agreements and option agreements we simply use the word *tenant*. Again, it's all about getting as many tiny weights on your side of the legal scale as you can so if you ever have to go before a judge, the scales tip in your favor. It is very unlikely that you'll ever have to go to court, but we want you to have the scale stacked on your side in case you do.

Also, one of the federal laws you have to follow when you lease or sell a property are the lead-based paint disclosure laws. Rather than trying to figure out when the house was built, we recommend you comply with these regulations with every buyer and tenant-buyer. It's easy to do. You simply give them a brochure titled, "Protect Your Family From Lead In Your Home." It's available for free from <www.hud.gov>. Also, on that same Web site you can get the federally approved lead-based paint disclosure forms. These laws are a formality when selling or leasing a property, but they are an important one to make sure you comply with because the penalties are stiff.

There are two formats of the lead-based paint disclosure form. We recommend that with your tenant-buyer you use the "tenant," (i.e., lessee/lessor) disclosure form up front and then repeat the document at the eventual closing when they exercise their option using the seller/purchaser disclosure form. You want to establish the paper trail indicating that they are renters not buyers.

Final Note on Disclosure Forms with Buyers

In many states, you need to fill out all the property disclosure information when you put a tenant-buyer in the property (e.g., California) even though no sale has taken place. In other states, you only need to do this disclosure information upon your tenant-buyer's actual purchase of the property.

We strongly recommend that you speak with a good real estate attorney in your area who can give you good guidance. The disclosure forms, available at a local stationary store, are simple to do. Also check with your real estate attorney about any other waiver/disclosure forms or clauses you may need, like a mold waiver/disclosure and registered sex offender (i.e., Megan's Law).

The final step you take to protect yourself with your tenant-buyer with respect to your paperwork is that you make sure your tenant-buyer does *not* record his option against the property. Why are we saying this? After all, didn't we say in Chapter 4 that you always record your option or a Memorandum of Option to protect your interest? That is true when you are buying, but *not* when you are selling to someone else. Don't let your tenant-buyer put a cloud on your title.

There are three ways to make sure the tenant-buyer does not record the transaction. First, just don't tell them about the need to record the document. Very few people know that this is a good idea. Second, don't put the legal description of the property on the option agreement. It is a requirement in most areas to have the "legal description" of the property on the document you are recording to ensure it gets recorded correctly. If the legal description isn't on the document it is much harder for them to get it recorded. And third, put a clause in your option agreement with your buyer that states:

> *The recording of this option or any memorandum thereof will result in the automatic revocation of this option, and all monies paid to Landlord by Tenant shall be retained by Landlord as liquidated damages. In addition, Tenant will be liable to Landlord for all incidental and consequential damages for slander of title, including, but not limited to, attorneys fees and court costs for correcting title.*

Would this clause stand up in court? It's a bit gray. But, knock on wood, by using all three of these techniques, we've never had a tenant-buyer record his or her option to purchase.

After having gone through all these strong-arm ways to protect yourself, we need to make three things very clear. First, you need to honor your word with your tenant-buyer. Second, you need to honor the *spirit* of your word with your tenant-buyer. Third, you need to honor the *intent* of your words with your tenant-buyer. But you want to be the one in control of the situation if your tenant-buyer should ever not live up to his or her word.

In a nutshell, this is our basic philosophy of investing: Do everything you said you would do no matter what the cost and make sure the paperwork protects you in the event that the other side doesn't behave in a similar fashion.

Seven Simple Steps to Sell Your House on the Spot

Okay, so you have eight different couples all coming to see your house at 6:15 PM on Wednesday. How do you handle this? First, don't panic. The more people you get to come at the same time the easier things will be for you to sell the house right there on the spot. Remember, the more people who are there, the more of a feeding frenzy for the property you will be creating. So take a deep breath, relax, and let's do this step by step.

Step One: Get to the Property Early and Make Sure It's Ready

The three keys to having the house show well are: big, bright, and clean.

Big. Clear out all the clutter and make sure the house looks as open and spacious as possible. If the sellers are still in the house, enlist them to help you do this. Tell them, "Mr. Seller, I am going to need your help to make this house sell fast. And the sooner I find my future buyer, the sooner I can start making your monthly payments." Get the seller to move his boxes into the closet or garage; make sure the clutter is cleared away.

Bright. Turn on all the lights. This makes the house seem warmer and larger. We even suggest replacing weak light bulbs with fresh 75-watt bulbs.

Clean. The only dirt anyone ever is willing to put up with is their own! Make sure you get the house looking clean, paying special attention to the front entryway, the kitchen, master bedroom, and bath(s).

You will have thoroughly prepped the property to make it show well. Still, get to the property at least 30 minutes early. Bring paper towels, vanilla air freshener, and a multipurpose cleaner with you. Make sure that the house is clean and smells nice. If it is daytime, open up all the curtains and blinds. Turn on *all* the lights. The brighter the house, the bigger it looks.

Without question, the three most important views for you to make sure look great are the curb view from the street looking at the front of the house, the view when the prospective buyer is standing on the porch looking at the front door, and the view when they first step into the house. All three of these views melt together inside the minds of the prospective buyers and become their first impression.

Step Two: Greet Everyone at the Door and Give Them Your Welcome Speech

Do your best to personally welcome every prospective buyer into the house as soon as they come to the door. You want to make sure they feel wanted and comfortable. Then give them the following welcome speech:

> Welcome, Mrs. Buyer, I was looking forward to meeting you. What I need you to do is just sign in there over by that counter, then wander around the house. If you love the house, come back, see me, and I'll talk through the pricing with you. If that is a fit for you, then you'll simply take five or six minutes to fill out an application right here. Then, I'll have some questions for you about what you put down on your application. If after that I feel you are the person I'm looking to choose to sell this house to, then you'll simply put a deposit down to hold the property here today. Okay?

And off they go to sign in (See Figure 5.4). You'll notice that on the sign-in sheet, you will ask them to put down the amount of upfront payment they have to work with. This is another way to get your potential buyers to be in competition with each other.

■ **David's Story**

A subtle technique I use is to presign in the person I talked with who had the most option money to work with. The reason I do this is that it creates the context to help me get the absolute most upfront money possible. When this person shows up, I simply say, "Oh, John, I've already got you signed in. Why don't you just go ahead and wander through the house.   ■

You also have probably noticed that they still don't know the price of the house. We recommend that you never tell your prospective tenant-buyers the price *until* they have gone through the house and let you know they love it! We do tell them the rent amount, but if you're ever tempted to tell them the price up front, read step three below *first*.

Step Three: Find Out Why They *Love* the Property *Before* You Talk Them through the Numbers

Remember in Chapter 3 on negotiating how you learned to never talk about the money with a seller until you have spent time on their motivation? The same thing applies with your buyers. You never talk about price until they have shared with you why they want the property.

" ■ **David's Story**

Whenever one of our students comes to me and tells me how he wasn't able to get a buyer to commit on the house even though several people were at the showing, I know he probably forgot to find out all the reasons the potential buyer had for buying the house before he spent time trying to get them to agree to the price and terms. This step is analogous to the Motivation Step of the Instant Offer System we covered in our first book. In my opinion, it is the single most overlooked step in selling a house on a rent-to-own basis. ■

Here is exactly what this sounds like:

Prospective Tenant-Buyers (John and Sarah): So how much is it? (They just looked through house and have come back to where you are waiting to talk through the numbers.)

Investor: First things first, John. Did you love the property?

FIGURE 5.4   Sample Sign-In Sheet for Prospective Tenant-Buyers

Name	Phone #	Amount of Upfront $	How You Heard About Property? (check one)
Paul Jones	*555-3124*	*$12,000*	☒ Classified Ad ☐ Signs ☐ Other _____
Sarah/Mark Tin	*544-1332*	*$ 9,000*	☐ Classified Ad ☒ Signs ☐ Other _____
Robert/Susan Maple	*544-7112*	*$10,000–$12,000*	☐ Classified Ad ☒ Signs ☐ Other _____
Eric Hafter	*553-2106*	*$ 8,000*	☐ Classified Ad ☐ Signs ☒ Other *Friend saw sign*
Melinda Kraft	*537-9888*	*$8,000–$10,000*	☒ Classified Ad ☐ Signs ☐ Other _____

John: Yes, we liked it a lot.

Investor: Did you just like it or did you love it? Because if you didn't love it, then I don't want to waste your time or my time going through the numbers.

John: No, we loved it.

Investor: Oh, good. How about you, Sarah, did you love it or did you just like it?

Sarah: I loved it too.

Investor: What did you specifically love about it, Sarah?

Sarah: I loved the view from the kitchen sink. It makes the kitchen so bright and open.

Investor: Can you share with me why this is important to you, Sarah?

Sarah: I do a lot of cooking and have always wanted a view like that out of the kitchen window with all the trees and flowers.

Investor: Oh, that makes sense. How about you, John, what specifically did you love about the house?

John: I loved the oversized garage. I can already see where I'm going to put my workbench in there.

Investor: Oh, what about the oversized garage with room for your workbench is so important to you?

John: I'm a model train fanatic. And I like a quiet place I can go to and be alone working on my trains.

Investor: Oh, that makes sense. Well, let me talk you through the numbers.

See how you have whetted your buyers' appetites and helped them both commit to you and each other that they love the property. Later on, they won't be able to come back with objections like the house didn't have this or that. The implication to all of this is that you are getting them to agree that this is the house they want, provided the numbers work out, of course.

Notice that you need to involve both the husband and the wife in this conversation. Don't let one of them be a silent watcher. If you do, then they will be the one who objects to the house later. Instead, turn and ask them direct questions just like you read a moment ago. This not only draws them into the conversation, but it also gives them a sense of ownership and participation in them buying this specific house.

Step Four: Talk Them through the Numbers

Before we show you exactly how to talk your potential buyers through the numbers, let's go over how you create your pricing first.

How to Price Your Properties for Maximum Profit and Minimum Effort

When you are creating your pricing for your properties, it is important to balance your desire to make the most money possible with your need to keep your work load low. If you price the property too high, that is, too aggressively, you will have to work very hard to move it. If you price the property too low, then you lose part of your profit. The following example is the simplest way we know to explain exactly how you come up with your pricing on your rent-to-own properties.

First, here are a couple of the background facts of this deal that can make this role-played example go smoothly for you. The house you are selling is valued at $245,000 to $250,000. The market rent for a four-bedroom house like this one is $1,500 per month. The area has been appreciating at between 4 percent and 5 percent for the past two years. You agreed with the seller on a four-year lease option where you pay a monthly rent of $1,400 per month and an option price of $225,000. You got the price down by using the negotiation strategies you learned in Chapter 3.

In case you forgot how to get the seller to lower their price, here is how the conversation probably went:

Investor. What were you asking for the property?

Seller: $250,000.

Investor: And what did you realistically expect to get?

Seller: Around $240,000.

Investor: Oh, $230,000 to $240,000. Okay.

Seller: Not $230,000, I expected to get at least $240,000.

Investor: Oh, Okay. A question for you, if a real estate agent came to you and said they could guarantee you a sale at the full $240,000 would you let them sell it for you at that full $240,000, or you'd what, probably turn them down?

Seller: No, I guess I'd let them sell it just to be done with this.

Investor: Oh, that makes sense. Then their 6 percent commission would be . . .

Seller: Roughly $15,000.

Investor: Okay, so that means that bottom line you would be getting . . .

Seller: I'd get $225,000. (Bingo! See how you let a few powerful questions lower the price by $25,000.)

Let's take this information and create your pricing for the property. Your goal is to find a price for your tenant-buyer that is below the anticipated future value of the property but high enough above your price so that you make a healthy profit. In our example, we are going to sell the house on a two-year rent-to-own basis.

First, you take the highest current value of the property and label that the current value of the house. Remember, properties are valued by how much other comparable houses have sold for, and it is impossible to put an exact dollar amount on any given house. Because you are selling with great financing in place, you should always start your current value of the property at the highest justifiable comparable property. In our example, that means the current value is $250,000.

Next, you calculate what the house would be worth at the end of the two years at its current rate of appreciation. In our example, the market was appreciating at between 4 percent and 5 percent. So again, we choose the higher end of that range. In this case, we use the 5 percent rate of appreciation. A key point here is that you do need to be realistic on your rate of appreciation. If you talk with five different real estate agents in an area and they tell you the rate of appreciation for that area is: 4 percent, 4 percent, 5 percent, 5 percent, 12 percent, you need to use some common sense that the 12 percent is not accurate.

To calculate the projected future value of the house, simply multiply the current value by 1.____ rate of appreciation as a decimal ____. In our example, multiply the $250,000 house by 1.05 to give you a one-year value of $262,500. Because you are selling this house on a two-year rent-to-own basis, you need a two-year value. You get this by taking the one-year value and again multiplying it by 1.___ rate of appreciation as a decimal ___ . In our example, we take $262,500 and multiply it by 1.05 to come up with a two-year value of $275,625. (See Figure 5.5.)

Now, we just need to choose a "sale" price that is below this two-year projected value, above your option price of $225,000, and still a great deal for your tenant-buyer. We recommend $259,980 for this house. We could have been real aggressive and gone after a price like $269,980. But because this is your first deal, we thought we would make it easier for you to sell. You can be more aggressive on the pricing of your next property!

Next, we need to decide what rent to charge your tenant-buyer. You start by charging the market rent. In this example, the market rent is $1,500. So you start your rent for this property at $1,495 (which is the more attractive way of writing $1,500). Then you use an idea called "rent credits" to bump up the amount of rent you are collecting. A rent credit is when you credit your tenant-buyer with a portion of his rent towards his purchase of the property. For example, if your tenant-buyer pays you $1,600 a month in rent, you might credit him with $150 per month off the purchase price. This is your way of both helping your tenant-buyer get a great deal and helping yourself get a larger cash flow out of the property. Remember, if your tenant-buyer decides not to buy, you keep all the extra rent.

As for the option money you want to charge your tenant-buyer, there is a simple formula that goes AMAYCG—As Much As You Can Get. Typically, you'll collect between 3 percent to 5 percent of the value of the property as a nonrefundable option payment from your tenant-buyer. In our example, you would be fine with an option payment of $10,000, but you wouldn't complain if someone volunteered to give you $15,000.

This is how you create your pricing for your properties. Ultimately the only way to know if your numbers are good is to have real

Calculating Value with Two-Year Appreciation	
e Current Value of the Property: (Current Value)	$250,000
Highest *Realistic* Rate of Appreciation for Area: (Appreciation Rate per Year)	5%
Turn Appreciation Rate into a Decimal: (Decimal Value of Appreciation—simply divide percentage value by 100.)	.05
To Calculate Projected One-Year Value:	$250,000
Current Value Multipled by 1.___ Decimal Value of Appreciation ___ :	1.05
Equals Projected One-Year Value:	$262,500
To Calculate Projected Two-Year Value:	$262,500
Projected One-Year Value Multiplied by 1.___ Decimal Value of Appreciation___ :	1.05
Equals Projected Two-Year Value:	$275,625

buyers come through the house. If you aren't getting people to say they want the property at your prices, there is something wrong with your pricing or the house shows poorly.

Here is a key point: Most tenant-buyers are *not* buying price; they are buying monthly payments they can afford and an upfront payment they can handle.

Now let's go back and learn how to talk through the numbers with your potential tenant-buyers, John and Sarah. We'll be using the sample Rent to Own worksheet you see in Figure 5.6.

Investor: Do you know how the rent-to-own program works?

John: A little bit, could you explain it to us though?

Investor: Sure, you simply put down an upfront payment which will all go towards your purchase of the house if you buy. Then you rent out the house. You have a set price you get upfront that you can buy the house for at any point over the two-year lease. It's kind of a one-sided agreement. I have to sell

---

FIGURE 5.6   Rent to Own Worksheet

Current value of property: $250,000

	Option 1		Option 2		Option 3
Rent:	$1,495	Rent:	$1,595	Rent:	$1,695
Rent Credit:	0	Rent Credit:	$150/month	Rent Credit:	$400/month
Total Rent Credit	0	Total Rent Credit	$3,600	Total Rent Credit	$9,600
Purchase Price:	$259,980	Purchase Price:	$259,980	Purchase Price:	$259,980
Rent Credits:	0	Rent Credits:	<$3,600>	Rent Credits:	<$9,600>
Option Payment:	<$10,000>	Option Payment:	<$10,000>	Option Payment:	<$10,000>
FINAL PRICE:	$249,980	FINAL PRICE:	$246,380	FINAL PRICE:	$240,380

Compare this to the value if the house appreciates at just 5%:
Future Value: $275,625

Six Reasons Rent to Own Works for You

1) **Rent Credits:** Each month a big chunk of your rent could get credited toward the possible purchase of your home, allowing you to build equity in your home faster than with a traditional mortgage—no more wasting all of your rent money.

2) **Improving Your Property:** Because you may own this property soon, any improvements you do
that increase the value of the property may help you build more equity for yourself.

3) **No banks** to deal with—no more bank hassles!

4) **Own Your Own Home!** You enjoy the benefits of owning your home *before* you technically ever
buy it!

5) **Flexibility:** You have total flexibility: You have the *option* to buy your home, not the obligation!

6) **Your Credit:** You are creating a strong credit reference while you are renting to own!

Note: All future values of property are projected estimates and may or may not come to pass.
No one can accurately predict the future value of any given property, and you understand the risks related to this
fact.

---

it to you at the agreed-upon price, but you don't have to buy it.
You have the option to buy or not buy. It's up to you. Depending on which option you choose, a portion of your monthly
rent gets credited toward your purchase of the property. Did I
make sense there, Sarah?

Sarah: Sure.

Investor: Okay, let me go through the pricing with you. The house is currently valued at $250,000. As you probably know, houses in this area have been going up in value at about 5 percent each year. If this house goes up at just this same 5 percent, it will be worth $275,625 at the end of the two years. We set our price at below this to give you a large chunk of that future growth and to build in a profit for us as investors. Does that make sense?

John: Yes, it does.

Investor: The price you have is just $259,980, which is over $15,000 less than the projected future value. You have three options to choose from. Option 1 is with a rent of $1,495. If you choose this option, then none of your rent gets credited toward your purchase of the property. Option 2 lets if you pay an extra $100 per month in rent, and you'll get $150 per month credited toward the purchase price. Over two years, that's $3,600 of money being saved up to help you buy the house. And Option 3 allows you to pay $200 extra per month. With this option, you get $400 per month credited toward the purchase price. Over two years, that's $9,600 credited towards your purchase. How much upfront money did you have to work with again?

John: $9,000.

Investor: Oh, $9,000 to $10,000. Okay. (Using the range technique)

John: I guess we could manage $10,000.

Investor: Let's just use that number for the moment as I go over how this works for you. As you can see, your final price left to pay on Option 1 is $249,980. Your final price left to pay on Option 2 is $246,380. And your final price left to pay in Option 3 is just $240,380. That's over $35,000 less than the projected two-year value! Did I explain that okay?

John: Yes.

Investor: Well, John, which of these three options is most comfortable for you?

John: Hmm, what do you think, Sarah?

Sarah: I think we should choose the second option. I like the idea of the rent credit, but I am not comfortable paying more than $1,595 per month right now.

Investor: Okay, Sarah. How about you John?

John: I'll go along with Sarah and choose Option 2.

That's how you walk your tenant-buyers through the numbers. When you are talking them through the numbers, make sure you go slow and let them be faster with the math than you are. It is important that you maintain the good feelings you have worked so hard to create earlier in this process. We recommend that if you have a calculator handy, let them use it to work the numbers—with you telling them exactly what buttons to push along the way.

Step Five: Get Them to Fill Out a Rental Application on the Spot

After you get your prospective tenant-buyers to choose which option they want, get them to fill out a rental application on the spot. If they balk at filling out the rental application, then they aren't serious buyers. Any person who really wants to buy your property will be willing to fill out the application right then and there. (See the sample application we use in Figure 5.7.) Note: We charge a $20 application review fee from each person who applies. This is an easy way to qualify your potential buyers. If a potential tenant-buyer is not willing to give you a filled-out application with $20 fee on the spot, then he or she is not really a serious candidate.

Here's exactly what you say to John and Sarah, your potential tenant-buyers:

> Investor: Okay, Option 2 it is. Now, what I need you to do is to take five or six minutes right now and fill out this rental application. Fill in all the information you can right now, and we can worry about any other information later, okay? I need to go talk to the next couple, but I'll be back in a few minutes. I'll go over your application and have some questions for you based upon the information you put down. If I feel comfortable with you and want to choose you to sell the house to, then you'll simply put a deposit down here today to hold the property. Any questions?

Notice how you positioned the application process. First, it only takes five or six minutes (fast and easy). Second, you are going to either choose or not choose them (fear of losing out on the house). And third, they will need to put a deposit down today to hold the property if they expect to get the house (sense of urgency). You have arranged things in your favor when you are selling the house.

Step Six: Qualify Them While Reviewing Their Application

Once your prospective tenant-buyers have finished filling out their rental applications and have given you the application fee, review their application and ask them some pointed questions. Here are seven questions that you should always ask your prospective tenant-buyers at this point:

1. What is the absolute most money you could come up with as your upfront payment?
2. Where do you have that money . . . in a bank account?

FIGURE 5.7 Sample Tenant-Buyer Application Form

Address of property _____

To guarantee compliance with the Federal Fair Housing Acts, a separate application and a $20.00 nonrefundable processing fee is required for each person over the age of 18 who will reside at the property.

Current monthly rent or house payment _____ Date you would like to move _____

My Current Monthly Income Is $ _____ per month

Name _____ Soc Sec # _____-_____-_____

Home phone _____ Work phone _____ Drivers Lic. # _____

How long at present address? _____ Occupancy dates _____ Why moving _____
Landlord's Name _____ Phone # _____

Before that I lived at _____
Occupancy dates_____
Landlord's Name _____ Phone # _____

Current Employer _____ Dates _____ Phone _____
Address _____ City _____ State _____ Zip _____
Position/Job description _____ Monthly take-home pay_____
Superior's name and position _____ Phone #_____
How long have you been working there? _____

In Case of Emergency Contact

	Name	Address	Phone	Relationship
1.				

CREDIT REFERENCES AND BANK ACCOUNTS

1. BANK ACCOUNTS _____
2. _____
3. CREDIT REFERENCES _____
4. _____
5. CREDIT CARDS_____
6. _____

Applicant hereby authorizes Landlord to verify this application through an Investigative Report and a Credit Report. A nonrefundable fee of $20.00 for processing is required before verification can begin.

_____   _____   _____
DATE   APPLICANT'S SIGNATURE   DATE OF BIRTH

Thank you for your interest in our home. If you are not accepted this time, you are welcome to reapply when we have another home available.

3. When did you want to move into this house?
4. When I talk with your past two landlords, what do you think they are going to tell me about their experiences renting to you?
5. What is your total monthly take-home pay?
6. What type of pets do you have?
7. When I check your credit, what should I expect to find?

At this point, you aren't doing all your due diligence to screen your tenant-buyers. You are simply qualifying their desire to buy and doing a preliminary screening. Let your tenant-buyers know that you will look at four criteria when reviewing their application:

1. Their past rental history
2. Their income
3. Their credit history
4. Their upfront payment

Of the four criteria, number four (upfront money) is the most important quality of solid tenant-buyers. More on this in a moment. We feel comfortable putting in tenant-buyers who have shaky credit as long as they give us enough money up front. One of the things you will do is to see if what the tenant-buyers tell you about themselves is true or not. While we will lease to people with bad credit or who are new on their jobs, we are very hesitant to select people who lied to us in any significant way on their rental application or during their interview.

Now, it is time to get your prospective tenant-buyers to make a real commitment to the property.

Step Seven: Collect a Nonrefundable Deposit to Hold the Property Right Then and There

The only real way to see if someone is a serious tenant-buyer or just a looker is to collect a nonrefundable deposit to hold the property. We recommend that you do this right on the spot. Here is the way you ask for it:

Investor: John, I'm happy with everything you and Sarah have told me so far. Provided everything checks out and my partner is as happy as I am with the arrangement we've made, the place will be yours. How much of a deposit did you want to put down here today?

John: I don't know. How much do you need?

Investor: Well, many people go ahead and just pay their full upfront payment, which in your case would be the $10,000. Typically, though, most people give me $2,500 to $5,000 to hold the property. If for any reason my partner doesn't agree with me to accept your application, then you'll get a full refund within 48 hours of him saying no. Also, we'll just make a plan for when you would get me the rest of the upfront money and your first month's rent that you and I both feel good about. What would you feel comfortable with as a deposit to hold the property?

John: How about $2,500?

Investor: That's fine. Were you just going to write me a check for that?

Sarah: Yes.

Investor: Okay, just make the check out to . . .

What should you do after you get one of the people at the showing to give you a nonrefundable deposit to hold the property? See how many more deposits you can get. Obviously, you will promptly return the money of any person you do not choose to put in the property, but it is always much better to have too many buyers than too few. You'll notice on the Deposit to Hold Property form (Figure 5.8) the language that makes this deposit fully binding on your prospective tenant-buyer but still subject to your final review of their application.

■ Peter's Story

Getting your tenant-buyers to make a financial commitment is the key to getting your properties filled quickly. I had a nice three-bedroom house that was only four years old that my tenant-buyer had moved out of at the end of two years, and now I needed to find another tenant-buyer. The problem was that because this property was over 90 minutes drive away from my house, I decided to use a property manager to help fill it. I ran the ads, took the calls, and set up the appointments just like I did when I showed the property myself. The only thing the property manager needed to do was show up and collect a deposit from one of the prospective tenant-buyers that I was sending to the property.

After the property sat empty for two months, I finally decided to handle it myself. I ran the ads, took the calls, and set up the appointments just as I did for the property manager. I had everyone showing up at 4:00 PM and by 4:10 PM there were four or five people walking around looking at the house. I made it very clear to the people there that if they wanted the house they needed to make a deposit today.

"This house is going to go fast, and I'm only going to consider those people who make a deposit today to let me know that you are serious," I said.

A local minister named Paul and his wife, Laurie, were the first to step up. "How much do you need?" he asked. "It's up to you," I responded. "Anywhere from $1,000 to $2,000 would be fine," I said giving him a range that used the amount I wanted as the lower number.

As Paul was writing out his check for $1,000, I asked who else there knew that they wanted to be considered for the house by giv-

FIGURE 5.8   Sample Deposit to Hold Property Form

Deposit to Hold Property

_____ (Prospective Tenant) is agreeing to a deposit of $_____ paid to hold Prospective Tenant's position to rent to own the property located at: _____

_____ .

This deposit shall be paid as follows:

_____

_____

_____ .

ALL of Prospective Tenant's deposit will apply towards the purchase of said property (it will be considered as part of Prospective Tenant's Option Payment) provided Prospective Tenant lives up to all other terms of his/her/their agreements with Landlord. This deposit is nonrefundable, and Prospective Tenant must pay additional $_____ option consideration by _____ and his/her/their first months rent of $_____ before moving into the property on _____ . If either of these payments is not received by Landlord on time then Landlord may at Landlord's sole discretion cancel agreement with Prospective Tenant and all money paid to Landlord by Prospective Tenant shall be kept as liquidated damages to cover application review, marketing costs to fill property, and lost opportunities. This agreement is subject to Landlord's final approval of Prospective Tenant's application. In the event that Landlord does not approve for any reason, Landlord may at his/her sole discretion refund all of Prospective Tenant's deposit and cancel this agreement. All option payments and first months rent must be in the form of either certified funds or money order except as noted below.

Prospective Tenant understands that Prospective Tenant does NOT have a valid lease or option to purchase said property UNTIL Prospective Tenant makes both other payments described above on time and signs all further paperwork with Landlord, including Lease Agreement, Option to Purchase Agreement, Disclosure Forms, etc. In no case may the Prospective Tenant enter or otherwise occupy said property until ALL conditions and terms in this agreement have been fulfilled. TIME IS OF THE ESSENCE!

_____   ____/____/____

Prospective Tenant

_____   ____/____/____

Landlord and/or Agent for Landlord

If initial deposit is to be paid by check, initial next to this paragraph to show both parties understand and agree to the following: Tenant understands that he/she/they are making a nonrefundable deposit on this day to hold the property. Furthermore, Tenant hereby states that there are sufficient funds available to cover this check and that Tenant understands Landlord is relying upon the fact that this check will in fact clear. In the event this check does not clear for any reason, Tenant understands that Tenant shall be liable for prosecution and collection to the fullest extent of the law. Furthermore, Tenant understands that all remaining option money and first months rent must be in the form of either certified funds or money order.

ing me an application and deposit. A young couple named Tom and Karen told me that they did. They explained that they had missed out on the last rent-to-own home they had looked at because they didn't move quickly enough. I also took a $1,000 deposit from them and let both couples know that I would process their applications. If they weren't approved for the house, they would get their deposits back right away.

In less than four hours, counting three hours driving time, I was able to get two prospective tenant-buyers to give me $1,000 each. This was the same house that the property manager spent two months trying to find a tenant-buyer for. The difference was that I asked for the deposit in a way that created urgency; the property manager did not.   ■

One question we always get is what form of payment do you want the deposit from your tenant-buyer to be in? Ideally, it would be in the form of a money order or cashier's check. You can take a personal check if you need to, but be sure that you have them initial by the clause on the Deposit to Hold Property form that says:

> Tenant understands that he/she/they are making a nonrefundable deposit to hold the property. Furthermore, Tenant hereby states that there are sufficient funds available to cover this check and that Tenant understands Landlord is relying upon the fact that this check will in fact clear. In the event this check does not clear for any reason, Tenant understands that Tenant shall be liable for prosecution and collection to the fullest extent of the law.

Even with this strong language, if you do have to take a personal check for the initial deposit to hold the property, we strongly encourage you to visit the prospective *tenant-buyer's* bank as soon as possible to cash the check so you know right away if there are any problems.

Now, you review all the rental applications. You verify th formation on the application and choose your best tenant-buye Don't get too caught up in looking for the perfect tenant-buyer. Speed is the key here. In most cases, all things being equal, you will choose the tenant-buyer who gives you the most money up front. All things not being equal, you will just need to use your best judgement to choose the best party. But whomever you choose, there is an urgency to finish things up fast. Time creates doubt, and doubt kills more deals than anything else.

The Three Hows of Selling Your Property

When you are selling your property using the Purchase Option strategies, you have three questions to ask yourself. Your answers will determine your pricing strategy for your property. The three questions that follow are a way to gauge the relative importance to you of three factors:

1. *How Much?* How much money do you want to make?
2. *How Long?* How long are you willing to wait to get all your profits as cash in hand?
3. *How Hard?* How hard do you want to work to increase the amount of profit you can make?

What follows are four different options that you have when selling a property that will allow you to use the three variables above to determine your pricing strategy. Which do you want? Quick cash but less of it? Maximum long-term profits with a minimum of work? One great thing about Purchase Option real estate investing is that you decide how you want to offer your properties for sale. This means your are the one in control of your real estate investing future.

Option One: Quick Cash

If you want to make fast cash and are willing to make less of it, you can turn over your properties right away. Typically, this involves "flipping" your deal to another investor. Flipping your deal to another investor means you sign up a deal with a seller, but rather than doing all the work to prep the property and find a retail buyer you simply sell your contract, and all the rights it contains, to another investor. The benefit to you will be a quick cash payoff. But the downside is that you will never make another penny off of that property ever again, and you will need to be looking for your next deal right away. For more information on flipping deals read *Flipping Properties: Generate Instant Cash Profits in Real Estate* by Bronchick and Dahlstrom (Dearborn Trade).

Here is a quick example of how to flip a deal. We did a deal with a student of ours, Michael, in New Orleans. We found a seller who wanted to unload a house that needed a major rehab. We locked up the house for a cash price of $25,000. The property needed $15,000 in work, and then it would retail for $65,000 to $70,000. Michael went to his local real estate investors club, something we'll talk more about in Chapter 6, and found another investor who did rehabs. We sold this investor our contract for $3,500 cash.

We've done this with other deals. Another house we had in Los Angeles needed a great deal of fixup. Our student, Greg, found another investor who advertised in his local paper with an I Buy Houses ad who paid us $2,000 for that contract. Again, all we did was sign up a good contract on the property and then sold our contract.

■ **David's Story**

When I watch investors flipping deals exclusively I think to myself, "Boy, they are sure working hard for a quick fix of money." Don't get me wrong. I've flipped deals before when I signed up a property that was going to take a major rehab to make it sell and I didn't want to put the time or money into it. But what I always caution beginning investors who say they just want to flip deals is that it's a treadmill. If you stop looking for properties, you stop making money. You are always having to scramble for your next deal. To me this sounds like a commission sales job. The biggest reason to invest in real estate is because it is the simplest way to create a *passive* money stream for yourself. To do this, you need to hang onto some of the properties you put under contract.   ■

Another way to make fast cash is to lock up a property at a great price and turn around and sell it to a retail buyer right away to make a cash profit. This is called "retailing" your property. One of our students, Stephen, found a highly motivated seller in Florida. Stephen signed up a contract to buy the house for $78,000. This price was well below the current market value of the home. Stephen put in about a week's work and $1,000 in cleaning up the house. He then went out and found a buyer for the house at the price of $109,900. All totaled, he netted $29,900 in a 45-day period.

Option Two: Sell to Your First Tenant-Buyer

Another option you have is to set your pricing to make it very likely that your first tenant-buyer will exercise his option to purchase. To do this you charge a larger option payment up front. Not only does this mean the tenant-buyer has more to lose if he doesn't buy, but it also qualifies him as a much more serious buyer and makes it easier for him to get his financing down the road because his option payment and rent credits, if any, will convert into a down payment at that closing.

As for the price you'll set, if you want your first tenant-buyer to buy, you should set the price lower than you would if you didn't care if he bought or not. Obviously, the lower the option price the more likely your tenant-buyer will be to buy. Some investors we know sell on a 6-month to 12-month rent-to-own basis at a price that is the fair market value as of the day the tenant-buyer moved in. These investors figure this is an easy way for them to get top dollar for their house without having to pay any real estate commissions.

If we had to sell a property and wanted to make sure our tenant-buyer bought, we'd sell it on a term of no longer than a year at a price that was very appealing to them as a buyer.

For example, we sold one of our houses we did with John, whom you'll meet in Chapter 6, exactly this way. Because we negotiated a great price on the property going into the deal, we sold the house on a one-year lease option for a price that was only $5,000 more than the current value of the house. This made it very appealing to the tenant-buyer who ended up closing on the house 13 months after moving in and at a price of $165,000, which was over $10,000 below the market value at the time of closing. We made a little over $23,000 on the deal, and our tenant-buyer got a great house. To be frank, we regret selling so cheaply because that house is now worth over $240,000! That's why we think you should pay particular attention to the next pricing strategy.

Option Three: Hold Long Term with Minimum Turn Over

If you pick up a property on a six-year lease option and sell it to your first tenant-buyer after two years, will you get the full benefit of that six-year term with your seller? No, you won't. You will only get two-years of cash flow, two-years of amortization, and two-years of appreciation. You'll be sacrificing the other four years of growth. That's why this pricing option is our favorite. If you don't need instant cash and are looking more long term for your investments, then this is the pricing strategy you'll choose.

Option three says to set your pricing to encourage your tenant-buyer to *not* exercise their option to purchase, but to also make sure you don't have too much turnover in tenant-buyers. Remember, the more turnover in tenant-buyers, the more work you'll have cleaning up the property and marketing it to another buyer. With this pricing strategy, you will charge a medium amount of money up front in order to make sure your tenant-buyer behaves but also to make it less painful for them to walk away from the deal without exercising their option to purchase. The key is to set your tenant-buyer's option price very aggressively, i.e., as high as possible. That way it lowers the odds that they'll buy. And if they do buy, you'll make enough money that it won't hurt you so much. As for the term you should set, choose a longer term of two or three-years.

Strange as it seems, we've found that the longer the term is, the less likely the tenant-buyer is to buy. This is merely a tendency, not a hard and fast rule. Over two or three years, life seems to just happen to tenant-buyers, and they often choose not to buy. Sometimes they have a relationship end, and other times they get a better job offer in another area. The net result is that they'll take care of your property for a long time, letting the values go up and the loan balance go down, and then give it back to you at the end.

A very important point to understand is that we never give our tenant-buyers more than a three-year term. We don't want anyone to tie up our property for longer than that. On occasion, we'll renegotiate an extension for a fourth or fifth year with our tenant-buyer, but we never commit to them in advance that we will extend. After all, if they don't pay their rent on time and are a hassle, we want them to leave. Now, if they are as good as most of our tenant-buyers turn out to be, then we will be thrilled to give them an extension—obviously, with a higher rent and price. Plus, if you give your tenant-buyer a term of five years or ten years and they don't pay you the rent, it will look to a judge presiding at the eviction hearing like you really have a buyer not a renter. The judge will say you probably *sold* them the house on something known as an "agreement for deed" or "land contract." This is not something you want to happen because you would then have to foreclose rather than evict.

We still have one of the houses we picked up on the original San Diego Challenge, mentioned in Chapter 2. It is a three-bedroom house that we got on a five-year lease option for $140,000. We have had three tenant-buyers in the property over the last four years. Our first tenant-buyer paid us $795 per month in rent and had an option price of $159,900. Our current tenant-buyer, number three, pays us $1,195 per month in rent and has an option price of $179,900. We're hoping they don't buy because the market rent for the house is now $1,400 per month and the home is valued at $230,000!

■ **Peter's Story**

I sometimes structure some of my long-term keeper houses on lease options. I put in a tenant-buyer who gives me a large option payment that is fully *refundable* provided they stay in the house for three years, pay their rent on time each month, and maintain the property. In the event they don't, they lose their option payment. The reality is that by making it so easy for my tenant-buyers of these high-end homes to walk away, they usually do. In the meantime, I have a large chunk of money that is several times greater than a normal security deposit to protect my interests. I don't use this concept on very many houses, but when I do it has made me a lot of money.   ■

Option Four: Squeeze Out the Maximum Profit Possible

It never fails: Whenever we are teaching a workshop, there are always some people there who want to make the absolute most money possible and are willing to put in the work to do it. When selling on a rent-to-own basis, the way to do this is to have a lot of turnover of tenant-buyers. Why? It is because each time you put a new tenant-buyer into the property, you collect another nonrefundable option payment. These option payments add up fast.

So, if this is the option you want to choose, then sell to your tenant-buyer on a one-year term. Make sure you collect a small to medium option payment, remembering that if you charge too much up front, they will probably buy. Also, you need to make sure the price you set is at the high end of what you project the property to be worth when they go to buy. Now we don't use this option because it is setting your tenant-buyers up for failure, but we feel that we need to at least make you aware that this choice does exist. If you do, in fact, choose this option, make sure you let your tenant-buyer know very clearly what you expect from them and the consequences if they don't end up being able to buy. Also, you need to know that you will be spending a lot of time cleaning up the property and marketing it each time your tenant-buyers move out.

You Choose How Much You Make and When

One of the nicest things about Purchase Option investing is that you chose how much you make, how much work you are willing to do, and when you will make your money.

What Now?

All right, you've learned all about the Purchase Option system for making big money by investing in real estate. Now what? How do you begin to put into practice all the ideas, strategies, tactics, and techniques you have been learning?

It seems wherever we go to teach investor workshops, the most common question we get is, "How do I get started?" These people, like you, are totally sincere in their desire to be successful in real estate investing. Like you, they are willing to invest the time, effort, and, if need be, the money, to launch their investing business. But they are unsure about how to start. All the information they are accumulating seems overwhelming at times. They ask us to cut out all the fancy stuff and give them the bottom line they need right here and right now in order to start making money by investing in real estate.

Would you like to read our bottom lines? Well, lean forward and pay close attention. We are about to share with you the critical information you need to get started. And then, you'll learn about five ordinary people who used real estate investing to make their lives extraordinary.

Three Techniques to Find Your First Deal in 45 Days or Less!

You've already read in Chapter 2 about the dramatic press challenge we made good on several years ago. We had staked our reputation that we could show three beginning investors how to find their first deals not just in 45 days but in 72 hours!

While it was a stressful, scary, and chaotic three days, it was worth it. We couldn't have been more thrilled with the results. Let's face it, results are what people care about, not fancy promises. Even better than the promotional value of those three days was the way the market has driven the value of these properties we handled then through the roof. These ten properties are now worth well over $2.5 million.

Since that time, we have been asked many times how we did it. How did we *really* find all those deals in such a short time. Well, it's time to pull the curtain back and reveal the wizard. Here are the three strategies we used to find those deals. Are these the only ways to find great deals? Of course not; they are just the fastest ways to find your first deal. If we were thrown cold into a city again and asked to find a deal, these are the strategies we would use to make things happen.

Technique 1: Calling For Sale By Owner and For Rent Ads

While making calls to people who have advertised their properties for sale or for rent may not be glamorous or thrilling, it is effective. On the original San Diego Challenge, we made hundreds of calls to people with properties advertised for sale or for rent to set up the nearly 30 appointments we went on to meet with sellers and see their properties. You can get a look at the word-for-word scripts that we used when calling these property owners; they are included in our first book.

One insider trick is to *age* the classified ads you call on to let time do much of the sorting of motivated and nonmotivated sellers for you. Rather than call on current For Sale By Owner ads, call on ads that are one month to three months old. With For Rent ads, call on ads that are one week to three *weeks* old. While many of the properties will no longer be on the market, the owners with properties that are left will be much more willing to deal.

If you haven't been stacking up your Sunday paper's real estate classified ads to make an aging file, go to your local library and get numbers you need from the back issues of the newspapers they have. Probably the biggest mistake we see people make who are calling on classified ads is to search for the perfect ad to call on. They seem to think they should look for an ad that reads, "Motivated seller must sell within the next 24 hours. Will deed my property to you for $1 gifting you the $50,000 of equity I have. Please call now, I promise to only say yes to your offer!" Okay, so we are getting a bit carried away. The point is that most of the perfect ads you will come across are written by other investors who are using words they know will generate a lot of interest. Besides, the real reason people look for the perfect ad is usually fear. They want to delay the act of picking up the phone and dialing as long as possible. We understand it can be scary, but how else are you going to learn to talk with property owners except by actually doing it?

Also, the more scared or uncertain you sound on the phone, the better! Most people who advertise their house with For Sale By Owner ads get flooded by agents' calls looking to pick up listings. And most agents are trained to sound professional, enthusiastic, and confident on the phone. After many years of investing and teaching our students to be successful in real estate investing, we've learned that you need to do the exact opposite of these agents (and the telemarketers who are out there calling up these sellers about other matters). You want to be a bit helpless and unsure for the first 30 to 60 seconds of the conversation. This helps you get over the big question mark in the mind of the seller, "Do I want to talk with this person?"

We know this is not the conventional approach to sorting through leads on the phone, but our negotiating strategies aren't conventional either. In our experience, this approach simply works best. We've personally picked up dozens of properties using this approach.

■ Peter's Story

I remember talking with a student named Craig. He and his wife had found five of their first nine deals by calling ads out of his local paper. His wife does the calls and sets up the appointments, and Craig goes and signs up the deals. They have a great partnership in place.   ■

■ David's Story

When we have our mentorship students at the three-day intensive training workshop, one of the very first things we do during the morning of the first day is to get them to call sellers of property. We form small groups of three or four people and get on the phones. Peter and I make a lot of the calls with them. We use a speaker phone, and when the student gets stuck, we press the mute button and tell them what to say next. Everyone starts off nervous on the phone. But at the end of the three days, when they have made 50 to 60 calls, they realize it's not such a big deal.   ■

One of the biggest mistakes many investors make is to try to explain their offer over the phone. Don't do it! Instead, if the seller presses you for an offer tell him, "Look Mr. Seller, I don't know if we have a fit here or not. I may not want to buy the house. May I ask you a few questions to see if I even want you to invite me over to see the inside of the house?" Notice how you are being a reluctant buyer here. The other benefit you get from this approach is that you never have to try to explain your offer over the phone before you've met with the seller. Remember, you are *not* negotiating over the phone, you are simply sorting.

Technique 2: Get Your "I Buy Houses" Ad in the Paper!

Go back and read through our earlier instructions in Chapter 2 on getting your I Buy Houses ad in the paper. Done properly, your classified ad will be good for several deals every year. It is fairly inexpensive and a very high-leverage way of finding motivated sellers.

■ David's Story

I've found about 30 percent of the deals I've done through classified ads that I've placed in various papers. Some weeks, I get no calls, and other weeks, I get five or six great leads. I wouldn't even think about removing my ads from the paper. I've got it on an autopay program through my credit card. It goes in every week. It's an automated process for me.   ■

Technique 3: Put Out 200 "I Buy Houses" Signs around Your Farm Area

Your farm area is simply a neighborhood or part of your city where you want to focus your buying efforts. While you'll still probably buy properties in other areas, the lion's share of your marketing efforts will be focussed on this area. You will become an expert on property values and rental values in this area. When something comes up for rent or for sale you'll know right away.

One of the best ways to farm this area is to get your I Buy Houses signs out. You can do this yourself or hire someone to do it for you. Make sure you are aware of local ordinances in your area about putting out signs.

■ **Peter's Story**

I don't know of any investor who has put out 200 signs who hasn't bought at least one house! They work that well. The best part is that the cost is just a few hundred dollars for the signs. What a bargain in marketing costs to get a great buy on a house.   ■

A Simple Five-Step Action Plan to Launch Your Real Estate Investing Business

Step One: Commit to Your Continuing Education in Real Estate

There is only one way to learn in life—experience. And experience can be a rough teacher at times. You have the choice of learning from your own experiences or supplementing your own experiences with insights from other people.

But don't think you need to know it all before you get started because you'll never know it all. That's a trap that catches many would-be real estate investors and freezes them cold. Just commit to steadily learning more and more over time as you are out there doing your investing. The best way to lower your risk is to invest in your knowledge base.

" ■ **David's Story**

I still read about 40 to 50 books a year to make me a better ...
I also go through at least five home-study courses a year. I'm not
looking for a flood of new information. I just want to pick the very
best ideas from everything I read and listen to. I take these ideas
and put them to work to make money. For example, I recently
learned about how to legally cut my tax liability when I sell certain
types of properties by over 15 percent. That one idea that has
literally saved me tens of thousands of dollars!   ■

Following are four must-read books to help you become successful by investing in real estate:

1. *Think and Grow Rich,* by Napoleon Hill, is the granddaddy
   of all self-help books. This is a must for your success library.
2. *The Aladdin Factor,* by Mark Victor Hansen and Jack Can-
   field, will teach you the critical skill of asking for what you
   want in life.
3. *How to Create Multiple Streams of Income Buying Homes
   in Nice Areas with Nothing Down,* by Peter Conti and David
   Finkel, is, we know, a shameless plug. But in our opinion, it's
   still a great book on how to find motivated sellers.
4. *Rich Dad, Poor Dad,* by Robert Kiyosaki and Sharon Lech-
   ter, will open your eyes to the big picture of financial freedom.

Step Two: Find a Mentor to Work with

Find a successful investor who is willing to help you learn the
ropes. Our friend, Darcy, recently completed an Ironman Triathlon.
While we think she's crazy for volunteering to suffer through that
event, she did share something very interesting with us. It seems
that during the 110-mile bike ride portion of the event, there are

strict rules that forbid any participant from drafting behind another cyclist. Because a rider uses up to 30 percent less energy by letting another rider block the wind for them, the officials don't allow it. But in your real estate investing, drafting is not only allowed, it is encouraged and rewarded. There is no better way to learn than by having someone take you by the hand and do it with you.

Step Three: Develop Three Independent Sources of Motivated Sellers

In order to make money in real estate investing, you need to work with motivated sellers. The number one priority of your investing business is to create three reliable sources of finding highly motivated sellers. Whether you use the ideas in this book or in our first book, you need to invest the time and energy to systematize your lead generation so you consistently turn up good leads.

■ Peter's Story

Just this year, we put seven of our mentorship students through an experimental program. One of the main focuses of this program was to fine tune their the deal-finding systems so that within three or four months they had done what most investors spend three or four years doing. What are the results? Three of the students gave up after a few weeks; they couldn't handle the reality of putting in 15 to 20 hours a week in this highly structured program. The other four students did ten deals over their first four months, with average profits of over $20,000 per deal. These four students now have their deal-finding skills down cold. You too need to reach the point where finding deals becomes second nature. ■

Step Four: Meet with at Least One Seller a Week—Every Week!

Magic things happen when you are sitting in the presence of a motivated seller. While you never know what the outcome of any one appointment with a single seller will be, you do know that if you meet with enough sellers you will sign up deals. You can't help but have this happen. It's just a numbers game.

Once you have your three deal-finding systems in place, you can expect to spend between three and five hours each week to get one high-quality appointment to go visit. On average, that appointment will take two hours, including driving time there and back, which means you have five to seven hours per week to put into your investing at an absolute minimum. Note: You'll have more time to put in when you are selling a house you have picked up. This will take you an average of 15 to 20 hours per week for two or three weeks. But no one seems to mind this part because it means you get to collect a fat check for your work!

Meeting with one seller a week means you'll meet with 52 sellers a year. Don't you think that after meeting with 52 sellers you are going to sign up at least one deal? And after you've done your first deal, don't you think you'll get better and better at negotiating and closing more deals?

■ **David's Story**

When our students first get started they go on an average of 12 appointments before they sign up their first deal. Obviously, this improves over time. I close one deal out of three-and-a-half appointments. To my lifelong dismay, Peter closes one out of three. Alas, it's a fact he never lets me forget. Sometimes having a best friend and mentor isn't all it's cracked up to be.   ■

Step Five: Create a Feedback System

You need a system in place that helps you step back from your day-to-day investing and fine tune your efforts as you go.

■ David's Story

Back when I used to play on the United States National Field Hockey Team, my coach used to have this saying. He said, "Are you getting one game's experience a hundred times, or are you getting a hundred games' experience?" The point sunk in with us players. After every game, we'd sit down with our training journals and write down what we learned from the game. We made sure to capture the best learning points from each match so that we would learn and grow as players. When I got started investing in real estate, I used the same idea. After each appointment with a seller, I'd sit down with my real estate journal and make sure I captured every important lesson from that experience I could.   ■

Create a real estate journal for yourself. After each session of talking with sellers or buyers on the phone, or meeting with them in person, ask yourself the following questions and record your answers in your journal:

- What went really well about that experience?
- What will I do different the next time I am in the same situation?
- What questions did the experience raise that I will need to find the answers to?
- Where will I go to find these answers?

Another way to get feedback on your investing is to tap into the power of your local Real Estate Investor Association (REIA). These groups are scattered across the country and typically meet once a month to share ideas, network, and support each other in their investing. They are a great resource for you as you get started in real estate investing. To find a list of different groups around the country simply look on the Web at <www.americanreia.com>.

How Five Ordinary People Created Extraordinary Lives by Investing in Real Estate and How You Can Too!

We'd like to introduce you to five of our past graduates. They came to real estate investing from a variety of backgrounds. We hope that their examples of what ordinary persons can accomplish when they step out there on faith and go after their dreams will inspire you to put to use all the strategies and techniques you have learned in this book.

The next time you feel that there is no way you could ever be successful by investing in real estate, we want you to remember their stories. If these five people could succeed investing in real estate, you can too. All it takes is the conscious decision on your part to get started, to keep going, and to remain open to learning along the way.

How an Ex-Hairdresser Built Up a Multimillion Dollar Property Portfolio and How You Can Too

Our first story is about Marcia, an outgoing investor with a heart of gold from the Midwest. Besides being a woman of great integrity, Marcia is the kind of person who you would turn to if you were ever in trouble. At age 30, Marcia set the goal of buying real estate part time around her hairdressing business to be able to retire at age 40. She went to a one-hour class in real estate and learned enough to get started. Her first purchase was the small commercial building she had her hair salon in.

Over the next five years, Marcia saved up enough money for a down payment to buy one property per year using conventional financing. At this point, she took stock on her progress and realized if she kept this pace she wouldn't hit her goal. She took some drastic action. She went out on a crash course of real estate investing classes and workshops. She studied everything she could get her hands on that dealt with creative financing and negotiating deals. Putting these ideas into action was scary for her.

The first property she ever did creatively was at an auction in her town for some farm land. She told us how she purposely sat in the front row of the auction because she knew there were "real" investors there and was scared to look at them. She ended up being the successful bidder that day on a 60-acre piece of land with three houses on it for $300,000. She had to write a check right on the spot for a 10 percent deposit. She got this $30,000 from a home-equity mortgage on her house. She was scared, but it was manageable because she had already lined up a money-partner to fund the deal. Then she got the devastating news: Her investor had backed out on her! Here she was with $30,000 at stake, a huge sum of money for Marcia at that point in her life, and no idea how she would make this deal happen.

Moving forward on faith, Marcia teamed up with an aggressive real estate agent who helped her sell $150,000 of property from her 60 acres. She then negotiated with the seller to give her a 30-day extension on the closing for the land in exchange for a $5,000 additional earnest money deposit. Using this extra time, Marcia and her agent sold off another $100,000 of property. Marcia again went back to the seller and this time gave the seller an additional $6,000 to extend the closing for 30 more days. In this final 30 days, Marcia managed to get the final $50,000 to the seller by selling off more of the property. When all was said and done, 90 days later, Marcia had bought the land for $300,000 that she had paid for by selling off most of the land, leaving her with 13 acres worth $110,000 which she now owned free and clear! Marcia used this profit to eventually buy five houses, worth a total of $250,000. She still owns these five houses today, and they give her $3,000 a month in positive cash flow.

The first year that Marcia started using the creative strategies you've learned about in this book, she bought 7 properties. The next year, she bought 10 properties. The next year, she bought 25 properties. And the next year, she bought 45 properties. As you can imagine, she did indeed meet her ten-year goal, with time to spare.

When asked what her favorite Purchase Option buying strategy is, she says, "My favorite is getting the deed [i.e., buying subject to] because then I don't have any lender costs, I don't have to qualify for the loan, the loan doesn't show up on my credit report, and having the title in my name makes it much easier when I sell."

One recent lease option deal Marcia negotiated was with a young couple who owned free and clear an immaculate brick, lakefront house. Marcia explains, "I talked to them about a lease option. Just as Peter and David had taught me, I asked for a long-term deal of ten years. We ended up at seven years with $10 down and $550 a month in rent payments. The price was $139,000, which was market value."

Marcia then marketed the house on a rent-to-own basis. She says, "Because it was in great shape, I didn't have to do a single thing to fix or clean the property. I put out some signs, ran some ads, and within 30 days I had $10,000 from my tenant-buyer, who had a two-year rent to own at a price of $159,000."

She told us about another deal she put together with a family who had a house that was vacant when they had moved out of the area. The sellers didn't even have enough equity to pay for a real estate agent to list and sell the house, unless they paid out of pocket for the closing costs and agent's commission. Marcia agreed to buy the property subject to the $195,000 mortgage. The monthly payments were $1,200 per month plus taxes and insurance.

The house itself was located right on a river and had a pool out back. In fact, Marcia liked it so much she decided to move in and live there. She put in $25,000 in improvements, and now that house is valued at $300,000. Marcia has an $80,000 profit in the property. Because she is single, she rents out the lower level of this 3,000 square-foot house and gets $800 a month in rent that covers over half of her monthly payment.

Marcia says, "Real estate investing gives me the flexibility and freedom to travel. Last year, I went to Australia and New Zealand for six weeks, and this was in addition to taking another six weeks of vacation. I couldn't do that as a hairdresser because when I was away from my chair I wouldn't make any income. Now, when I'm traveling, the income still comes in."

How a Young Construction Worker Went from Laying Carpet to Investing Full Time

■ David's Story

I remember when I first met John at a workshop I was giving in San Diego. He spoke so softly that I could barely hear what he was saying. He stuck around after everyone else had gone home and in his own way asked me to mentor him in his investing. At the time, I remember thinking to myself, "Why am I saying yes to him? He'll quit after the first no he gets from a seller." Was I ever wrong! ■

During his first three months investing John went on appointment after appointment with no luck. On several occasions, John would call us up and share a great appointment he had, and we would ask him to fax over the contract he had signed up. "Oh, I didn't sign up anything. I thought I better call and talk to you first." Inevitably, by the time John went back to meet with the sellers, they had found another buyer.

"John," we would say, "just sign it up even if you do it all wrong. As long as you leave the 'subject to' clauses in the agreement you'll be fine." Can you understand the real reason John didn't bring out his agreement with the seller? It was fear. He was scared that no seller would take a 22-year-old carpet layer seriously.

Then one day something clicked for John. He was meeting with the seller of a three-bedroom house about seven minutes from where he lived. The seller was moving out of state and hadn't been able to sell the house. From looking through the property, John knew the problem was the ugly carpet in the house. Maybe it was the fact that he knew he could replace the carpet at cost, or maybe it was the fact that this house was so close to his own, or maybe John had just gotten sick of letting deals slip through his hands, John moved ahead. When the seller agreed to his offer, John finally pulled out his agreement and got it down in writing.

He faxed into our office the three-year lease option he had signed at about $10,000 to $15,000 below market value. He also estimated that it would take about $3,000 to replace the carpet and paint part of the inside of the house. He said he would do it with a buddy of his from work over the weekend.

■ David's Story

I remember looking at the agreement and being so proud of what John had done. Still, the investor in me knew from everything he told me that we could make this deal even better. So I told him to go back and ask for one small thing—a "one time renewal" of the agreement if we wanted it. This meant that our three-year deal would turn into a six-year deal. I could tell John was nervous about how the seller would react, but John went ahead and did it any way. And the seller did say yes!   ■

John sold this house on a 12-month rent-to-own basis. He made $100 a month from the cash flow and another $26,000 when his tenant-buyers cashed him out at the end of a year. He was on his way.

Another house he bought near where he lived was from a call off of an ad he had placed in his local paper. He bought the house for $5,000 down and subject to the sellers existing $125,000 loan. At the time he bought it, the house had $18,000 to $20,000 of equity in it. He put a tenant-buyer in the property for $8,000 option money at a price of $159,900. Fortunately, for John, his tenant-buyer didn't buy because a year-and-one-half later John got a cash offer for the house for $165,000. John ended up giving his tenant-buyer back $6,000 of his option payment because of all the improvements the tenant-buyer had made to the property. At closing, John collected a check for $35,000.

About 12 months ago, John took the leap into investing full time and quit his construction job. When asked about his decision to invest full time he says, "I just couldn't do it anymore. I was working 10-hour to 12-hour days, and then I would get home and be too tired to make my sales calls or go meet sellers. Jackie and I talked it over, and we decided I should quit and start full time on my investing. This has been incredible. I knew I didn't want to be in construction forever. I used to watch the guys who had been doing it for 20-plus years. They had so many health problems from all the demanding work. Real estate has been my ticket out of all that."

If you met John today you would see him as he was meant to be—a soft-spoken man in his mid-20s who is quietly confident about his and his family's future. Gone is the old uncertain construction worker. In his place is a sharp and highly expert investor who is comfortable negotiating with just about any seller and signing the deal up on the spot, with a few "subject to" clauses, of course.

How a Real Estate Broker Cashed In by Investing *not* Brokering

Our next story is of one of our students named Gary. Gary is a real estate broker who spends all of his time investing, not representing other buyers or sellers. He lives in Southern California and focuses only on properties that are right near the ocean. He knows that these homes have excellent long-term appreciation.

Gary buys most of his homes subject to the existing financing with the seller carrying back a second mortgage for the balance of the purchase. Because most of his sellers don't want their name on the loan forever, Gary typically agrees to completely cash out the existing loan and the seller-carry second mortgage within five to seven years.

Gary figures he talks with about 50 to 75 sellers for every one deal he finds. He finds most of his leads out of the multiple listing service (MLS), the proprietary database that real estate agents use to advertise properties for sale. He searches through the MLS for comments like:

- Found another house
- Foreclosure looming
- Out-of-town owner
- owc (owner will carry)
- AITD (all-inclusive trust deed—a fancy name for a type of "subject to" purchase)

Gary also gets some of his deals from referrals from other agents in the area who know what he is looking for. He's found that most sellers are stuck on their price. So he gives them full price in exchange for them giving him good terms. He says, "I work only with agents who are willing to talk with their sellers about all-inclusive trust deeds or subject to's. I sometimes even give my buyer's side of the real estate commission to the listing agent as an added incentive to them to make the deal happen. I can put 6 percent into the deal up front and still make a bunch of money. I've found that you can't be greedy in this business." Gary goes on to say, "For some reason I've found that sellers are more stuck on getting their asking price than with terms."

He won't buy a property that needs much more than a simple painting and carpeting. He says he tries to make sure it takes him less than a week to get the property ready to sell to his tenant-buyer.

His cookie-cutter approach to selling the property on a rent-to-own basis is to give the tenant-buyer a one-year lease option with the right to renew for one more year. At a minimum, Gary marks up the price to at least $30,000 over what he paid for it. He usually offers a rent credit for the first year only of a few hundred dollars per month, but only if his tenant-buyers pay on time. For the second year, he bumps the price by 50 percent of the average increase in value for that area. So, if the area went up in value 10 percent, he bumps the tenant-buyer's price by an additional 5 percent. He also collects a second option payment of $3,500 to $12,000 from his tenant-buyer for the right to this renewal.

Here's an example of one deal Gary put together. He paid motivated sellers $5,000 down and bought the sellers' $150,000 condo subject to the existing financing. The sellers carried back a second mortgage for the balance of their equity. Three years later Gary sold that condo for $299,900. While most of his deals don't end up making this much money, he still does quite well for himself. Gary says, "We may only do five or six deals a year like this. That means on paper we're making a minimum of $125,000 a year. Now, in reality, we've done a lot better than that because they [his tenant-buyers] haven't all exercised their options. At the end of a tenant-buyer's time, if the tenant-buyer doesn't exercise their option and moves out, we do an appraisal of the property. Then we add at least $30,000 on top of that appraisal and sell it to another tenant-buyer. It ends up we're making over $300,000 a year."

Back from Real Estate Bankruptcy

Frank, who lives on the east coast, had been a real estate appraiser for close to 20 years. In the beginning, he had invested in real estate using traditional techniques. Says Frank, "I used to buy properties at good prices, often below market value, even putting money in my pocket at closing on occasion. I was getting bank loans and signing personally on them. I then rented out the property. I had 21 properties when I was 23 years old. At this time, the market changed, and the tenants weren't able to keep paying the rent. I was stuck making payments on 21 properties plus my own house, and it was too much. I ended up going bankrupt."

Six years ago, Frank started to invest again. Only this time he was smarter about it. "When I restarted, I went after houses I could buy and resell right away, or I used a lease option or 'subject to' financing to get in. These I sell on a rent-to-own basis."

When we asked him what the biggest difference between what he used to do when he invested and what he does now after integrating all those expensive lessons, Frank said, "20 years ago I was putting my name on every mortgage when I bought. I try [now] to get in on a lease option or to buy it subject to so that I can keep the property longer and still feel comfortable about it. If my tenant-buyer puts up $5,000 as option money that will be credited later as a down payment, I've found that 80 percent of my problems go away. They tend to pay their monthly payment on time; they take care of the maintenance and repairs. You don't hear from them as often, and you don't have the headaches that you do as a normal landlord."

Frank now does an average of two deals a month with average profits of $10,000 to $15,000 per deal. When we asked him what words of advice he has for someone who is just getting started investing in real estate he shared this: "Based on my experience from 20 years ago when I ended up going bankrupt, I realized that while you can make a lot of money investing you can also lose a lot if you don't do it right. There is a lot of good information out there based on other people's learning and mistakes. This can save you a fortune. I lost more money than I want to think about. The main thing is to read the books, go to the seminars, learn from the people who have done it. Then just be consistent when you go out and do it yourself."

One Last Story to Tell

Reddy moved from Hong Kong to the United States back in the early 1990s. When she first came here, she lived on the east coast and worked as a CPA. In 1997, Reddy quit her job and moved to Atlanta. She settled in, took every real estate class she could find from real estate law to "nothing-down" seminars. Says Reddy, "I probably spent $20,000 for all those classes, but they gave me the very strong confidence I needed."

When she got started, Reddy used lease options exclusively for the first two years. She liked them because she didn't have to come up with much, if any, money up front for the seller. In 1997, she picked up seven houses. In 1998, she took five months vacation and still picked up eight more houses. In 1999, she started to add buying properties subject to the existing financing. That year, she took three months off and added nine houses to her portfolio. And in 2000, she took a whopping nine months off and bought four more houses.

Reddy focuses on the upscale houses in her area. She says she used to be just like a lot of investors who aren't comfortable with the really nice homes when they get started. When we asked her how she overcame this fear, here is what she had to say, "I did some expensive homes my first year. I don't know what made me feel like I could do this. I never had owned or lived in an expensive home. So what I did was to get myself psyched up. I went to an Open House in an expensive area with $250,000 homes and talked with the agent. I told the agent I had just moved to the area and was interested in purchasing homes in this price range. I had her chauffeur me around for the day. We looked at 10 or 15 very expensive homes. A couple of days later, I met with another agent and did the same thing. I was fair to both agents; I paid them for their time. I told them that I wasn't buying yet, but I wanted to be familiar with the area for when I started to buy. From that point on, I was not afraid to walk into a $250,000 to $300,000 home because I had been there 30 times!"

We had the good fortune to be in Atlanta a while back giving a keynote talk to the Georgia Real Estate Investors Association. Reddy and another student of ours named Bill took us out on a victory tour of some of the houses they had bought using the Purchase Option techniques. We spent several hours shuttling from one house to another. Unfortunately, we never got to see the 16-unit apartment building Bill had bought using "subject to" financing. At one house, Reddy's tenant-buyer peeked out from her window as Reddy posed on the front steps for a photo. A moment later her tenant-buyer realized it was Reddy and came outside to give her a warm hello. As we watched all that Reddy had done over the past three-and-one-half years, we thought to ourselves no one has any excuse why they can't make this work. Here is Reddy, a woman who came to this country speaking English as a second language in a completely foreign culture. Yet she doesn't let any of that stop her.

One of the greatest assets Reddy brings to her investing is her willingness to just be who she is with sellers. She doesn't pretend to be some huge nationwide company that buys thousands of houses every month. She is just herself, and sellers respond to her sincerity.

A Few Closing Thoughts

We've tried to share with you the best of what we have to teach you about making money by investing in real estate. If you are an experienced investor looking for just one or two ideas to help you fine tune your investing, we hope you have found them. If you are at the beginning of your real estate investing, then we hope we have not only given you the tools to help you start but hope we have cleared away some of the uncertainty too.

■ Peter's Story

My wife, Joanna, started up a nonprofit group, <www.allfor youth.org>, that helps orphans and street children in Africa and Asia. One day while I was helping her in a shelter for troubled families, I found the following handwritten note tacked up on the bulletin board:

Our deepest fear is not that we are inadequate. Our deepest fear is that we are powerful beyond measure. It is our light not our darkness that most frightens us. We ask ourselves, "Who am I to be brilliant, gorgeous, talented, fabulous?"

You are a child of God. Your playing small doesn't serve the world. There's nothing enlightening about shrinking so that other people won't feel insecure around you. You were born to manifest the glory of God that is within you. It's not just in some of us, it's in everyone. And as we let our own light shine, we unconsciously give other people permission to do the same. As we're liberated from our fear, our presence automatically liberates others.—*Nelson Mandela*   ■

We both think these words are the right way to close this book. We know that you can do this. You weren't meant to settle for less. Take action and step toward your dreams. Let the world see the beauty in all that you can accomplish. Let your inner light shine forth. We wish you much success on your journey.

A

Acceleration clause, 66–73
Accrued interest, 104
Action plan
    continuing education,
      236–37
    feedback system, 240–41
    mentor, 237–38
    motivated seller sources,
      238
    seller meetings, 239
Aging file, 233
American Real Estate Investor
    Association, 76
Amortization, 14–15, 52–54
Annual payments, 104
Appreciation
    future, 37, 210–11
    long-term, 15
    rate of, 32
Assignment, 96–97
Attorney objection, 138–40
Authorization to release
    information, 158
Automatic renewal clause,
    101–2

B

Balloon note, 101–2
Beneficial interest, 71, 72
Beneficiary, 71–72

Buyer
    benefits, 182
    exit strategy, 147–49
    motivations, 206–8
    reluctant language, 113–16

C

Caller ID, 76
Capital gains, 12
Carrying costs, 3
Cash close, 85–89
Cash flow
    creation of, 14
    positive, 87
    rental property, 32–33
    from tenant-buyer, 47–48,
      187–88
Cash purchase, 3
Classified ad
    for sale by owner, 232–35
    motivated sellers, 76
    placement of, 77–78
    for rent, 232–35
    rent-to-own, 188–89, 190
Closing, 109
    costs, 85
    delayed, 171, 173–74
    higher authority technique,
      124
    language, 118–21
    motivation before money,
      116–18

    offer as seller's idea,
      123–24
    two chair technique,
      124–26
    what if technique, 121–22
Community property state, 159
Competition, 194–97
Compound interest, 104
Consistency, 130, 188
Continuing education, 236–37
Contract clauses, 94–103
Contractors, 159
Corporate shield, 100
Corporation, 177–78
Credibility, 120–21
Credit check, 159
Credit issues, 61
Current value, 210

D

Deadline, 126–27
Deed, 173
Deed of trust, 159, 174–75
Deposit to hold property,
    219–23
Descriptive language, 118–21,
    128
Disclosure, 179–80, 201–2
Document escrow, 171, 173–74
Document recording, 170–71

Down payment
    objection, 31, 141–43
    risk management issues,
        164–68
    traditional investment, 32
Due diligence
    checklist, 150–51
    comparable property, 149,
        151–52
    market rents, 152–55
    neighborhood, 162–63
    profit calculations, 163–64
    property inspection, 162
    responsibility, 148–49
    title, 155–61
Due on sale clause, 66–73

E

Eager role, 125
Emotional response, 112–13,
    116–18
End user, 28, 168
Equity, 52–54
Equity pay down, 14–15
Equity splits, 54–59
Escrow, 73, 171, 173–74
Eviction, 199
Exit strategy, 145–49
Extension clause, 101–2

F

Farm area, 235–36
Fear factor, 5
Feedback system, 240–41
Fictitious buyer technique,
    135–36
Financial details, 109
Financial failure, 5
Financial independence, 9–10
Financial payoff, 130–32
Financing
    assumption of, 93
    carry back, 90–105
    contract clauses, 94–103
    100 percent, 87
    qualification, 61
    seller, 20–21, 69, 87–88,
        90–105
    subject to, 93–94
    terms, 13
First deal techniques, 232–36
First impressions, 204–5
First mortgage, 85–86
First right of refusal, 97–98
Fix-up costs, 3
Flexibility, 6–7, 96–97
Flipping, 24–25, 224–25

For sale by owner ads, 232–35
Foreclosure, 67–68, 80–81, 199
Freedom, 9
Funding sources, 29, 39–41
Future value, 210–11

G

Go long technique, 126–27
Goals, 4
Graduated payments, 105
Group showings, 195–97,
    203–9

H

Handyman's special, 25
Home owners association, 158
Hybrid equity split, 57–59

I

Impound account, 73
Income-producing property, 14
Income stream, 9–10, 27
Information source provider, 81
Instant offer system, 107–9
Insurance, 71–72, 178–79
Integrity, 180
Interest-free loan, 87–88
Interest-only payments, 88
Interest rates, 61–62

J–L

Journal, 240
Landlord/tenant relationship,
    198–99
Landlord trap, 25, 33, 44–45
Land trust, 71–72, 178
Language patterns, 113–16
Lead-based paint disclosure,
    201–2
Lease option
    down payment negotiation,
        141–42
    equity pay down and, 15
    equity splits, 54–59
    examples, 49–52
    explanation, 34–49
    hidden profit, 52–54
    maintenance costs, 44–45
    risk management, 174–75
    subject to clause, 43–44
    upfront money, 37–41
    withdrawal from, 48
Legal consideration, 38
Legal description, 160, 202–3

Lender, 66–73
Leverage, 11, 29
Leveraged repairs, 64
Liability, 61, 99, 168
Liens, 73, 100–101
Limited liability company
    (LLC), 177–78
Limited power of attorney, 74,
    75
Liquidated damages clause,
    95–96, 147–49
Loan
    assumption of, 70
    balance confirmation, 158
    costs, 60
    interest-free, 87–88
Long-term capital gains, 12
Lump sum payment, 88

M

Maintenance costs, 169–70,
    185–86
Market
    rents, 152–55, 211
    segment, 25
    stagnant, 37
    value, 12–13
Master lease option, 166–67
Mechanic's lien, 159
Memorandum of Agreement,
    171
Memorandum of Option, 171,
    172
Mentor, 16–18, 237–38
Mismatching, 111–12
Mortgage, 85–86, 174–75
Motivated seller
    description, 28, 35
    lease option, 37, 49–52
    life issues, 23
    market conditions, 12–13
    maintenance costs, 44–45
    price negotiation, 36–37
    reasons why, 30
    sources, 238
    upfront money, 38–39

N

Names, 157, 160
Negative cash flow, 32–33
Negative phrasing, 58, 112–16
Negotiation
    best price techniques,
        132–36
    close, 109, 116–26
    concept then details,
        128–29

financial details, 109
financial payoff, 130–32
good fit, 129–30
language patterns, 113–16
mismatching, 111–12
motivation building, 109,
    111–12
objections, 136–43
offer as seller's idea,
    123–24
phrasing techniques,
    112–16, 126–32
play dumb, 130–32
psychological payoff,
    130–32
seller rapport, 107–8,
    109–11
upfront agreement, 108–9
what if technique, 121–23
Neighborhood inspection,
    162–63
Neighborhood signs, 79–80
Neuro-Linguistic Programming,
    111
90 day notification clause,
    48–49
Nonassignment clause, 97
Notice of default, 80
Notice of sale, 80

O

Occupancy, 39
Offer, wording of, 86–87
Option payment
    amount of, 41, 185
    formula, 211
    tax issues, 41
    tenant-buyer withrawal
        and, 45–46
Owner carry back financing,
    83–84, 90–105
Owner occupants, 61–62
Ownership and encumbrance
    report, 155

P

Passive income, 9–10, 14
Personal liability, 99–100, 168
Phrasing techniques, 112–16,
    126–32
Positive cash flow, 33, 87
Postcards, 80–83
Preliminary title report, 155
Price, 2–3
Pricing strategy
    for first tenant buyer sale,
        225–26

for long term hold, 226–28
for maximum profit,
    228–29
negotiation techniques,
    36–37, 132–36
for quick cash, 224–25
Professional inspection, 162
Profit
    hidden, 52–54
    lease option, 52–54
    maximum, 228–29
    numbers, 163–64
    purchase option system,
        41–42
Program objection, 136–37
Promissory note, 159
Property
    appreciation, 15, 32, 37
    income-producing, 14
    inspection, 162
    legal description, 160
    manager, 36
    ownership, 157, 159
    purchase, 2–3
    tax, 158
    value, 3
Psychological payoff, 130–32
Public records check, 159
Purchase agreement, 173
Purchase option system, 24
    cash close, 85–89
    equity splits, 54–59
    focus, 26
    income streams, 27
    lease option, 34–54
    owner carry financing,
        90–105
    profits, 41–42
    steps, 28
    subject to financing, 59–84
    traditional investment
        comparison, 42–45
Pyramiding, 169

Q

Qualified resident clause, 43
Quarterly payments, 104
Quitclaim deed, 173

R

Range technique, 134–35
Rate of return, 11
Real estate agent, 137–38
Realistic expectation
    technique, 134
Recording, 170–71, 202–3
Recourse debt, 99, 168–69

Rehab property, 24–25, 26
Reluctant buyer, 113–16
Reluctant role, 125
Rent
    above-market, 40
    ads, 232–35
    credit, 211
    setting rates, 211
    survey, 152–55
    tenant buyer, 45–46
Rent-to-own, 22–23
    application process,
        215–23
    benefits, 187–88
    cash flow, 187–88
    classified ad, 188–89, 190
    competition, 194–97
    disclosures, 202
    explanation, 185–87
    group showing, 195–97,
        203–9
    option payment, 201
    pricing property, 209–15,
        224–29
    property, 25, 185
    recorded message, 191–94
    recording issues, 202–3
    safety, 198–99
    security deposit, 200–201
    signs, 189–91, 192
    worksheet, 213
Rental application, 215–16, 217
Rental property, 25
    benefits, 183
    cash flow, 32–33
    down payment, 32
    downside, 183–84
    risk, 32
Repair allowance, 21
Repairs. See Maintenance
Retailing, 225
Risk
    hedging, 11
    limiting, 29
    of traditional investment,
        32
Risk management
    corporation, 177–78
    delayed closing, 171–74
    disclosure, 179–80
    due diligence, 149–64
    exit strategy, 145–49
    insurance, 178–79
    integrity, 180
    lease option, 174–75
    nothing down, 164–68
    presell property, 168
    property maintenance,
        169–70

Risk management *continued*
   recording, 170–71
   recourse debt, 168–69
   seller, 175–77
   trusts, 177–78
Routines, 6
Royalties, 10

S

Sale price, 211
Sales comparables, 149, 151–52
Second mortgage, 85, 86
Securities, 10
Security, 9
Security deposit, 21, 200–201
Self-confidence, 7–9
Seller
   attitude, 188
   cash close, 85–89
   credit check, 159
   deadline, 126–27
   equity, 52–54
   equity splits, 54–59
   exit strategy, 147–49
   guarantees, 100–101
   maintenance costs,
      169–70, 186
   meeting with, 28, 175–76,
      239
   motivated. *See* Motivated
      seller
   motivation building, 109,
      111–12
   objections, 136–43
   public records check, 159
   rapport with, 107–8,
      109–11
   recommit, 175–77
   remorse, 175
   second mortgage, 85, 86
   signature issues, 73–74
   sources of, 238
Seller financing
   accrued interest, 104
   down payment negotiation,
      142–43
   graduated payments, 105
   pure principal payment,
      104
   quarterly/semiannual/
      annual payments, 104
   strategies, 20–21, 69,
      87–88, 90–105
   thank you payments, 103–4
Semiannual payments, 104
Signatures, 157
Signs
   city ordinances, 190–91

farm area, 235–36
handmade, 190, 192
neighborhood, 78–79, 81
professional, 189–90, 191
rent-to-own, 189–91
Simple interest, 104
Specific performance, 95
Stagnant market, 37
Straight owner financing,
   90–93
Subject to clause, 43–44,
   95–96, 140, 146–49
Subject to financing
   advantages, 59–62, 83–84
   credit issues, 61
   deal sources, 74–83
   due on sale clause, 66–73
   examples, 63–66
   existing liens, 73
   explanation, 62–63
   interest rates, 61–62
   liability, 61
   loan costs, 60
   pitfalls, 66–74
   qualification, 61
   seller's signature, 73–74
   tax issues, 60
   transaction summary, 65
Subordination clause, 98–99
Substitution of collateral clause,
   103
Support professionals, 94–95

T

Take away close, 112–16
Tax issues
   advantage, 11
   lease option, 185
   option payment, 41
   shelter, 12
   subject to financing, 60
Technical language, 118–21
1031 exchange, 22
Tenant-buyer, 22–23
   application process,
      215–18
   benefits, 185
   cash flow, 47–48, 187–88
   deposit to hold property,
      219–23
   description, 35
   landlord/tenant
      relationship, 198–99
   leads, 188–99
   lease option, 40, 49–52
   maintenance costs, 44–45,
      169–70, 185–86
   mentality, 25, 185

multiple, 46–49
90 day notification clause,
   48–49
option payment, 41, 45
presell, 43
prospects, 203–9, 215–23
purchase price, 40
qualifying questions, 216,
   218
rent, 40, 45–46
renter distinction, 200–202
screening, 218
term, 40, 227
transaction summary, 67
turnover, 226–28
withdrawal of, 45–49
Terms, 2–3
Testimonials, 241–51
Thank you payments, 103
Title
   checklist, 157–61
   due diligence, 155–61
   insurance, 100, 155–57
   report, 155, 156–57
Toll-free voice-mail system,
   74, 76
Traditional investment
   barriers to, 31–34
   purchase option system
      comparison, 42–45
Trust, 177–78
Trustee, 71–72
24-hour recorded message,
   192–94
Two chair close, 124–26

U

Umbrella liability policy, 179
Undisclosed lien clause,
   100–101, 156
Upfront agreement, 108–9
Upfront money, 32
   lease option, 38–41
   liquidated damages clause
      and, 96
   from tenant-buyer, 41
Upside leverage, 11, 29

V

Value, 210–11, 212
Voice-mail system, 74–75,
   191–94

W

Walk-through inspection, 162
Welcome speech, 205–6
Workshops, 17

Self-made millionaires Peter Conti and David Finkel are two of the nation's leading investment experts. They are successful business owners, investors, and co-authors of *How to Create Multiple Steams of Income Buying Homes in Nice Areas with Nothing Down,* which was selected as one of the all-time top three investing books by the American Real Estate Investors Association. Their syndicated column in *Creative Real Estate Magazine* is read by over 65,000 investors across the country.

Each year Conti and Finkel hold workshops and seminars, at which thousands of investors across the country discover the realities of making money by investing in real estate. Their personal real estate holdings are valued at over $8 million, and their students have bought and sold close to $100 million worth of real estate over the past decade.

Conti and Finkel were also the masterminds behind the original San Diego Challenge, in which they guided a group of three novice investors in picking up over $1.5 million worth of properties—with only $37 down.

For more information, visit their Web site <www.resultsnow
m> or contact them at:

Mentor Financial Group, LLC
7475 W. 5th Ave., Suite 100
Lakewood, CO 80226
e-mail: mentor@resultsnow.com

A Special Bonus for readers of *Making Big Money Inv...*
Real Estate without Tenants, Banks, or Rehab Pr...

A FREE 12-Month Subscription to
The Purchase Option Investor's Newsletter

This free newsletter is filled with insider tips and techniques to help you make money using the powerful Purchase Option strategies you just finished reading about. Your newsletter issues will be e-mailed to you at the beginning of each month.

It's our gift to you, a reward really, for reading this book. To get your free subscription started, simply follow the instructions below.

Two Easy Ways to Get Your FREE Subscription Started Right Now:

1. Go to <www.resultsnow.com> and register online.

2. Fax this form toll-free to 1-877-689-4602.

Name _____ Phone ( ) _____

Address _____ City _____

State _____ Zip _____ E-mail _____@_____

Making Big Money Investing in Real Estate

For special discounts on twenty or more copies of *Making Big Money Investing in Real Estate without Tenants, Banks, or Rehab Projects*, please call Dearborn Trade Special Sales at 800-621-9621, extension 4307.

Dearborn™
Trade Publishing

A **Kaplan Professional** Company